SKIP INTRO

Flash Usability and Interface Design

Duncan McAlester & Michelangelo Capraro

New Riders

201 West 103rd Street   Indianapolis, Indiana 46290

SKIP INTRO: FLASH USABILITY & INTERFACE DESIGN

International Standard Book Number: 0-7357-1178-x

Library of Congress Catalog Card Number: 2001095495

Printed in the United States of America

First Printing: April 2002

06   05   04   03   02   7   6   5   4   3   2

Interpretation of the printing code: The rightmost double-digit number is the year of the book's printing; the rightmost single-digit number is the number of the book's printing. For example, the printing code 02-1 shows that the first printing of the book occurred in 2002.

Trademarks

Warning and Disclaimer

Publisher
David Dwyer

Associate Publisher
Stephanie Wall

Executive Editor
Steve Weiss

Production Manager
Gina Kanouse

Managing Editor
Sarah Kearns

Acquisitions Editor
Deborah Hittel-Shoaf

Development Editor
Linda Laflamme

Project Editor
Michael Thurston

Copy Editor
Keith Cline

Technical Editors
Daniel Keeler
Chris MacGregor
Todd Marks

Product Marketing Manager
Stephanie Layton

Publicity Manager
Susan Petro

Manufacturing Coordinator
Jim Conway

Cover Designers
Duncan McAlester
Michelangelo Capraro
Aren Howell

Interior Designer
Wil Cruz

Compositor
Wil Cruz

Proofreader
Marcia Deboy

Indexer
Lisa Stumpf

Media Developer
Jay Payne

CONTENTS AT A GLANCE

Foreword

Introduction

1   Bad Flashers Anonymous

2   Basic Training

Section I: Höpart Bothur Exhibit Site

3   Overview—A Comfortable Situation

4   A Good Experience from the Start

5   Scrolling Without Boundaries

6   Less Cluttered and More Usable

7   A Point of Flexibility

Section II: GroceryClick.com Site Design

8   Overview—Convenience in a Flash

9   Tabbed Windows—Convenient Access to Supplementary Information

10   Needles and Haystacks—Site Searches

Section III: Wind-Automata Developer Site

11   Overview—A Familiar Setting

12   A Simple Hierarchy

13   Tool Tips—Know Before You Go

14   The End...

Appendixes

A   What Every Interface Designer Should Know

B   Usability Resources

C   Flash and Design Resources

Index

TABLE OF CONTENTS

Foreword   xv

Introduction   1

   Who This Book Is For   2

   Who This Book Is Not For   3

   What's the Goal of This Book?   3

   How This Book Works   4

   Terminology   4

   Typographical Conventions   7

1   Bad Flashers Anonymous   9

   The Problem   10

      Admit You Have a Problem   *10*

      Now What?   *11*

      A Little Bit of History   *11*

      Identifying Bad Design   *12*

   Brains Versus Beauty   14

      Keep Things Simple   *14*

      Know Your Client   *14*

      Know Your Users   *14*

      Know Your Market   *15*

      Know Your Goals   *15*

      Know Your Tools   *16*

      Know the Rules   *16*

      Know Thyself   *17*

   It's Not About Faster or Easier, It's About Better   18

2   Basic Training   19

   The Flash Environment   20

   The Coding Environment   21

   Common Mistakes, Debugging, or What to Do When Code *Doesn't* Work   23

   How We Build Our Projects   26

   Other People's Code   27

   Mac or PC?   27

   Conclusion   27

Section I: Höpart Bothur Exhibit Site

3   Overview—A Comfortable Situation   31

   Case Study: The Digital Museum   33

     Character Profile   *35*

   Defining Your Own Goals   35

4   A Good Experience from the Start   37

   Solutions—Giving Nancy Time   38

     Seeing It in Action   *39*

   Implementation   41

     Information Object   *41*

   Construction   42

     Setting the Stage   *43*

     Test It!   *45*

     Taking Control   *46*

     Crunching the Numbers   *47*

     Finishing Touches   *52*

     Progress!   *56*

   Conclusion   58

     Key Points/Don't Forget   *58*

5   Scrolling Without Boundaries   61

     Solutions—Making the User More Efficient   *62*

     Seeing It in Action   *63*

   Implementation   64

   Construction   66

     Setting Up the Movie   *66*

     Hiding the Clip   *67*

     Public Functions   *67*

     Handling the Offset   *68*

     Creating a Clip Array   *69*

     Organizing Your List Clips   *70*

     Initializing Your Variables   *72*

     The Over State   *74*

The Heart of the System		*76*
Test Your Work		*80*
Making the Component		*85*
Conclusion		86
6	**Less Cluttered and More Usable**	**87**
	Solutions	89
	Seeing It in Action	*90*
	Implementation	91
	Construction	91
	Setting Up the Movie	*91*
	Creating the Component	*92*
	Code	93
	Initialization	*93*
	Building the Menu	*94*
	Mouse Handling	*95*
	Open to the Public	*98*
	Fading	*100*
	From Movie Clip to Component	*102*
	Conclusion	104
	Key Points/Don't Forget	*104*
7	**A Point of Flexibility**	**105**
	Seeing It in Action	*106*
	Implementation	107
	Construction	107
	Building the Cursor Libraries	*109*
	Setting Up the Events	*110*
	Installing the Cursor and Preparing It to Move	*110*
	Making the Cursor Move	*111*
	Handling Mouse Overs	*112*
	Handling Mouse Outs	*113*
	Cursor Cleanup	*114*
	Hogging the Cursor	*116*
	Modifying the Cursor	*118*
	Components and Detection	*123*
	Conclusion	124
	Key Points/Don't Forget	*124*

Section II: GroceryClick.com Site Design

8	Overview—Convenience in a Flash	127
	Case Study: GroceryClick.com	129
	Character Profile	*130*
	Defining Your Own Goals	131
9	Tabbed Windows—Convenient Access to Supplementary Information	133
	Solutions—Giving Sanjeev Access	134
	Seeing It in Action	*135*
	Implementation	135
	Construction	137
	Setting Up Your Movie	*137*
	Creating the Content Window	*137*
	Creating the Content Areas	*137*
	Setting Up the tabbedWindow Movie Clip	*138*
	Code	140
	Buttons	*140*
	Movie Clip Code	*141*
	Making It Move	*142*
	Setting the Initial Position	*144*
	Open the Tab Function, Getting It Ready to Move	*144*
	Accessing the Move Function	*145*
	Closing the Tab	*146*
	Adding the Auto-Hide Feature	*151*
	Making Your Code Portable	*152*
	Adding the Clip Parameter Variables	*152*
	Adding the Last of Top Variables	*152*
	The Initialize Function	*153*
	Last Step of Code	*159*
	Setting Up a Component Clip	*159*
	Conclusion	160
	Key Points/Don't Forget	*160*
10	Needles and Haystacks—Site Searches	161
	Seeing It in Action	*162*
	Implementation	163

Construction 163

Creating the Search Field 163

Creating the Clip 164

Code 165

Conclusion 170

Key Points/Don't Forget 170

Section III: Wind-Automata Developer Site

11 Overview—A Familiar Setting 173

Case Study: Wind-Automata Knowledge Base 174

Character Profile 176

Defining Your Own Goals 177

12 A Simple Hierarchy 179

Seeing It in Action 181

Implementation 182

Construction 183

Setting Up the Movie 184

Skinning the Menu 184

Building the Component 187

Conclusion 198

Key Points/Don't Forget 198

13 Tool Tips—Know Before You Go 199

Overview 200

Solutions 200

Seeing It in Action 200

Implementation 201

Construction 202

Setting Up the Movie 202

Drawing the Tool Tip Graphic 202

Converting to a Movie Clip 202

Create the Text Field 203

Convert It to Another Movie Clip 203

Code   204

    Buttons   204

    Passing the Function   205

    Hide and Seek   206

    Setting the Height and Width   207

    Setting the Placement of Your Tool Tip   210

    Timed Tips   214

    Finishing Up!   218

    Components   219

Conclusion   222

    Key Points/Don't Forget   222

14 The End…   **223**

  Key Points   224

Appendixes

A   What Every Interface Designer Should Know   **225**

  Ten Usability Heuristics   226

  Interface Design Principles   227

    Anticipation   227

    Consistency   227

    Explorable Interfaces   228

  Proper Task Analysis   229

  Cognitive Walkthrough   229

  Testing, Testing…   229

B   Usability Resources   **231**

  Books   232

  Web Sites   236

  Newsgroups, Email Lists, Organizations   238

C   Flash and Design Resources   **239**

  Web Sites   240

  Books   242

Index   **245**

ABOUT THE AUTHORS

Duncan McAlester lives at the beach and endeavors to one day be retired; until then he makes a living doing things that he is still astonished people are willing to pay him for—namely designing and programming various things through his company, Breathe (www.breathedesign.com). When he's not creating interactive designs, he can be found teaching interface design at the University of California Irvine Extension, sitting in on life drawing classes at the Art Institute of Southern California (his alma mater), or hosting a very informal Flash user group at the local tavern (stop by and say hi). He also speaks on various topics relating to design, multimedia, and interface design and very occasionally finds time to sleep.

Photo by Bryan Medway, creative@razorlab.com

Michelangelo Capraro has been designing user interfaces and interaction for more than seven years. Throughout his career he has worked for many different clients ranging from big-name corporations and movie studios to smaller mom-and-pop establishments. He began his career designing multimedia CD-ROMs in Macromedia Director and moved into the entertainment industry web site design for movies and television. After founding and helping to run a design and development firm located in Los Angeles (and partaking in countless other entrepreneurial adventures), Michelangelo moved to the Bay Area of northern California where he worked on the User Experience team at Be Inc. He is currently Visual Experience Designer at PalmSource, Inc.

Michelangelo attended the Art Institute of Southern California where he studied fine arts, ran the computer lab, and left school to pursue a career in graphic design and multimedia. He believes in designing interfaces that are not only comfortable to use, but also entertaining, and hopes to fulfill his dream of being a rock star one day very soon.

ABOUT THE TECHNICAL EDITORS

Daniel Keeler is a journalist and editor with a distressingly long career. When he's not editing, rewriting, and generally butchering Duncan and Michelangelo's prose, he is managing editor of an international financial magazine. In the gaps in between these two jobs, he creates and manages editorial content through his company Celerity Media. At the time of writing, he was still wrestling with a dilemma over whether to remove the entirely worthless and un-user friendly Flash intro from his web site (www.celeritymedia.com).

Todd Marks jumped ship from teaching high school in the public sector in 2000 and joined forces with his kayaking partner, Brett Rampata, and Walt Rampata to fill in the left-brained activity at digitalorganism. Currently the Vice President of Research and Development at digitalorganism, Todd has worked extensively with Flash ActionScript, Lingo, and various middleware, placing cutting-edge code in several projects, including digitalorganism's own site. With Todd's contributions, digitalorganism has received three Flash Film Festival nominations, among other honors. Todd is a Certified Flash Developer, an editor and contributor for several Flash books, and has lectured on ActionScript, PHP, and C++ at Georgetown University and several Macromedia organizations.

Chris MacGregor is an interaction designer with MacGregor Media in Houston, Texas. He consults with clients across the world to improve the usability of their Flash and web projects. In addition to his award-winning work, MacGregor is recognized as a leading proponent of Flash and usability. He is the publisher of Flazoom.com, a popular Flash critique site and author of a number of articles focusing on Flash and usability. Last year Macromedia published MacGregor's Flash usability white paper entitled "Developing User-Friendly Flash Content."

ACKNOWLEDGMENTS

Duncan McAlester

First, I would like to thank my writing partners. Michelangelo, a friend for going on 10 years now, and we go way back to our very first class at the Art Institute of Southern California. Daniel Keeler, another good friend and a real writer, is listed here as a "technical reviewer," but he was more than that. Truly the most enjoyable collaboration, thanks in no small part to you two.

Next to the wonderful people at New Riders, a group of people that I can pay no higher compliment than to say that "they just get it." Steve Weiss, who actually took the proposal seriously and scheduled that first meeting in Los Angeles. Deborah Hittel-Shoaf and Theresa Gheen, our wonderful acquisitions editors, who were ultra-supportive and kept us on our toes. Linda Laflamme, our editor, was so full of great ideas and encouragement and patience. David Dwyer, publisher at New Riders, for being a great guy, signing the contract, and putting *that* photo on the web. Chris MacGregor and Todd Marks, who aren't part of New Riders, but were our technical editors and did a superb job.

Special thanks to Dennis Bock, my third through sixth grade computer teacher, who introduced me to the Apple IIe, AppleBASIC, and my fascination with computers. Ernie Welke, my junior high and high school art teacher, who taught me there was more to art than tiny space ships on college-ruled notebook paper. Gary Birch, my college multimedia professor, who gave me inspirational guidance; I know I wouldn't be writing this today if not for you. To Shahram Aarabi, Andy Scott, and Indi Trehan for taking the time to teach me the math and physics I should have learned in school, but didn't because I was too busy drawing Batman comics. The gang at were-here, especially Jessica and Aaron, for setting up such a wonderful place to be. You guys are mmmMMMmMMMMmmmGreat!

To David Beckham for that fabulous free kick, Michael Owen for those three goals, Sven Göran-Erikson and the rest of the England team for keeping me out of the post-football lethargy that sets in after a loss.

Thanks to Henriette Cohn and Peter Santangeli from Macromedia for saving me while I was on the road.

Most importantly thanks to my family. To Jill, my mum, for being my artistic inspiration and best critic—the right side of my brain. To Trevor, my dad, for giving me the ability to reason, for being a usability guru before your time, and for letting me learn through observation—the left side of my left brain. To Jessica, my sister, who is more gung-ho than the three of us combined. You inspired me to pursue this book with your confidence.

Finally to you, the reader. Thank you for taking the time to listen to what we have to say.

Michelangelo Capraro

First things first: I want to thank Duncan not only for choosing me to write this book with him, but for being an inspirational artist and friend throughout the many years of our friendship. Thanks to Daniel Keeler, for turning our highly messy, unorganized thoughts in to actual, readable text, and for being such a cool person to work with. Thanks to my friends and family who I have not seen much of for the past several months; you have been so tremendously patient with me while I worked on the book. Thanks! Thanks to my parents for teaching me the value of hard work. To Deb, Linda, and Theresa at New Riders, you really kept us going and motivated me beyond what I thought I was possible of doing. Thanks David and Steve from New Riders for believing in the idea for this book and letting us designers do what we like to do best: design. Todd Marks, thanks for going through the chapters, trudging through the stuff that didn't work, and suggesting stuff that did. Chris MacGregor, thanks for reviewing the book and all the usability assistance you've given us; you are really part of the reason we are writing it in the first place. To Jakob Neilsen, your article is the other reason we are writing this. Thanks to Cooper and Norman for teaching me what usability is through your books, and to Genevieve Bell, your talk inspired me beyond words. Chris, thanks for your usability opinions, and Dan, thanks for your influence of good, clean coding practices. Tinic, Jeremy, and all of Macromedia, you guys rock! Bryan, aside from your wonderful photography and the head shot for the book, thanks for inspiring me. To the Artist's Roundtable, you all gave me that extra motivation when I needed it. A very special thanks to my wife, Karen, whose support throughout the writing of this book was what kept me going. Thank you for believing in me and for sacrificing your own time to help me with my goal for this project. And finally, thank you, the reader, for buying this book. I really hope you enjoy it and that Duncan and I can inspire you to create a great experience for someone today.

A MESSAGE FROM NEW RIDERS

As the reader of this book, you are our most important critic and commentator. We value your opinion and want to know what we're doing right, what we could do better, in what areas you'd like to see us publish, and any other words of wisdom you're willing to pass our way.

As Executive Editor at New Riders, I welcome your comments. You can fax, email, or write me directly to let me know what you did or didn't like about this book—as well as what we can do to make our books better. When you write, please be sure to include this book's title, ISBN, and author, as well as your name and phone or fax number. I will carefully review your comments and share them with the authors and editors who worked on the book.

Please note that I cannot help you with technical problems related to the topic of this book, and that due to the high volume of email I receive, I might not be able to reply to every message. Thanks.

Fax: 317-581-4663

Email: steve.weiss@newriders.com

Mail: Steve Weiss
          Executive Editor
          New Riders Publishing
          201 West 103rd Street
          Indianapolis, IN 46290 USA

Visit Our Web Site: www.newriders.com

On our web site, you'll find information about our other books, the authors we partner with, book updates and file downloads, promotions, discussion boards for online interaction with other users and with technology experts, and a calendar of trade shows and other professional events with which we'll be involved. We hope to see you around.

Email Us from Our Web Site

Go to www.newriders.com and click the Contact Us link if you

- Have comments or questions about this book.
- Want to report errors that you have found in this book.
- Have a book proposal or are interested in writing for New Riders.
- Would like us to send you one of our author kits.
- Are an expert in a computer topic or technology and are interested in being a reviewer or technical editor.
- Want to find a distributor for our titles in your area.
- Are an educator/instructor who wants to preview New Riders books for classroom use. In the body/comments area, include your name, school, department, address, phone number, office days/hours, text currently in use, and enrollment in your department, along with your request for either desk/examination copies or additional information.

FOREWORD

Two years ago a book about Flash usability would have been unheard of. At that time most Flash on the web was more about showing off a designer's skills than actually meeting the needs of users. In the heyday of the web, that was all fine and good. Designers were being paid to create impressive web sites that looked cool. Flash developers did not know about usability or did not care. With priorities in the wrong place a designer who could create really "flashy" sites was in higher demand than one focused on user experience.

Then the bubble burst. The particular pinprick that exploded the bubble of ultra-excess in Flash design was the AlertBox column "Flash is 99% Bad" by usability pundit Jakob Neilsen. In his article, Neilsen blasted Flash developers and Flash as a format for propagating poor usability on the web. That article had a big impact on Flash content development. All of a sudden clients started asking for justification from Flash developers. The excesses of the past were now the Praia's of the present. Our clients started equating Flash content on the web with failure.

The situation today is getting better. Flash developers are learning about usability and making Flash content easier to use. Instead of jumping right into the excesses of the past, Flash developers are thinking more about their users and the needs of their clients.

This book is part of that effort. Inside these pages you will find a treasure trove of usability concepts, tips, and code to make your Flash content more usable. The authors, Duncan and Michelangelo, have done an excellent job breaking down many of the problems with Flash usability and offer well thought out, and exceptionally coded, solutions.

Think of this book as a Swiss Army Knife for making better Flash content. Instead of scissors, saws, and files, you now have a collection of SmartClips to enhance the sites that you use. The book itself is an instruction manual that shows you how, and more importantly when, to use each SmartClip to improve usability. By reading and using the suggestions in this book, the experience of your Flash content can improve. It is up to you, and buying this book is an excellent first step.

—Chris MacGregor
www.MacGregor.net

INTRODUCTION

Skip Intro covers the concepts and theories of user interface and usability design as they relate to Flash. It not only explains why usability is important, it goes a step further by diving into Flash and ActionScript and shows you how to implement the different concepts in your own projects. All the modules discussed in this book are available as drag-and-drop Flash Components on the CD-ROM.

Be aware, however, that this book is not about making life easier for the designer; it's about making life better for the web site user. The good news is that well-designed Flash code will make your sites easier to design in the long run.

WHO THIS BOOK IS FOR

This book is for Flash developers who want to make their Flash projects more user-friendly. Perhaps you've heard some of the criticisms about Flash and how it is poorly used on so many web sites. Maybe you've read a few of the growing number of usability books out there and you want to know how Flash can be built keeping the user in mind. Perhaps you've seen the word *usability* start to pop up more and more in the Flash forums you hang out in and want to know what it's all about. Or maybe you know what it is and you know that designing for usability can help users of your work have better experiences on the Flash sites you build. This book will help you in all these circumstances.

> One very important thing to keep in mind is that the concepts covered here are applied in the Flash MX authoring environment, but this is *not* a Flash MX book. The theory here can be taken and applied to almost any multimedia authoring application—Java, Director, DHTML, or future versions of Flash.
>
> **Note**

> By the time you read this, the next generation version of Flash should be readily available. If you are at all interested in creating Flash web sites that are more usable, Flash MX continues to offer you the ability to create refined, user-centric web sites.
>
> Traditionally, as developers move to the new version of Flash, user experiences begin to suffer when users go to a web site and the first thing they see is a "Get Flash 5" or a "You need Flash 5 to view this site" button on the site.
>
> You, as part of the Flash developer community, must make a concerted effort to educate your users not only about *what* they need to view the web site, but *why* they should get the new plug-in. We have in the past done a very poor job of this, simply putting up a note explaining "You will need the Flash 5 Player." Well, most users don't know Flash 5 from Flash 2 and couldn't tell you what version they have. Beyond that there is no clear indication why the user should update to the latest plug-in.
>
> Flash MX contains more tools than ever before with which developers can design great, usable web sites. Because Flash MX is such an important release, go above and beyond what has typically been done in the past and take the time to explain to users the benefits of the new plug-in and why they should take the time to download it. If you need help or aren't quite sure what to say, visit our web site and download our "Why should I upgrade?" note for your users.
>
> **Note**

If you're an ActionScript whiz but want to understand better what user interface design is, this book can help. You want to know what usability or interaction design mean? This book will help you gain that understanding and help you take those theories and goals and apply them to your own coding practices.

You work for a company that hires Flash developers, either full time or on contract? This book will help you to be an educated client and intelligently select a Flash designer or design firm that knows what usability means, because you will learn what it means and how it can impact the success of your projects. This book will help you communicate with designers in their own language. You'll find the case study chapters (Chapters 3, 8, and 11) particularly interesting.

Additionally, if you're a client it's important for you to know what usability is. To be an educated client, you need to understand that what you might want and what your designer might want won't necessarily be what your customers want. This book will help you see how usability can help you make your project more successful. Chapter 1, "Bad Flashers Anonymous," will be of most value to you.

If you relate at all to any of the above descriptions, this book has got you covered! Stop reading in the aisle, rush right up to the cashier, and take this book home with you.

Still not sure this book's right for you? Read on...

WHO THIS BOOK IS NOT FOR
This book is not for people who want to learn ActionScript. Dozens of books on the market teach it better than we can. This book is about usability and interface design in Flash. If you are a designer wanting to learn ActionScript, check out Brendan Dawes's *Flash ActionScript for Designers: Drag, Slide, Fade* (New Riders).

This book also isn't for hardcore ActionScript code gurus looking for some super efficient object-oriented code to play with or add to their collection of amazingly amazing algorithms. You won't find that here. In fact, we made the decision at the beginning of the writing process to keep the code at the intermediate level. We avoid the simplistic nature of Normal mode and steer clear of some of the more esoteric concepts of object-oriented programming to offer something that is easily readable and gets the point across. Although we both really dig OOP and have a few surprises planned for the *Skip Intro* web site (did we say that out loud?), we decided not to include OOP to ensure the usability of this book.

WHAT'S THE GOAL OF THIS BOOK?
The aim of this book is to give you a clear understanding of a few really important concepts. To do this, we

- Explain why your target user should be the center of your project design from the beginning.
- Show you good practices in usability and interface design and how to apply those to Flash projects.
- Provide you with solid examples of user interface design focused on usability.
- Show that it's not always about following all the rules and laws of usability all the time.
- Help to educate both the Flash community and the anti-Flash community so that together we *can* build a better experience for everyone.

HOW THIS BOOK WORKS

The book's first two chapters delve into the theory of interface design as it pertains to Flash and the Internet community as a whole. Sections I through III, listed here, provide project tutorials:

Section I: Höpart Bothur Exhibit Site

Section II: GroceryClick.com Site Design

Section III: Wind-Automata Developer Site

Each project starts with a brief but important case study in which we identify the need for the project and the goals it should achieve. This is the first chapter in each project section and is essential reading. Working through the tutorial without having read the case study chapter for each project will give you only the "how" and not the "why." We then split the project into separate tutorials, each of which tackles how to achieve those goals from a usability standpoint, the features that must be included, and how to build them in Flash. The book concludes with our final observations and suggestions for improved Flash usability. The appendixes offer supplementary reference and inspirational materials.

Before jumping into the theory and hands-on projects, we're going to take a few pages here to familiarize you with some of the terminology and the way that we present information in this book. Many of the topics covered may already be second nature to you, but we still encourage you

"Give a man a fish and he eats for a day. Teach a man to fish and he can eat for a lifetime." This might seem like a strange analogy, but it is entirely appropriate here. If you don't read the case study section of each project, you will only be learning code without knowing why you are learning it.

Note

to take a few minutes to read through this material. More than anything, we just want to make sure we're all on the same page, so to speak. And who knows, you might actually find out something you didn't know before.

TERMINOLOGY

A good place to start is making sure that we're all speaking the same language. Depending on where we learn our craft, we may use different terms for the same thing or the same term may have different meanings. Take a moment to familiarize yourself with some common terms and how we will be using them throughout the book.

- **Cursor.** The cursor is the graphic representation of the user's mouse location within the graphical world of her computer. The cursor and the mouse are not the same thing. A cursor, for instance, cannot "click" and a mouse cannot "roll over" a button. Always make sure you are very clear when referring to the person using an input device, the input device itself, or the representation of the device onscreen. These are very different things and should be considered separately when designing for your user.

- **GUI.** An acronym for *graphical user interface*, pronounced "gooey." GUIs replaced the command-line interface (most commonly seen as the DOS prompt, or the Shell in the UNIX world) with the ability to interact with a computer using an input device such as a mouse or trackball. Through a clever use of icons and menus, users could complete relatively complex tasks in a much more comfortable and familiar visual manner. GUIs were pioneered by Xerox PARC with the STAR system, popularized by Apple on the Macintosh, and made commonplace by companies such as Microsoft.

- **User interface.** A more generalized term than GUI, user interface (or UI) can refer to "real" objects in addition to the metaphorical world of computer user interfaces. For example, the buttons on your microwave are the interface to control the settings of the microwave. In this book, user interface refers to the visual portion of the software that the user interacts with, to interact with the computer—in other words, the buttons or icons on the screen that enable you to affect the software on your computer.

> **?**
> For an absolutely fascinating look at the more esoteric development of GUIs, we highly recommend reading Erik Davis' excellent essay "Techgnosis, Magic, Memory and the Angels of Information." In a scant 25 pages, he goes from Gnostic mystics, to Xerox PARC, to William Gibson's *Neuromancer*. The essay can be found online or in a collection of equally intriguing writings called *Flame Wars: The Discourse of Cyberculture*, Mark Dery Editor. Duke University Press, Durham and London 1994. ISBN 0-8223-1540-9.
> **Note**

- **User interaction.** User interaction is a term made popular in recent years that refers to the physical actions users must perform, most likely with a mouse, in the user interface of the software they are using. Some examples of this would be the act of double-clicking a folder icon to see the contents of that folder, or clicking and dragging an object from one location on the screen to, perhaps, the trash can icon on your desktop. These are examples of the interaction of the person using the software on a computer. Although this term is sometimes thought to be synonymous with user interface, it differs significantly. It describes how a person *uses* the user interface. When software companies spend time refining the user interface to change the user interaction, it can be said that they are refining the user interaction model.

- **Usability.** This word represents the level of comfort a person feels when using software. Examples of this would be whether the software was easy to use, or perhaps more efficient for the user and less frustrating. This would mean the software has a high level of usability. This level is directly affected by the attention paid by the software developer to the user interaction model. More usable software may have had more effort put toward refining the interaction model of the software; overly complex and hard-to-use software may not have had any time spent honing the interaction model.

- **Personas.** This is a user interaction development term used by author and usability expert, Alan Cooper. This is a very effective "role-playing" method used when designing a user interface. The basic concept behind a persona is that instead of developing for a demographic (say, 18 to 29-year-old women), you create an in-depth character study of perhaps three women of ages ranging from 18 to 29. To be effective the character study should be as detailed as possible, down to minute details such as hair color and favorite movie. Things such as daily activities, number of immediate family members, job position, even a photograph taken from a magazine ad or someone they might know can all prove extremely helpful in defining this persona and ultimately in deciding what kind of interface to design for this target audience. One of the main reasons this method is useful is because after you have developed this persona, it won't change its mind as quickly as a regular person does. It always remains at the same experience level (whereas real persons can easily learn an activity after they attempt it once), and the persona is available at all times. Therefore the development project is not at the mercy of your target audience's schedule. Using this method helps you empathize with your audience and target your work to what a real person would expect from your design. You'll find yourself replacing "target audience" and "user" with your persona's name, humanizing the process. When you design for a person, you will find your designs become more usable. Keep in mind, however, that developing an accurate persona is not a replacement for testing your work at many different stages of its design (from paper sketches to actual working product) with real people representing your target audience.

  Each project chapter has a new persona, and when we use the term *persona* it refers to the specific persona in that chapter.

  > Unfortunately we don't have enough space to give the persona approach the time it deserves, but we highly recommend that you read Alan Cooper's *The Inmates Are Running the Asylum*, for a full breakdown of the use of personas, in addition to many other excellent user interface and user interaction critiques and concepts. You might find that after reading this book, you have a whole new perception of the people who use the sites you design.
  >
  > **Note**

- **Scenarios.** These are example use cases for a project. Typically, you will develop your personas and then develop many different scenarios for how that persona will use the site you are designing. From these many scenarios, you would typically pick the few probable cases and make sure your interface makes these the most efficient for the users.

- **User.** We use this throughout the book to refer to the people who use or will use the user interface of the project you are working on. Also known as the *target user* or *target audience*.

- **You.** In an attempt to differentiate between the "user," our "persona," and you, the reader, we'll be calling you, well "you." Very impersonal, we know, but at the least you'll know whom we are talking about!

TYPOGRAPHICAL CONVENTIONS
In addition to a common set of terms, we will be using some typographical conventions to help you visually identify and differentiate special types of text, such as variable names and code fragments. The following list identifies those conventions and what they mean:

- `Code`. All code appears in a monospace font. This should look very similar to what the code looks like in the Flash Actions window.

- ***Variable.*** Variable names are in bold and italic.

- *Movie clip instance*. Instance names of movie clips on the stage are italic.

> An interesting thought occurred to us while writing this portion of the book: The typographical conventions we use can improve the *usability* of the book itself—that is, we can make it easier for you (the reader) to differentiate between different elements that we may reference. If variable names looked the same in this book as regular text, you would have a hard time figuring out what we might be trying to explain. Just thought we would point that out.
>
> **Author Note: Michelangelo**

- Main menu>submenus. Menus and submenus are written out using a right-facing arrow (>) to indicate a submenu (for example, Window>Common Libraries>Skip Intro vol. 1).

- (Ctrl-shortcuts). Keyboard shortcuts appear between parentheses. Due to slight differences between keys on the Macintosh and PC platform, keyboard shortcuts are presented twice, once for the Mac and once for the PC (for example, Cmd-N/Ctrl-N).

- **Layer**, **movie clip**, **scene.** Layer names, movie clip names, and scene names are all in bold.

- **Reader entry.** Any text you should enter is shown in a bold font.

That does it for terminology, introductions, and typographical conventions. The next section actually delves into usability theory, and all the terms just discussed are used extensively throughout. If you get stuck on an abbreviation or term, don't hesitate to come back here for a refresher. Now, let's dive in!

CHAPTER 01
Bad Flashers Anonymous

Computing is not about computers anymore. It is about living.

—Nicholas Negroponte

We confess: We love Flash! It's a fantastic tool, it's flexible, powerful, easy to use, inexpensive, and, well, just great. There can't be many software programs that are so much fun to play with *and* that can produce such stunning results in the right hands. Right? And that's the problem. Sometimes it's just too much fun.

It's so easy to get carried away. You have all this power at your fingertips, how can you help but use it? So what if the site takes a little longer to download? The users will just love it when they see the design! Well, actually, no. They might not wait that long. Users are fickle, impatient creatures—just like you, in fact. And if you lose them before they even get into a site, you'll probably find your clients are none too pleased, no matter how impressed they were when they first saw your designs.

THE PROBLEM
There's no denying it, there's a lot of bad Flash out there: the irrelevant Hollywood blockbuster-style intro, the complex, drawn-out transformations triggered by a simple click of a button, the noise and the drama. It might make the designer feel good, but it sure as heck isn't making the user's experience better. True, there is a time and a place for a long Flash intro movie and for complex interactive interfaces. Generally, however, web site visitors are looking for some information and more often than not that super-cool Flash movie stands between them and their goal, instead of helping them reach it.

Sadly, this kind of design makes Flash and those who promote it an easy target for the knockers, and it diverts attention from all the great, effective Flash work being produced. In an era when the usability of Internet sites is such a hot topic, all that flashy Flash is a sitting duck. Imagine the fun the usability gurus have every time they come across a 2MB Flash movie on the home page of a site. Picture them gleefully switching over to 28K modem connections so that they can time how long it will take the so-called average web user to download this piece of cyber-frippery. For them it's just another Flash designer banging yet another nail in the coffin of the program they love to hate.

Flash critics have got a point. However, they're also missing the point. Flash is one of the most effective interface design tools ever created. This book shows you how you can turn this awesome power to your advantage—and how to silence the critics once and for all.

Admit You Have a Problem
The first, and possibly the hardest, step to recovery from a problem is admitting you have one. The fact that you are reading this suggests you are looking for a way to improve the usability of the web sites you're working on, which is pretty much the same as admitting you have problem.

It's a problem we all share—designers, programmers, and engineers alike. How do you balance your desire to create the best, most beautiful, coolest, cleverest Flash movie with the needs of the person who will ultimately be using the web site it's on? Your heart is all for producing an award-winning stroke of genius, and your creative juices are urging you to push the boundaries of design so that your peers will just bow their heads in awe when they see your work. At the back of your mind, however, a small voice is telling you there's more to it than that: Someone has to use this site. And that someone, not the people you want so dearly to impress, is who you're ultimately working for.

The great thing is that usable design doesn't need to be boring. You can flex your creative muscles just as effectively—or maybe even more so—to produce a solution that is usable *and* cool. That's the wonderful thing about Flash: It's the perfect tool for creating beautiful and effective interfaces. One goal of this book is to inspire you to produce work that excels in both areas.

Now What?

So, if you're admitting there may be a problem, you're already half way to solving it. Just being conscious of the ease with which the end users will get around your site will put you in the right frame of mind to create a product with great usability. Keep the focus on the aims of the user while you pull in all the design features you love.

Later in this book, you'll learn about some features you can create in Flash that epitomize the beauty of this program: They are not only cool, they also can dramatically improve a user's experience on a web site. As you walk through the creation of these features, you'll find that designing with the end user in mind becomes second nature.

> **(dm)**
>
> Think of it like automotive design. If you want to pander to your ego, you might want to design the new Lamborghini. If you want to design a car that will provide the best service for the most number of people, however, you'll probably find that applying your skills to creating the next Honda Accord will be much more gratifying, if less glamorous.
>
> **Author Note: Duncan**

A Little Bit of History

Why is there so much bad usability and interface design on the web and in Flash? It's hard to know where to start! There are so many reasons, but, of course, no excuses.

The rapid growth of the web hasn't helped. One minute it was a haven for computer geeks, college students, research scientists, and the military. The next minute it had become the best place to buy the latest Harry Potter book. Unfortunately, much of the style and design established in the early days, when the web was created by and for techies, has filtered through into today's Internet.

The development of the Flash designer mirrors that of Flash itself. In its first incarnations, Flash was a simplistic tool designed to create better, faster, simpler alternatives to GIF animations. Even through the development of Flash 4, it was still a relatively primitive tool. Understandably, designers used it as such, but the temptation to play was so great that many succumbed to building Flash animations and putting them on web sites—not because they were necessary, but just because they could. In its latest incarnations, Flash has so many cool features it seems like a crime not to use at least some of them on a site, even if they're not strictly necessary.

Clients share the responsibility for promoting some of the more egotistical examples of Flash on the web. Web site owners pay designers to produce cool Flash "riffs" because they believe that's what their users want.

Now that the Internet balloon has deflated somewhat, site owners have begun to look at what works and what doesn't work. They're realizing that sites with a user-focused design have a much better chance of attracting, satisfying, and hanging on to visitors. News and information-rich sites were probably the first to really crack this by going back to old rules of usability derived from print media. No Flash was needed.

> **(mc)**
>
> Staying with the automotive metaphor, it's like the concept cars you see at motor shows: They look incredible, but in reality most of them can be completely impractical. From those outrageous machines, however, designers will filch little tricks, techniques, and ideas that they will apply extremely effectively to cars designed for the real world. It's how they get ahead of the competition.
>
> Flash is just like that. Keep trying to push the envelope: Within those mind-blowing but essentially purposeless showcase pieces, you might discover the technique you need to lift your real-world Flash work to the next level.
>
> **Author Note: Michelangelo**

Or was it? Some of the most successful online media sites use Flash extensively, but discretely. Flash is turning out to be the perfect tool for interactive graphics, maps, and navigation devices. There are no spinning logos or extended intro movies, but Flash is right there, making those sites more useful—and more usable.

Identifying Bad Design

If you want to really understand and address the problem of bad usability design, start by learning how to spot it. That's not necessarily a simple task because so many factors could be involved. It creeps up on us slowly and stealthily, and we often don't notice it until it's too late. You can, however, keep an eye out for it, and during a few key stages in the development process you can find it and stop it from spreading.

Don't Design for Design's Sake Have you ever started a project wanting to use some great new design you've been working on or some awesome new code you threw together? Watch out! This is one of the prime sources of bad usability design. You probably want to push the envelope and show the world what the possibilities are; but as an interface designer, your first task, your first thought,

> **(dm)**
>
> We have borrowed the "persona" concept from the usability expert Alan Cooper, who uses the concept to great effect in his book *The Inmates Are Running the Asylum*. Cooper argues that by giving your target audience a name, a job, a lifestyle—an identity—you can begin to empathize with them. They are no longer a mere statistic; they're more like a friend. You can ask them questions, imagine their needs more clearly, and, in the end, design a better experience for them.
>
> **Author Note: Duncan**

should be to satisfy the needs of the target users so they can have the best experience possible.

Approach the design with the user in mind. We're not talking about just keeping a rough idea of the target audience in the back of your mind. User-centered design involves getting into the heads of your potential users and developing character studies, or personas, that closely represent your users. After you have that, you can then start to make design decisions based on what your chosen persona needs or doesn't need.

As tools such as Flash become easier to use and more powerful, less time is spent developing on paper. It is still worth taking the time to do paper "wire frames" of your interfaces, however, and to develop tests for target users to go through. Removing the computer from the process can be a highly effective way to trap usability cracks in your project without investing hours in developing that Flash interface… in Flash.

mc

I once worked on the design of a user interface that had one-click access to everything, much like a web browser. We would use it and click the buttons and links and click to open items in a list. It worked great. Then we held some user tests and found that the majority of users wanted to double-click everything. Everything! We were so convinced that the single-click approach was the way to go, but the audience we were dealing with wanted double-clicking. So we had to put aside our design egos and adjust the interface so that it worked better with double-clicking.

Author Note: Michelangelo

Constantly Challenge the Usability of the Design Another point where you can catch bad usability is in the production process. Test yourself along the way: "Is this a site Nancy can use?" "Does it help Judy fulfill her goals on the site?"

As you design more projects with the user in mind, you will start to develop a treasure chest of usability rules—general things that will apply to almost every project. These include seemingly obvious but often overlooked points, such as making the type readable or keeping clickable areas large and easy to spot.

Many usability experts perform something called "heuristic" evaluations. They go through the design for an interface and, using a similar treasure chest of usability rules, they can make a determination about the usability of the interface and things that can be done to make it more usable. (For more detail on heuristic evaluation, see Appendix A, "What Every Interface Designer Should Know.")

mc

When evaluating interfaces using your accumulated store of usability rules, don't be too strict. If you've done your homework and made sure that your target audience is comfortable with a new design or tool—and you're certain the users' experience will be enhanced by it—it may be fine to bend the rules.

A lot of usability is based on the notion of intuitiveness for the end user. For something to be intuitive, it may need to be familiar to the user (the menus described later in this book, for example). It doesn't mean you shouldn't design new controls, however. If a new type of control will improve the user's experience, use it.

Author Note: Michelangelo

Test Early, Test Often Testing is one of the best ways to spot bad usability in a design. Try to test with real users. For some projects you may have to go all the way and hire a usability company to carry out formal testing. For others, you might find testing it with selected friends or coworkers is enough to put your interface through its paces. The key is to make sure your testing is effective and appropriate.

BRAINS VERSUS BEAUTY

Good interface design for usability is not about aesthetics alone, nor is it about functionality alone: It's about both working in harmony. You need to look at how the site's aesthetics work for the target persona. It means the usability may completely define the visual design process.

To design effectively for the user, you need to make user-centered design a habit. Instead of beginning an interface design project with a challenge to build the coolest site on the web, make your challenge to design a site with the best experience for its target market.

> Poor usability design stems from a flaw in the design process in general. Mostly, the visual design process starts as soon as you know what look or feel the client wants. If you're designing for usability, however, the visual design should be created for the same personas as the interaction design. The designer should begin by taking into account the target audience's needs and the client's needs, and then develop personas that accurately represent the target audience and the union of these needs. Only after this has been settled can the visual design process really start to take shape as it follows the lead set by the interaction design.
>
> **Author Note: Michelangelo**

Keep Things Simple

When working on the interaction or visual design for your interface, remember to keep things simple. All too often designers want to add tons of little details, but these may distract users from their goal. If an area of your design is feeling difficult and it's becoming hard to determine the user's path through the site, tear things down and simplify the design. This is one of the areas where keeping control of your ego is highly effective.

Establishing the usability guidelines for a particular project can be extremely tricky. If you break it down so that you think of the different people involved in the project, it can help you get a clearer idea of the task you are trying to complete.

Know Your Client

Sometimes, clients aren't exactly sure what they want, or more importantly, what their target audience wants. Your first step should be to get a clear handle on what the client wants the project to do for the end user. Help your client to understand the need to narrow the focus to the actual target user for the site, and then focus the design on that user.

This not only helps you maintain focus when designing, it also helps the client understand what they are trying to achieve.

Know Your Users

This is really the biggie. Taking what you know about the client's goals, you must clearly identify the target audience for the site. This should be a pretty detailed specification. From this description, you will start to develop your character studies, or personas.

Use the personas you've developed to create scenarios for how these different personas will use the site. You will find that as you start to work out several different scenarios, certain ones become more probable than others; these are the scenarios that you want to make the first priority in the design of your interface. Similarly, the least common scenarios should represent features that are of lowest priority and shouldn't get up-front billing in your interface. The more scenarios you work out, the better.

Although personas offer a lot of the answers to the usability questions when designing your interface, you'll want to have real people you can call on to answer the other questions. A parent, an old high-school buddy, maybe a person from a discussion group you visit online: Find people who can give you intelligent feedback on your design. Try to ensure these people are similar to the target audience for your project.

> **mc**
>
> I love developing personas at the beginning of a project. There comes a time when you just know you've got a persona that could really exist. It's really up to the design team to decide how detailed the persona needs to be, but make sure the character study covers all the intricacies you'll be basing your interaction modeling on. And after you have created your personas, keep them around in case you need them for other projects.
>
> **Author Note: Michelangelo**

> **mc**
>
> Genevieve Bell, an ethnographer, was once working with a group of designers building an e-commerce site. The designers were trying to make the shopping experience on the site as quick as possible because, in their minds, people don't like to spend much time shopping. The team was surprised when Genevieve revealed to them that there are people who love to spend long hours shopping. Not all people shop the same way: There are some stores where you may spend more time perusing the selection and trying things on. At other stores, the faster you can zip in and out the better.
>
> It's a perfect example to show that you're looking to create an experience that is not necessarily faster or easier, but better for your intended audience.
>
> **Author Note: Michelangelo**

Know Your Market

The study of ethnography, or descriptive anthropology, is becoming more and more useful to the technology industry every day. This study of human cultures and societies focuses on finding out why a culture is the way it is—how the mailbox icon makes a lot of sense in the United States, but that same icon in India is lost on users because they don't use those types of mailboxes; how colors mean different things to different cultures. All these things can play a role in interaction design.

Details such as these help to bring you closer to the people for whom you are designing, and they can make the difference between an uncomfortable experience and a good and memorable one for the end user.

Know Your Goals

Now you know your client's goals and the goals of the client's target users, it's time to identify your own goals. Easy! Your main goal should be to make sure the client's and the target audience's goals are met to the highest possible degree.

Well, it sounds easy, but achieving it may be trickier. Take a bit of time to make sure the goals of the client and the users are compatible; you may need to do some rethinking at this stage. When you're sure about the final goal for your personas, you should have a clear target when designing your interface. Your goal should then be to design an interface that any one of your personas can use efficiently. Make sure you design for the persona, not the 70 percent of the web users who won't stick around on the site. This takes a surprising amount of discipline, and it will require you to really get to know your audience.

At this point you also can begin to compose the visual language of the interface. Develop a palette of colors and stylistic elements based on the tastes of the personas. Remember, you may have some whiz-bang new widget you've invented and really want to use, but the user needs to come first. If the whiz-bang little doodad helps the end-user experience, great! If not, don't use it.

Know Your Tools

Remember, not every situation will need the features of Flash. Be aware of the pros and cons to the different options you have for developing your user interface and how each one relates to what the users want. You may have had Flash in mind from the very beginning and it may well be the right choice, but before jumping in make sure it really is the correct choice.

Thankfully, the science of web site usability has progressed rapidly in recent years; there are plenty of sources of advice around. Some rules, skillfully applied, will help you design your Flash projects for usability. Remember, however, you get to choose which rules you use. You want to break them? Go ahead, as long as you are certain you're doing it for the right reasons.

Know the Rules

Many rules and mathematical formulas can be used to study usability and human-computer interaction, so many that it would take an entire book just to look at them. Many of these rules were developed for different software programs or other user experiences, but they can be applied equally well to user interaction design in Flash. Check out some of the references in Appendix B, "Usability Resources," for sites that cover usability rules. Don't apply rules slavishly, however. If a rule works to improve the user experience, apply it. If not, don't!

With a clear knowledge of your client, the user, the tools available, and the rules of usability, you're pretty much set to create an awesome user interface. The last element is… you.

Know Thyself

No, this isn't some induction into Plato's *Academy*, but it's very important to understand your own personality type. Are you obsessive or do you like to speed through a project? Are you detail-oriented or a big picture person? Once you know yourself, you'll be able to watch out for, and compensate for, your own weaknesses.

You might want to be on the lookout for a few of the following key traits:

- **Laziness.** A key contributor to bad user interfaces. Plenty of designers cut corners, breeze through planning, or fail to take those few extra steps to polish off an interface.

- **Focusing on the big picture.** If you're a big picture person, slow down while working on individual pieces. Take a step closer toward that piece and see how it really works. If everything looks fine to you, stop and pass it along to a coworker, colleague, or peer and have them check it out. Don't be afraid to give up parts of the project that you know you won't enjoy doing or to find someone with whom you can work who compliments your disposition.

- **Obsessing over the details.** This is just as dangerous as ignoring the minutia for the big picture. You can have the most thought-out button widget around, but if the user path through the web site is broken or branches too many times, a clever button probably won't help much. Try to step back from what you're working on and see how each piece of the puzzle must integrate with the others. Or find a partner who balances your skills.

That's about it for the rules, knowledge, focus, and background. Before you launch into designing for usability, however, there is just one last thing to remember: It's not about faster or easier, it's about better!

(dm)

In Chapter 6, "Less Cluttered and More Usable," you'll read about how much difference a little attention to detail can make. At one point, we write about dragging an object around the stage. It's a fairly simple operation that could be handled easily in two lines of code, using Flash's built-in `startDrag()` and `stopDrag()`. But Flash's built-in methods are inefficient and create some very noticeable lag between the cursor and the object being dragged. Most users may not notice it or may blame it on their own computer. We know better: With a little extra effort, namely writing 10 lines of code rather than two, we can create a much better, cleaner, smoother user experience.

You'll also be looking at the bigger picture. Every chapter works off a persona that was developed specifically for the sample site. These personas are used to design the interaction and visuals for the site and help identify the potential user's goals.

Taking a big picture approach married with attention to detail helps ensure an effective and enjoyable experience for the end user.

Author Note: Duncan

IT'S NOT ABOUT FASTER OR EASIER, IT'S ABOUT BETTER

It may seem as if all we've talked about so far is making your sites faster and easier. Most of the time that's exactly what we're about. However, those concepts are two crucial parts of a bigger concept: making your sites better.

There are two principal routes to San Francisco from Southern California by car. You can take Route 5, up over the Grapevine and on through Oakland and Berkeley. It's about 400-odd miles, not particularly attractive, and takes about 6 to 8 hours to complete the journey. The other option is to take the Pacific Coast Highway (PCH), which takes you along the Pacific coast and offers wonderful ocean views on the way. On a good day it takes about 10 hours to complete the journey. Objectively, you could make no argument that PCH was more efficient. Even if you were to throw in intangibles such as traffic, PCH will never be as efficient as Route 5. Yet droves people choose PCH. Why? Simple. For some, the journey is part of the experience. They'll be stopping along the way in San Louis Obispo, or Santa Barbara, idling in some small seaside cafe, or just pulling off the highway to play in the surf. None of this can be measured by any laws of efficiency, nor should it even be attempted.

This example shows that "better" is intangible, personal, and more nebulous than any other concept you have to deal with as a Flash designer. However, it's the core of the whole experience. Once you know your users and their goals and your client and their aims, you'll have an idea about whether you should be offering them a fast and direct experience or taking them on the scenic route.

CHAPTER 02
Basic Training

1. Out of clutter, find simplicity.
2. From discord, find harmony.
3. In the middle of difficulty lies opportunity.

—Albert Einstein

Now that you have had an introduction to the theory and philosophy of user interface design for usability, it's time to move on to actually implementing those concepts in a Flash environment. To make sure we're all speaking the same "dialect" of Flash, the following section gives you an overview of how we will be developing the projects found in the remainder of this book.

You're probably sick of hearing this by now, but the preceding section on user interface design and usability is only an introduction to the concept. We strongly recommend that you read Appendix B, "Usability Resources," for a list of books whose sole purpose is to explain usability and interface design. There's some great stuff out there!

Author Note: Michelangelo

THE FLASH ENVIRONMENT

When working in the Flash environment, you should organize your files consistently and logically. We use the following conventions throughout the book:

All files are labeled **chapterNumber_topicCovered.fla**, as in **04_loader.fla**.

In each file, elements are separated into their own individual layers, and each layer is given a descriptive label. This not only helps during production by enabling you to lock and hide individual elements, but also in debugging. As you'll see later, it is much easier to identify and locate the Scroll Button layer than it is to locate Layer 4.

Figure 2.1
An example of a Flash file saved with the naming convention of this book.

We also create two layers for nothing more than frame labels and ActionScript. In cases where you will have many key frames of ActionScript, you might want a separate layer for global functions and one for frame scripts. It's also a good idea to include a Notes layer where you can write information for yourself or subsequent developers. When you come across these Notes layers, make sure to take a quick peek at them; they will give you any details about the file the developer really wants to know about .

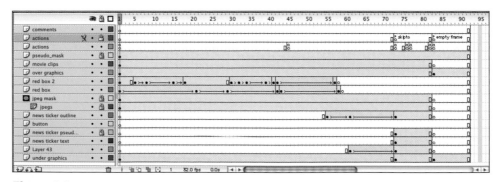

Figure 2.2
This figure shows an extreme use of layers, with two Actions layers, a Notes layer, and a Frame Label layer.

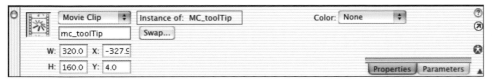

Figure 2.3
Notice that the movie clip symbol name and the instance name are nearly identical, the only difference being the use of lowercase letters with the instance name and the mc_ prefix.

By synchronizing the movie clip's symbol name and its instance name on the stage, we make building the project a much smoother process—we create a cognitive link between the visual appearance of the movie clip, its library name, and its instance name.

THE CODING ENVIRONMENT
Flash MX enables you to write code in two ways: Normal mode or Expert mode. Normal mode emulates the Flash 4 method of coding and offers novice programmers the ability to create less complex code through a simple point-and-click interface. However, it's nowhere near powerful enough to accomplish the goals of the code in this book. All the chapters in this book are written with the assumption that you're using Expert mode. If you aren't set up in Expert Mode you can change to it now by opening the ActionScript Editor and pressing Cmd-Shift-E/Ctrl-Shift-E .

You do have the option of switching between Normal and Expert mode on a case-by-case basis. Just click in the ActionScript Editor window and click the arrow in the upper-right corner and select Normal mode or Expert mode (Cmd-Shift-N and Cmd-Shift-E/Ctrl-Shift-N and Ctrl-Shift-E).

In addition to using the Expert mode in ActionScript, the code throughout the book is written in a style derived very loosely from Hungarian Notation. Hungarian Notation is a way of writing code that makes things easier to read, is more compact than other coding styles, and has

Don't forget that the ActionScript Editor is context-sensitive! If you click a frame in the timeline, you will be entering code for *that* frame. If you click a button, you will be entering code for *that* button. If you click a movie clip, you will be entering code for *that* movie clip. The ActionScript Editor does not give you much feedback in this area, so please be aware.

One habit you should definitely develop is checking the title bar of the ActionScript panel before you are about to enter any new code. This title bar changes from Object Actions to Frame Actions depending on what you have selected, so you can save yourself a ton of time by making sure you're not writing it into the wrong mode. For the most part, existing code in the panel will help you to figure out the other items you might have selected, but it's still always good to make sure you have the right mode selected. Just click the object or frame, check the title bar, and start coding.

C A U T I O N

Figure 2.4
To switch between Expert and Normal mode, use the menu in the ActionScript panel.

become a common standard among ActionScript and JavaScript programmers. If you have been working with ActionScript or JavaScript, this notation system should already be familiar to you.

The following list is a reference guide to our take on Hungarian Notation. For the most part, variables and functions are named using lowercase letters, denoting separate words with a capital letter. You can use your own variation of this style; just remember to keep it consistent throughout your project so that other developers who might need to look at your code can easily find their way around. (See Figure 2.5.)

- **normalVariables.** Normal variables should be written using lowercase letters, with words separated by capitalizing the first letter of the next word.

- **gGlobalVariables.** Global variables follow the same convention as normal variables, but are preceded by a lowercase *g* to indicate they're global. This means the variable is used throughout the movie or movie clip, by other functions and code, and perhaps even changed by that code. Therefore, any change that happens is "global" and affects other code that uses this variable.

- **CONSTANT_VARIABLES.** These variables are set once in the life of your movie or movie clip and should not be changed by other code in the movie or movie clip. These are written using ALL_CAPS with words separated by underscores (_).

- **mc_movieClips.** References to movie clips always start with a lowercase *mc_*. This is done to help differentiate between references to objects and references to movie clips in your code.

- **fieldVariableText.** Text box variables—variables referenced by dynamic or input text boxes—are named by their movie clip instance name (without the *mc_*) and the word *Text*.

When you create a dynamic or input text field in Flash and you give it a variable name, the field will display the contents of that variable. These are the same as any other variables we have created in our ActionScript code. To differentiate variables that are being used in text fields and other variables, we add *Text* to the end of the variable name. This makes it easy to know when reading through the code that a change to a variable will display in a field on the stage.

Author Note: Michelangelo

By the way, don't be bashful with the white space. White space is the blank area in your code that can help you to separate related parts of code and can generally make things easier to read.

Another important aspect you will want to address when dealing with code in Flash is the speed at which your code executes. Because a great deal of our code will run either in frame loops or on `enterFrame` clip

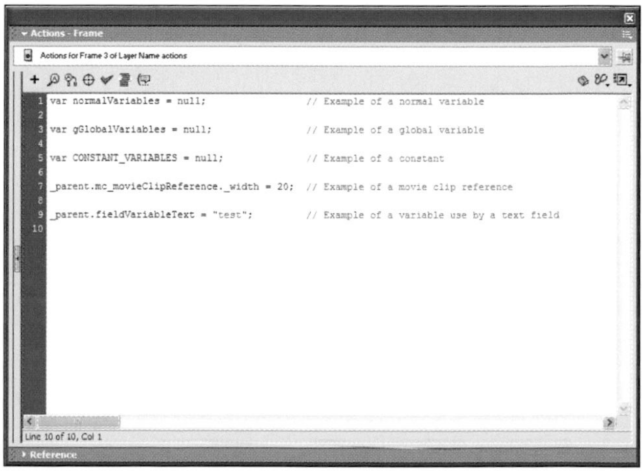

Figure 2.5
What our coding conventions look like in the ActionScript panel.

events, their execution time depends on the Frames Per Second (fps) setting of the movie. The default fps setting for a new movie in Flash is 12fps. This means that the code in a frame loop will execute 12 times every second. This really isn't fast enough for all operations, so, while the debate rages on as to what is the best catch-all setting for your Flash movies, we will be setting all of our projects to 20fps.

There are plenty of other rules or suggestions for *how* you code; but it really comes down to legibility and what you as the developer are comfortable with. The only other vitally important aspect to coding is commenting. Comment the heck out of your files, explaining what you did and why you did it. This can be especially helpful if you're taking a break and coming back to figure out what you were trying to accomplish with your code the previous night. You've probably read that in every programming book you've ever bought, but it's true and bears repeating. Comment your files. You'll be glad you did!

By using Expert mode and adhering to the notation system described earlier, you can avoid many of the common sources of bugs in your code. If you do happen to run into errors while working, take a look at the next section, which covers some of the basics of debugging.

COMMON MISTAKES, DEBUGGING, OR WHAT TO DO WHEN CODE *DOESN'T* WORK

First, don't panic! Code errors happen to every programmer, all the time, every day.

Debugging is a fairly in-depth concept and we don't have the space to cover it in any great detail, but we will look at a few of the most common sources of errors that you're likely to encounter while working through the book.

The most common bug is one of syntax—a missing comma, a misspelled word, an unclosed bracket. It's the silly little things that slip through the cracks while we code. Unfortunately computers aren't particularly smart. Although you could interpret a sentence missing a few key words, a computer will come to a grinding halt or produce an unexpected result if you forget to put a semicolon in the right place. You have to make up for this lack of sophistication by combing through your code looking for the error. Syntactical errors are very easy to fix and are the ones you will run into most. The only sure way to find these kinds of errors is to read through your code carefully.

A tougher bug to deal with is the error in logic. Logic errors are actual mistakes in the code (for instance, checking for a variable that hasn't been set). If the following code were in frame 1 of your movie, it simply wouldn't work:

```
gotoAndPlay(myVariable);
```

Because you haven't set the **myVariable** yet, the code won't work. What's worse is that although Flash will tell you when you may have a syntax error (this will show up in the Output window), Flash may give you no clues when you have a logic error. Logic gaps can be much more difficult to isolate because they often won't break the code, but just return an unexpected result. Rest assured: We've tested all the code in this book thoroughly and found it clean.

To help prevent, identify, and eliminate bugs, here are a handful of useful coding tips:

> Colin Moock's exhaustive *ActionScript: The Definitive Guide* includes an excellent chapter on debugging in the Flash environment. Pick it up; it's one of our favorite programming books!
>
> **Note**

- **Format your code consistently.** You don't have to format your code the way we do in this book, but you should use a legible and logical way of writing your code. All too often we have seen novice users program with no line breaks and all the code left justified, making it nearly impossible to read. Tabbing your code in properly and leaving white space around different areas of your code will help you to track down syntax errors and make your code more readable overall.

- **Trace your steps.** The Output window is an excellent helper in tracking down syntax errors, logic bugs, and anything else lurking in that big pile of code that took you three hours to write. Just throw in `trace()` calls around the area of code you think is problematic and watch the Output window when you test your movie.

- **Test often.** We can't emphasize this enough. Don't sit down and write 100 lines of code at a stretch. Break the process down into smaller, more manageable chunks and test often. You'll find this actually makes your code better, as well, because you will be making more modular code as a result.

- **Rewrite your code.** Honestly it's often much, much easier and faster to stop where you're at and start again. Unlike computers, we have this amazing ability to "fix" mistakes in our minds. Looking for a missing quotation mark in several dozen lines of code can be an exercise in futility. Rewriting the code will not only keep you a bit more focused, reducing the possibility of mistakes, but also will help you better understand the code.

- **Ask a friend.** Our technical editor and all around great guy, Chris MacGregor, had a really cool demonstration at a recent conference. He asked us to take out a business card and exchange it with someone in the audience we didn't know. He then said, "Now you have someone who can do usability testing for you." The same concept can be applied to code; it doesn't have to be a stranger, it can be your cubicle mate or your friend still at school. Have someone take a look at the code. Because they're not so close to it, they might be able to zero in on your problem straight away. They also might be able to point out where your code could be improved. Also, you'll find user groups and online forums are really helpful. The people you meet through these channels are great to keep in touch with. You can check out Macromedia's user groups at www.macromedia.com/support/programs/usergroups/.

- **Go online.** There must be hundreds of really great resources for Flash and ActionScript online. We have an amazing community of developers, unlike any other we've encountered. People are really happy to help with problems and share code, tips, and techniques. Take advantage of this (and give back!). You can find a list of some of our favorite online resources in Appendix C, "Flash and Design Resources."

- **Read the manual.** Shocking idea we know, but the ActionScript Dictionary is very helpful and may point out flaws in your logic.

- **Look at your Output window.** It's there for a reason! It might look a little bit scary at first, but if you take it one step at a time, the Output window is easy to read and is a very powerful tool. Also shown in Figure 2.6, the following is an actual error we received while developing the Tool Tips module (see Chapter 13, "Tooltips—Know Before You Go"):

```
Scene=Scene 1, Layer=button, Frame=1: Line 3: '{' expected
    on(rollOut)_level0.toolTip.hideMessage();}
```

Examine it one step at a time. The first few lines of the error message tell you where the error is located. In this case the error is in Scene 1, on the layer labeled button, in Frame 1 and on Line 3 of the code. After telling you where the problem is, the Output window tells you what the problem is. Here an open curly brace is missing ({). Flash also tells you where it's missing—in this case, before _level0.toolTip.hideMessage();.

With this information and looking at the code, can you see how to fix the problem?

```
on(rollOut)
  _level0.toolTip.hideMessage();
}
```

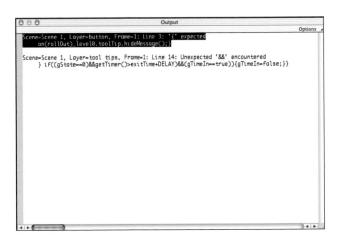

Figure 2.6
An actual glitch in the code for the Tool Tips module found while developing this book.

The Output window can get very cluttered very quickly, even if there's only one mistake in your code. The problem is, code can be like dominoes: If you knock one over, the rest will follow. So if your Output window looks like you have hundreds of bugs, scroll to the very first bug and fix that first. Often when you fix that, the rest of your "bugs" will disappear.

Tip

If you said, "Place a open curly brace ({) after `on(rollOut)`," you're absolutely correct.

■ **Take a break.** When all else fails, probably the best thing you can do is take a break away from the computer and think the problem over in your mind. This often leads to the best solution to the problem, because your mind has time to relax a bit and ponder. Most of our best ideas come out of thinking about trying to solve other problems in our mind. It's funny, but it works.

Keep a pencil and notepad or sketchbook by the side of your bed; you won't believe the number of solutions you come up with at 4 a.m. If you don't write it down immediately, you might spend half the next day just trying to remember what you figured out the night before.

Tip

Keep these points in mind while progressing through this book. If you encounter a problem, come back here and go through these steps to make sure you've examined all the possibilities. If it still doesn't work, take a day off. Heck, take a couple of days off! Put the code out of your mind for a while and work on something else; when you come back, you might find that the solution to your problem has formulated in the back of your mind, and what had you stumped for two hours is now fixable in two minutes!

dm

If you're a designer and just getting into code, you might find yourself getting frustrated with the limitations and rules that you must abide by. Don't be! With a slight change in perspective, I think you will actually begin to enjoy the boundaries that coding forces you to work within.

In design there is no real right or wrong. So often it's intangible: "It feels right," or "It doesn't work for some reason." It's quite funny when you think about it. How many times have you sat in front of your monitor changing the width of a rule from one size to another, over and over again for hours trying to get it to "feel" right? Probably more times than you care to recall.

Now with code, all of a sudden you have something that is either correct, and your code works, or incorrect, and the code does not work—how refreshing. Not only that, but with Flash it will actually tell you what's wrong.

Author Note: Duncan

HOW WE BUILD OUR PROJECTS
Whereas most books that delve into code take you systematically through the entire block of code, we don't. Why? Because no one codes that way. (Well, maybe Branden Hall does!) Most of the code in this book ranges from several dozen to several hundred lines of code, and no one sits down and bangs out that much code in one fell swoop. For us and many other designers, coding is very much an iterative process. We type a few lines, test the movie to make sure it works, and if it doesn't, we go back, look for mistakes, and fix them. If it does work, we go back, add a few more lines of code, and repeat the process. Although we cannot take you through the entire gestation of the code, we have labored to make it a process much closer to how you would design in the real world. In fact, you'll probably notice that sometimes we go

mc

Sometimes I find that "composing at the keyboard" doesn't work. You might find it difficult to get exactly what you want out of code when you just sit down and start typing away in the ActionScript Editor. Often what I do is sketch some initial ideas out in my sketchbook or on a white board to try and get a picture of how I see the code working. I try to think through it logically and break it down into little groups so that I can visually see how it all works. I even write some of the code out if it comes to me. This approach gives me a clearer target when I'm sitting down to finally write the code in Flash, and I usually end up with something that works a lot better logically.

Author Note: Michelangelo

back and revise code we may have written a few pages earlier. It might take some getting used to, but we think that it's not only more natural, but will also reduce the number of mistakes you make and the time spent looking for them.

OTHER PEOPLE'S CODE   Many times you'll be working with code that looks like a completely different language from the ActionScript with which you're familiar. It might have been written by a coworker or colleague, or perhaps you found it on one of the Flash sites mentioned in Appendix C of this book. Don't be scared! Even if you're just getting started with ActionScript, you can break down complex lines of code by taking some time and "translating" it into English. Step through each line of code, word by word, function by function, with the goal of understanding in plain English what the code is trying to do. This is a great technique that coders at all levels use and it really helps you to learn, as well.

MAC OR PC?   Ah, the eternal question. There must be more flame wars on the Internet between Mac and PC people than on almost any other topic. Nevertheless we decided at the beginning of the process to write code and concepts that were entirely cross-platform. Everything you see in this book will work just as well on Windows as it will on the MacOS (even OSX; we've tried it!). Half the screen shots are Mac-based, half are Windows-based, so hopefully that should keep you all happy.

CONCLUSION   Okay, the boring stuff is out of the way. Don't forget, we went easy on you. We could spend literally hundreds of pages on each of these topics, but there are countless books out there that cover them in depth. We've already mentioned a few, but if you want more, go to www.skip-intro.org, where you'll find some other recommendations.

And now, if you're ready, it's time to roll up your sleeves, get down in the trenches with ActionScript, and prepare to make your projects more usable!

SECTION I
Höpart Bothur Exhibit Site

Computers are useless. They can only give you answers.

—Pablo Picasso

CHAPTER 03
Overview—A Comfortable Situation

If you want to achieve a product satisfaction level of 50%, you cannot do it by making a large population 50% happy with your product. You can only accomplish it by singling out the 50% of the people, and striving to make them 100% happy.

—Alan Cooper
(The Inmates are Running the Asylum)

Figure 3.1
The MODA web site.

Have you ever found yourself lost on a Flash web site? Or discovered that you had no idea what you needed to do to get to what you wanted? Sure, some music kept you amused; but after you had waited several minutes for the site to download, all you found was a confusing and uncomfortable situation.

If this sounds familiar, you're certainly not alone. What site designers often don't seem to realize is that the consequence of not having comfortable users is not having users. Whenever users think their goal is unattainable, or find themselves waiting but not knowing why, they'll probably leave the site.

Luckily, you can do a few things to hang onto those users. For a start, offer feedback about what's happening (if they are being made to wait for a download). Remember, in Flash you have the luxury of being able to control the situation, even while files are still downloading.

Simplify the site to make the goal clearer and easier to achieve. This doesn't mean removing all the neat features you have in mind for your site: It does mean including only the features that enhance the user's experience. The simpler you can make the structure of the information, the clearer the user's path to his goals on the site. Making that path clear means you have created a solid, comfortable setting for the user.

Clarifying the information may mean simplifying the way the user controls the information. Fancy, multistate buttons with animated rollovers and playful click states are great, but make sure they are appropriate for the audience and appropriate for the content. If the goal of the site is to display artwork, the last thing you want to do is steal the show with your super click-and-drag concept button. Design the controls to make it easy for the user to navigate the information on the site, not to show off your own talents. Flash is great at enabling you to create smooth, organic controls that offer logical feedback. Use this capability to inject some smoothness into your user interface and you'll be well on the way to making the user's experience full, rich, and, above all, comfortable.

In this chapter, you study the case of a web site for a museum exhibit. Specifically, you will see how to create custom cursors with intelligent feedback, contextual or mouse-based menus, smart and informative preloaders, and a gestural scrolling interface element. The aim is to keep the user informed about what's going on and to provide a simple structure for the site that enables your users to reach their goals easily.

Don't forget that even though you'll be focusing on a specific market and target audience, the concepts and methods discussed in this section can be applied to *every* project you work on. This doesn't mean each particular detail of one solution is an appropriate solution for every Flash project, but the methodology used to arrive at that particular solution should be the same. Anything that does not support the user's goal for the site may not be appropriate for your project.

Note

Now take a look at the case study and find out more about the client's goals, the user's goals, and the issues you will need to resolve to make the user's experience comfortable.

CASE STUDY: THE DIGITAL MUSEUM

The Museum of Digital Art is showcasing a new 15-piece collection of work in a special section of its web site. One of the museum directors' primary concerns is to make the downloading of the images less apparent. Previous online exhibits forced users who wanted to see a particular piece to wait while the entire collection downloaded. Analysis of site traffic showed users were not prepared to wait, particularly because they were unable to view or do anything until the download completed.

Navigating the collection was another issue. The museum wanted users to have a rich experience. Visitors could view information on each art piece, and they could have the artwork categorized by style,

Figure 3.2
Nancy works all day at a pretty stressful job, so when she visits the MODA web site, she wants her experience to be easy and comfortable.

date, or artist, depending on the type of exhibit. The client also provides an introduction page and a general information category that describes the collection as a whole. This information may have been interesting, but it was scattered and potentially confusing. The site traffic reflected this, being heaviest in the areas with the actual artwork. The museum realized that many users don't take the time to download and read the other sections of the collection. Many users also complained that the navigation was too complex: They would just read about the artwork and look at the images rather than click through the several levels of categorization to get to an image.

The client's main aim is to encourage site visitors to sign up as members of the online museum. Members pay an annual fee that allows them access to special areas of the site, as well as giving them free admission to many digital art events. The client feels that if the online exhibits are easy to navigate and offer good exposure for the artwork by way of a positive user experience, then users are more likely to want to become members.

The main goal of the site's users is just to see the artwork and learn more about it. With this in mind, the user experience should be tailored in an effort to maximize the users' success in achieving this goal.

According to the client, the site's primary target audience will be museum members who will learn about new exhibits through the museum's monthly email newsletter. The museum believes a large number of members follow the links to the site, because there is a spike in traffic after the newsletter is sent out. For these users, the navigation should be simple and easy to understand. Taking into account the issues the client relayed, the site should also be responsive with a minimum of click-and-wait. These users should be aware of what's happening on the site, and there should be no occasion when these users are waiting for a download without knowing why.

The secondary target audience will be occasional visitors to the site. These user experiences should be simple and allow them to achieve their goal efficiently. The better the experience this group has, the more likely they are to sign up as members. This group also will include first-time visitors, so the navigation in the exhibit area should be very straightforward and offer enough feedback to make it easy to learn.

The museum also reports that there will soon be more Flash areas on the site. These include exhibit announcements and collection histories. Further examination of web server logs shows people seem to want to wait less for these richer parts of the site than they do for the static HTML pages.

> **(?)** If you haven't read "Know Yor User" in Chapter 1, "Bad Flashers Anonymous," you might want to do so now. That section explains in detail what personas are and why they are used.
>
> **Note**

With an initial grasp of the client's needs, the next step is to develop a persona for the target users, including all their specific likes and dislikes, to help tailor an experience that is right for them.

Character Profile

Name: Nancy Roberts

Age: 35

Occupation: Marketing Director

Nancy works for an ad agency that specializes in developing campaigns for fast-food chains. She is married with two children (aged 5 and 11). She and her family live in a 4-bedroom home in the suburbs outside the city where she works.

Back in 1990, right after graduating, Nancy was one of the first people in her new job to initiate the transition to a digital workplace. She convinced her boss to outfit the Marketing department with Apple Macintosh computers, like the ones she used in college. Nancy even volunteered to help train her colleagues. Since that time, Nancy has moved through the ranks of the company, eventually being named Marketing Director last year. She loves the city she lives in, partly because of the fantastic art scene, which she regularly checks out with her husband during the city's "Art Walk" night on the first of every month. They both share an interest in digital art and, when they can, visit The Museum of Digital Art (MODA) in the city.

With her promotion to Marketing Director, Nancy joined the museum as a "President's level" member. She really enjoys the special perks of membership, including the member's section of the site. With her new promotion and two grade-school children, Nancy doesn't always have the chance to make it down to MODA for every show and enjoys at least being able to see the show on the web at home.

Even at home, however, Nancy is still busy; so she does not enjoy waiting for the pages to download. The fact that there is no indication of what is happening and nothing to do while the images download just increases her frustration.

Now that you know more about Nancy and her background, you can start to tailor her experience by isolating your key design goals.

DEFINING YOUR OWN GOALS
From this persona description, you now know a few things about your user. First, Nancy is busy. Second, she's creative, and busy or not she visits the museum site to be entertained and informed. Third, Nancy is a connoisseur of the arts and she genuinely wants to support art and the art community. Fourth and finally, you can assess that Nancy is fairly computer-literate, because she uses a computer for work everyday, but she's certainly not a tech geek.

With these things you now know about Nancy and the client's own goals, you can begin to develop a set of goals for yourself that can help direct you in the design process. The following specific goals for this project can help create a positive experience for Nancy:

- **Loading awareness.** Nancy probably has five minutes between putting the kids to bed and preparing the next day's client pitch to look at the MODA web site. Presenting her with a dumb "Loading 320K" screen won't do her any good. Nancy needs to see some relevant information, something not in techno geek terms. In short, Nancy needs to know how long she needs to wait spelled out in plain English.

- **Controlling the situation.** Part of improving the user experience for this site involves simplifying the site structure so that Nancy wouldn't have to do a lot of clicking and digging to get to the works she wants to see. There can be many art pieces per collection, so they need to be displayed in an effective and space-conscious way that Nancy will find easy to use and informative. It should enable her to quickly assess the entire collection and choose which images she wants to see without a lot of clicking.

- **Keeping things in context.** Part of simplifying the structure of the web site involves reducing the visual clutter of the site's layout. Nancy is interested in the artwork, so you can remove a lot of the less-used site options and build contextual menus that contain relevant information and options without cluttering up the screen with additional interface widgets.

- **A smarter cursor.** Although Nancy is comfortable with the computer, she still needs some indication as to when and where these context menus are available or how to navigate the list of exhibit images. Providing Nancy with a smart cursor that alters its appearance when additional functionality is available would help in this case.

The next four chapters show you how each of the previously discussed elements contributes to improving Nancy's experience at the Museum of Digital Art web site and give you step-by-step instructions on how to build them in Flash.

Don't forget what the first two chapters covered: The way a site looks and how users interact with it are two sides of the same usability coin. The key to successful Flash design, however, is to build with true usability-enhancing goals and an appropriate aesthetic design built on that foundation.

Note

CHAPTER 04
A Good Experience from the Start

We've got the right to choose, yeah there ain't no way we'll lose it.

—Dee Snyder
(chorus from Twisted Sister's anthem
"We're Not Gonna Take It")

"Loading… please wait" must be one of the most contentious and aggravating phrases on the web. In one form or another, it appears on most every site that offers viewers significant-sized files. Unfortunately this simple device does nothing to either tell viewers how long the download will take, or to explain why they should bother waiting. It is just a weak stab at trying to keep users interested while they wait… and wait….

There's no reason why this should be the case: Flash enables you to do much more than provide an unlabeled progress bar or a pulsing "loading" graphic. With a little additional coding, you can provide a real-time, visual representation of the download status, such as a progress bar or pie chart, or an actual figure—"*x* MB of *y* MB downloaded." And with a bit of additional planning, you can stream the movie in logically so that the user becomes less aware of the wait. These more informative feedback devices adhere to one of the more important usability principles: to ensure your users are informed of what's happening at all times; Donald Norman refers to this as *situation awareness*.

Giving Nancy an estimate of how long she has to wait is a start, but you can further improve the downloading experience for Nancy by giving her pieces of the information as they are downloaded. Flash gives you all the power to stream your movies from the web so that some parts of the movie can start playing before the entire movie has even downloaded. So, using this technique, you can make Nancy's wait time less noticeable by streaming the movie in and letting her interact while the other parts of the movie continue to download.

This chapter presents ways of streaming a Flash movie so that Nancy can start to interact with the site and accomplish her goals without having to wait for a long download. It describes how Flash can provide Nancy with feedback about the download and shows you how you can offer the same feedback to your users by building a reusable Flash Component that can display feedback to the user about any downloading movie.

Having outlined the specific movie loading issues that affect Nancy's experience on the MODA site, the next step is to develop solutions to those issues.

SOLUTIONS—GIVING NANCY TIME
The keys to the success of this project will be to build the movie so that larger parts can download while Nancy is busy viewing parts that have streamed in already. At the same time, you'll want to provide live feedback on the progress of the download so that Nancy is aware of what is happening and how long she may have to wait. This exhibit will contain about 15 images of the artwork in the collection. The actual size of the artwork is small, and the rest of the movie artwork is all vector-based, so the movie should download fairly quickly.

In the next section, you'll take a look at the sample movie for the MODA site and see what Nancy's experience should be like.

Seeing It in Action

From the *Skip Intro* CD-ROM's **Projects** folder, open the **04_loader.fla** file and test it (Control>Test Movie). When the test movie begins to play, select Show Streaming from the View menu; this will let you view the movie as if it's being downloaded from a 56K modem or slower connection. (You can alter the simulated connection rate using the settings in the Debug menu.)

The first thing you'll have noticed is that objects load onto the screen quite slowly. First up was the text explaining a bit about the artist and his work. Next, a progress bar with some download information appeared at the bottom of the screen. Following this, an image of a piece from the collection appeared with a caption below it, and then the navigation buttons appeared semi-transparently. As each image loads, its corresponding navigation button fades into full opacity. Notice that while all this is happening, the progress bar at the bottom continues to update and display the estimated time remaining in the download. The order in which these load is governed by the structure of the Flash FLA file itself.

One of Flash's most useful and most often-ignored features is the Load Order command, which you'll find in the Publish Settings menu (File>Publish Settings>Flash>Load Order). This setting enables you to choose to load the movie from the top down or from the bottom up. These refer to the arrangement of the layers in the timeline. If the Load Order is set at Bottom Up when you export your movie to an SWF file, the movie will be loaded, layer by layer, starting with the bottom layer in the timeline and working its way up. You can change this behavior and have it load Top Down instead. Whichever you choose, pay attention to this in development so that you can control what loads first, and what your users will see first.

a good experience from the start

Don't be a Memory Hog!

You may think you've created a pretty small download with your new Flash file, but if you've crammed the movie full of bitmap images your users could be in for a shock when they play the file. Playing a Flash movie that contains a lot of bitmap imagery can actually take up a significant amount of RAM on the target user's computer. Flash can compress images inside a movie, so while your finished Flash file may be only a few hundred kilobytes in size when the movie is played back on the target computer, it'll take up far more RAM. Suppose, for instance, that the images you load are roughly 1MB each in size before they're compressed. Suppose further that you use 11 of these in your Flash movie. Even if the SWF file is only 150K to download, it will be taking up at least 11MB of the user's RAM by the time it has finished playing. That could make you extremely unpopular (not to mention crash the user's browser/computer).

Now when a Flash movie is loaded, the entire movie is in the computer's memory, even parts of the movie that you've already looked at or haven't yet seen. If the movie you've loaded has 3MB of uncompressed imagery in it, even if they are not all onscreen at once, it is still taking up 3MB of memory until you close the window containing that Flash movie. The solution to keeping the memory usage down is to use the `loadMovie` and `unloadMovie` commands in Flash. When you load a movie inside another Flash movie using this method, you still take up the same amount of memory; but when you call the `unloadMovie` function to remove the previously loaded movie, all the memory it takes up is returned to the operating system. Now you're managing memory!

So keep this in mind when deciding whether to separate images out in to individual Flash movies or include them all in one movie.

Tip

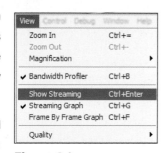

Figure 4.1
The load info sample movie in action. Be sure to turn on Show Streaming to simulate a remote connection.

For MODA's site, notice the order in which the items loaded was planned to accommodate Nancy as much as possible. The collection text gives her something to read, and then the progress bar indicates the download time of the collection pieces. Then the collection thumbnail images load and indicate when each of the bigger images they point to are loaded by undimming themselves.

No time has been wasted for Nancy. The movie gives her something to do almost immediately and slowly gives her more until the movie is completely downloaded. Nancy never has to see a "Loading…" animation that forces her to wait idly without knowing how long she might have to wait, and she can determine whether she wants to wait for the download because she can see the estimated time it will take to complete.

Close the test window and check out how each feedback element works. At the upper left of the Stage, you'll see a movie clip called **LoadInfo** with the instance name of *mc_load_info*. This innocuous looking little clip is the heart of the feedback system. It provides you with all sorts of useful information about the movie being loaded. If you look at the Component Parameters panel (Window>Panels>Component Parameters), you'll see it enables you to choose whether you want the movie to play while it's loading (streaming) or to be stopped until it has downloaded completely. You also can adjust the number of bytes, the number of frames, or what percentage of the movie to download before it starts to play. There's also an option that examines the amount downloaded and the running time of the movie. If the amount left to download can be downloaded in less time than is required to play the already downloaded portion of the movie, the code will tell the movie to start playing, so the downloading frames can finish downloading before they get played. Wow, this clip's thought of everything!

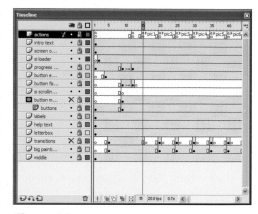

Figure 4.2
The layers in this movie have been told to load Top Down. Notice how only a few of the layers actually load anything on the first frame. This ensures the end user sees something quickly when the movie is streaming.

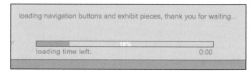

Figure 4.3
The progress indicator gives Nancy a good idea of how long the download will take. There is also adequate feedback telling Nancy what is downloading.

Figure 4.4
The LoadInfo Component. To help identify the Components, each has a custom icon. You can create your own or use the graphics provided on the CD.

IMPLEMENTATION
For the LoadInfo Component to be a truly powerful and reusable tool, the implementation needs to take into account all the possible information you may want to show the user at any given time the user might be downloading a movie.

The kinds of information and control you may want to have accessible through the LoadInfo Component are as follows:

- **The amount downloaded.** Returns a number between 0 and 1.0, representing the percentage of the movie downloaded. This number is used as the basis to display more useful information to Nancy, such as a progress bar or actual percentage downloaded. You also can extrapolate more technical numbers such as the bytes downloaded and remaining.

- **Estimated times.** A rough estimation, but very helpful for keeping Nancy informed and in control of her own time; now she can know how long she's waited, and more importantly, how long she might still have to wait.

- **Control over whether to download or to stream.** This option should help control Nancy's experience by either stopping the movie as it's downloading and playing the movie when the download is complete, or playing the movie as it is downloading (streaming it).

Information Object
The LoadInfo Component will act as a messenger of information, an information object that you can access in your code like any of the built-in ActionScript objects. Each of the variables of information should be accessible in a way similar to this:

```
_root.mc_load_info.estimatedTimeLeft;
```

You can then access this information from ActionScript attached to other movie clips or dynamic text fields to display textual information to the user or adjust the width of a progress bar.

Now define which specific variables of information the code should return. In all, the **LoadInfo** movie clip will make available 14 variables:

- *isLoaded.* Returns a true when the movie has loaded, or a false while the movie is loading.
- *totalBytes.* Returns the total size in bytes of the movie being downloaded.
- *loadedBytes.* Returns the total amount that has been downloaded so far.

- ***bytesPerSecond.*** Returns the download rate in bytes per second.

- ***totalSize.*** Returns the movie's size in a friendly format (such as 250KB, 1.2MB).

- ***loadedSize.*** Returns in a friendly format the amount of the movie downloaded so far (such as 250KB, 1.2MB).

- ***sizePerSecond.*** Returns the download rate in a friendly format (such as 250KB, 1.2MB).

- ***totalFrames.*** Returns the total number of frames in the movie being downloaded.

- ***loadedFrames.*** Returns the number of frames that have been downloaded so far.

- ***fractionLoaded.*** Returns a floating-point number representing the fraction of the movie that has been downloaded so far.

- ***percentLoaded.*** Returns the percentage of the movie downloaded so far.

- ***elapsedTime.*** Returns the amount of time that has elapsed since the download began.

- ***estimatedTime.*** Returns an estimate of the total time the movie will take to download, based on the rate at which the movie is downloading.

- ***estimatedTimeLeft.*** Returns an estimated time that it will take to download the remainder of the movie, which is especially useful.

- ***framesPerSecond.*** Returns the frames that are playing per second. This will not always return the fps that your movie is set to, but may return a lower number if the user's machine is unable to play the movie at the speed you set.

You also can specify the exact functionality this Component should exhibit on its parent movie in terms of allowing it to stream in or not:

- Stop until the entire movie has been downloaded, and then play the movie.

- Stop until a certain number of bytes has downloaded, and then begin playing the movie.

- Stop until a certain number of frames has downloaded, and then begin playing the movie.

- Stop until a certain percentage of the movie has downloaded, and then begin playing the movie.

- Play the movie after enough of the movie has downloaded so that the rest of the movie can download while the movie plays.

- Immediately play the movie as it is downloading.

Finally, you should make these settings adjustable in the Component Parameters window when the **mc_load_info** movie clip is selected on the Stage.

Now that the details of the Component are set, it's time to start the actual task of putting it together.

CONSTRUCTION

Start with a new movie and an empty library. Import several bitmaps and place each of them on the Stage, in their own frame in the timeline. This will help you test the code you'll write later on. If you can't find any images to import, you can copy the bitmaps used in the sample movie. After you have some images in your movie, draw a shape on the Stage; this can be any object but a square is fine for now. Make the square into a movie clip (Insert>Convert to Symbol) and give it a symbol name of **LoadInfo**. This will be the information object, and so will not be doing anything visible in the movie. Therefore, you can move this clip well out of the actual viewable area of the main movie Stage. Give this clip an instance name of **mc_load_info** and then double-click the movie clip or the movie clip's icon in the library to put it into Edit mode. Make a new layer in the timeline called **actions**, select the first frame on this layer, and open the Actions panel (Window>Actions).

Figure 4.5
Be sure to give the LoadInfo clip an instance name of mc_load_info.

Setting the Stage

This movie clip's sole purpose in life is to generate nuggets of information for your use in fields, movie clips, and so on, so the first thing you need to do is initialize those variables. Add the following code in the Actions panel:

```
var gLoading = true;
```

All the variables needed for this clip will be initialized within this frame. When they are all initialized, set **gLoading** to `true`. This will be used later when it's time to start updating the variables of information displayed to users such as Nancy.

Next, add two lines of code right before setting `gLoading` to `true`:

```
var totalBytes = _parent.getBytesTotal();
var loadedBytes = _parent.getBytesLoaded();
```

These two lines of code could be considered the most important lines in this whole clip. **totalBytes** calls the built-in Flash function `getBytesTotal()` on the parent movie (the one being downloaded, for which this movie clip is considered a child). This will return the total size in bytes of the movie being downloaded. **loadedBytes** performs a similar role, but it calls the `getBytesLoaded()` function, which returns the amount in bytes of the movie that have loaded so far. These two variables are used to determine the percentage of the movie downloaded and estimate the total download time. In fact, almost all the variables generated by this movie clip are derived from **totalBytes** and **loadedBytes**.

Now define some variables that will be used primarily to display directly to the user. Put these right after the variables you just defined:

```
var totalSize = formatBytes(totalBytes);
var loadedSize = formatBytes(loadedBytes);
```

These variables get their values by calling a function, `formatBytes()`. This function returns the number of bytes loaded and the movie's total size as a "friendly" version, which contains B for bytes, KB for kilobytes, and MB for megabytes. The `formatBytes()` function figures out whether the bytes you pass it in are a megabyte or a kilobyte and formats the number it outputs, so it follows the format 24.34KB. This is a key usability function: For users, 24.34KB is much easier to understand than 24340.

To define the `formatBytes()` function, add this code right after the last line of ActionScript in this frame:

```
function formatBytes(bytes) {
  var kb = 1024;
  var mb = kb * 1024;
  var tempNum = 0;

  if (bytes >= mb) {
   tempNum = String(Math.floor((bytes / mb) * 100) / 100);
   if (tempNum.substring(tempNum.indexOf("."), tempNum.length).length == 2) {
    tempNum += "0";
   }
   tempNum += " MB";
  } else if (bytes >= kb) {
   tempNum = String(Math.floor((bytes / kb) * 100) / 100);
   if (tempNum.substring(tempNum.indexOf("."),tempNum.length).length == 2) {
    tempNum += "0";
   }
   tempNum += " KB";
  } else {
   tempNum = bytes + " B";
  }

  return tempNum;
}
```

This function calculates the total size of the movie left to download and converts that number into a user-friendly format, such as kilobytes or megabytes remaining.

It's almost time to test the movie, but the script requires a few more lines of code that check that the **gLoading** variable has been set to `true`, and updates the variables previously defined. The `trace()` function will help you debug the variables so that you can see that something is actually happening. Add a key frame on frame 2 of the timeline and then add this code:

```
if (gLoading) {
  loadedBytes = _parent.getBytesLoaded();
  loadedSize = formatBytes(loadedBytes);

  trace("totalBytes = " + totalBytes);
  trace("loadedBytes = " + loadedBytes);
  trace("totalSize = " + totalSize);
  trace("loadedSize = " + loadedSize);
}
```

For this code to really do its job, make sure the movie clip loops on frame 2. To do this, add a key frame on frame 3 of this clip's timeline, and enter this code in the Actions dialog box:

```
gotoAndPlay(2);
```

This line will ensure the movie clip continues to loop over the second frame, in which the main code is located.

Test It!

It's time to test your movie. Save the movie, and then test it as before, making sure you turn on Show Streaming in the View menu. If you can, keep your Output window in sight so that you can see that the variables are actually getting updated (Window>Output).

```
Output                                          Options
  loadedSize = 36.58 KB
  totalBytes = 135698
  loadedBytes = 37564
  totalSize = 132.51 KB
  loadedSize = 36.68 KB
  totalBytes = 135698
  loadedBytes = 37660
  totalSize = 132.51 KB
  loadedSize = 36.77 KB
  totalBytes = 135698
  loadedBytes = 37855
```

Figure 4.6
Your Output window should look like this if your code is error free.

If something's gone wrong. Don't fret; this happens to even the most experienced programmers. Use this information to isolate the problem and fix it. If you're having difficulty, refer back to Chapter 2, "Basic Training," for further assistance.

If your values are not updating in your Output window, check your code for syntax errors. When you're happy the movie is working as it should, you can begin creating the code that controls the way the movie plays.

Taking Control

```
1  this._visible = false;                            // make sure the clip doesn't show up on the screen
```

Figure 4.7
Make sure you hide the clip so that it doesn't show up when the movie plays.

Select frame 1 of your movie clip and open the Actions window. At the very top of the first frame, on the line before initializing the ***totalBytes*** variable, add these lines:

```
this._visible = false;
var isLoaded = false;
```

The first line hides the movie clip. This is always a good idea when developing information clips that you don't want visible on Stage. The ***isLoaded*** variable is a simple Boolean variable used to indicate whether the movie is loaded. Now add the following code right before you define the `formatBytes` function:

```
var gPlaying = false;
_parent.stop();
```

gPlaying holds the state of whether the parent movie is playing. It is set to `true` later, after the parent movie has completely downloaded or one of the other conditions for playing the movie is met. The parent movie (the one that contains this movie clip) is then told to stop playing. As soon as the movie is loaded, the movie should start playing again. At the bottom of the second frame's ActionScript, add the following:

```
if (loadedBytes == totalBytes) {
 isLoaded = true;
}

if (isLoaded) {
 _parent.play();
 gLoading = false;
}
```

This code checks the ***totalBytes*** and ***loadedBytes*** variables that are updating. If ***loadedBytes***, which holds the amount of the movie that is loaded so far, is the same as ***totalBytes***, which is the total size of the movie, it is safe to assume the movie has completely downloaded, and the ***isLoaded*** variable can be set to `true`. The code then checks to see whether the ***isLoaded*** variable has been set to `true`, and then tells the parent movie to start playing. It also sets the ***gLoading*** variable to `false` so the containing `if` statement will no longer evaluate to `true` and this code will no longer be executed. Doing this ensures variables aren't being updated with the same information.

Save and test the movie again, using the Show Streaming setting. The movie should stop on the first frame until it's loaded, and then it should play. Notice as well that the variables being sent to the Output window with the `trace()` functions no longer update when the movie is loaded and playing.

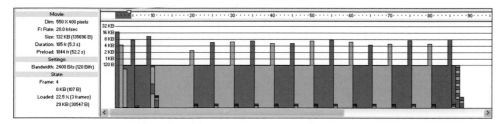

Figure 4.8
The Bandwidth Profiler can help you tune those first few frames of your movie so they download quickly and allow the rest of the movie to stream in.

Crunching the Numbers

Okay, you've done a lot already. Now you're on the home stretch: adding the remainder of the code, which includes more variables and statements to help you arrive at some estimates of the time it might take to download the movie.

Right after the code that initializes the ***totalBytes*** and ***loadedBytes*** variables (in frame 1), add the following:

```
var totalFrames = _parent._totalFrames;
var loadedFrames = _parent._framesLoaded;
var fractionLoaded = 0;
var percentLoaded = "0%";

var bytesPerSecond = 0;
var sizePerSecond = formatBytes(bytesPerSecond);
var elapsedTime = "0:00";
var estimatedTime = "0:00";
var estimatedTimeLeft = "0:00";
```

This code uses built-in Flash functionality to determine the total frames in the movie and the number of frames downloaded so far. This will be useful later when the ability to start the movie after a defined number of frames have loaded is added.

Next is the code that outputs progress feedback. All these variables will be updated as the movie loads. The **fractionLoaded** variable is used to set the width of the progress bar. The other variables will help you to keep track of the time elapsed.

To estimate the time the movie will take to download, you need to determine the bytes downloading per second. To do this, you need to have a good idea of when the movie started downloading, which can be retrieved using Flash's built-in timer function:

```
var gStartTime = getTimer();
var gCurrentTime = getTimer();
```

The `getTimer()` function returns the number of milliseconds since the movie began playing. Using this with the **loadedBytes** variable you can find the rate of download. This will be done with the help of the following variables, which should be added next:

```
var gSampleTimer = gCurrentTime - gStartTime;
var gSizeSample = loadedBytes;

var framesPerSecond = 0;
var frameCounter = 0;
```

These variables will later help determine when a second of time has passed and, when it does, to calculate the bytes that downloaded in that second.

The last group of variables you need to initialize are those dealing with the code that determines how much of the movie needs to be downloaded so that it can play while the rest of the movie downloads in the background. To figure this out, you need to know the playback speed of the movie. This will be held by the **framesPerSecond** variable. The **frameCounter** variable will be used in calculating the playback speed.

It's time to move on to the second frame, where all the real work gets done. Immediately following the line of code that updates the **loadedSize** variable, add the following:

```
loadedFrames = _parent._framesLoaded;

gCurrentTime = getTimer();
```

First the code will update the **loadedFrames** variable with the current number of frames loaded. Then it will update the **gCurrentTime** variable to the number of milliseconds that have passed since the movie started to play. This will be used in the next section of code, which determines the elapsed time, in minutes and seconds. Add the following:

```
var elapsedMinutes = Math.floor(((gCurrentTime - gStartTime) / 1000) / 60);

var elapsedSeconds = Math.floor(((gCurrentTime - gStartTime) / 1000) % 60);

if (String(elapsedSeconds).length == 1) {
 elapsedSeconds = "0" + elapsedSeconds;
}

elapsedTime = elapsedMinutes + ":" + elapsedSeconds;
```

From the **gCurrentTime** variable, this code subtracts the time at which the movie started downloading, which was captured when **gStartTime** was initialized. It then divides this difference by 1000 to convert from milliseconds to seconds, and then divides it by 60 to arrive at the actual minutes since downloading began. Finally, it uses the `Math.floor()` function to make sure the number isn't a fraction. This is captured, or stored, in the **elapsedMinutes** variable.

The line after that carries out nearly the same operation as the preceding line, except instead of dividing by 60 to retrieve the minutes of elapsed time, the modulo operator (%) is used to get the remainder of the number divided by 60. `Math.floor()` converts it to a whole number and inserts it as the **elapsedSeconds** variable.

The next line checks to see whether the **elapsedSeconds** variable is one character long, and if it is, appends a 0 to the beginning. Finally, the **elapsedTime** variable is set to the combination of **elapsedMinutes**, a colon, and then **elapsedSeconds**. This should return something like 2:24.

The next batch of code, which determines the estimated time for the download and the playback speed, is possibly the most complex in the clip. It calculates the download time by grabbing a "sample" of bytes every second and compares it against the total amount of bytes in the movie. This example starts off with the outer structure of the code first, and works its way in. Add this piece of code next:

```
frameCounter++;
if (gCurrentTime - gStartTime >= gSampleTimer + 1000) {
  framesPerSecond = frameCounter;
  frameCounter = 0;

  gSampleTimer = gCurrentTime - gStartTime;
}
```

The first thing happening here is incrementing the **frameCounter** variable. This variable increases by one every time a frame is played.

Next, the code checks whether the difference between the **gCurrentTime** (the number of milliseconds that has elapsed since playing the movie) and **gStartTime** (the time at which the movie began loading) is the same or greater than **gSampleTimer** (which was initialized in the first `if` statement) plus 1000 milliseconds. In a nutshell, if 1 second has passed since downloading began, the code inside the statement should be executed.

The next lines help to determine the frames per second, or playback speed, that the movie is playing. This is not necessarily the same as the value used in the Movie Properties dialog box because some machines will play movies back slightly slower than you specified. Because this code only gets executed every second that goes by, the **frameCounter** variable should return an accurate representation of the number of frames that play in a second, returning the actual playback speed. So **framesPerSecond** is equal to **frameCounter**. **frameCounter** is then set back to 0 so that the next time it is checked it will return its new value.

The line of code following sets the **gSampleTimer** variable to the current difference between **gCurrentTime** and **gStartTime**. This will ensure that the whole `if` statement gets called properly in the next second that follows, and every second after that.

Now start filling out the `if` statement with more code. Add this line of code right before setting the **gSampleTimer** variable:

```
gSizeSample = loadedBytes;
```

This updates the **gSizeSample** variable to the bytes of the movie downloaded thus far.

Next insert the following code after the line of code that sets **frameCounter** to 0:

```
bytesPerSecond = loadedBytes - gSizeSample;
sizePerSecond = formatBytes(bytesPerSecond);

var estimatedMinutes = Math.floor((totalBytes / bytesPerSecond) /60);
var estimatedSeconds = Math.floor((totalBytes / bytesPerSecond) % 60);

if (String(estimatedSeconds).length == 1) {
 estimatedSeconds = "0" + estimatedSeconds;
}

estimatedTime = estimatedMinutes + ":" + estimatedSeconds;
```

The first line of this code sets the **bytesPerSecond** variable to the difference between the current number of bytes loaded and the number of bytes loaded one second previously (in the **gSizeSample** variable). This gives a pretty good estimate of the number of bytes that are downloading per second. The **sizePerSecond** variable is a "friendly" version of this amount.

Next the total size, in bytes, of the movie is divided by the **bytesPerSecond** variable to estimate the time it will take to download the entire movie. Using the same method employed earlier to format the elapsed time of the download, you end up with an **estimatedTime** variable, which contains the estimated amount of time to download the movie.

Now you will determine the estimated time left in the download process. Add the following code next:

```
var estimatedMinutesLeft = Math.floor(((totalBytes - loadedBytes)
➡ / bytesPerSecond) /60);

var estimatedSecondsLeft = Math.floor(((totalBytes - loadedBytes)
➡ / bytesPerSecond) % 60);

if (String(estimatedSecondsLeft).length == 1) {
 estimatedSecondsLeft = "0" + estimatedSecondsLeft;
}
estimatedTimeLeft = estimatedMinutesLeft + ":" + estimatedSecondsLeft;
```

This code performs a very similar function to what was done to estimate the time for the whole download. However, instead of dividing the total size of the movie by the bytes per second, the total movie size is determined by the difference (**totalBytes**) and

```
38    // this is the estimated time...
39    var estimatedMinutes = Math.floor((totalBytes / bytesPerSecond) / 60);
40    var estimatedSeconds = Math.floor((totalBytes / bytesPerSecond) % 60);
41    if (String(estimatedSeconds).length == 1) {
42        estimatedSeconds = "0" + estimatedSeconds;
43    }
44    estimatedTime = estimatedMinutes + ":" + estimatedSeconds;
45
46    // ... and an estimate of how much time is left
47    var estimatedMinutesLeft = Math.floor(((totalBytes - loadedBytes) / bytesPerSecond) / 60);
48    var estimatedSecondsLeft = Math.floor(((totalBytes - loadedBytes) / bytesPerSecond) % 60);
49    if (String(estimatedSecondsLeft).length == 1) {
50        estimatedSecondsLeft = "0" + estimatedSecondsLeft;
51    }
52    estimatedTimeLeft = estimatedMinutesLeft + ":" + estimatedSecondsLeft;
```

Figure 4.9
The time and frame estimates are calculated every second that goes by.

amount of the movie that has been downloaded so far (**loadedBytes**).

Phew! That rounds out the crucial estimating part of the code.

Next add these two lines immediately following the } after the **gSampleTimer** variable gets set:

```
fractionLoaded = loadedBytes / totalBytes;
percentLoaded = Math.floor(fractionLoaded * 100) + "%";
```

This code sets the **fractionLoaded** variable to the fraction of the movie that has been downloaded. This is the floating-point number that was used previously to resize the progress bar while the rest of the movie was downloading. The **percentLoaded** variable takes **fractionLoaded** and converts it to an integer value before appending a % to it. This is just a more user-friendly version of the fraction.

Now save what you have so far. Next you will be diving into the final details of the code and setting up the Component.

Finishing Touches

You're now ready to add several additional `trace()` function calls that will enable you to see the results of the new variables you added. Below the `trace()` functions you added previously, input the following:

```
trace("totalFrames = " + totalFrames);
trace("loadedFrames = " + loadedFrames);
trace("elapsedTime = " + elapsedTime);
trace("estimatedTime = " + estimatedTime);
trace("estimatedTimeLeft = " + estimatedTimeLeft);
trace("fractionLoaded = " + fractionLoaded);
trace("percentLoaded = " + percentLoaded);
```

After adding the `trace()` calls, try testing your movie again. Remember to use Show Streaming. You should see the Output window updating with a lot of variable calls.

Almost there now. All that's left is to make your movie into a Component and add the supporting ActionScript. This will enable you to select the number of bytes or frames at which the movie starts playing. To do this, open the movie's library and select the **LoadInfo** movie clip you've been working on. Then from the Options menu on the Library window, select Component Definition.

Using the plus sign (+), add the following variables to the Component Definition window:

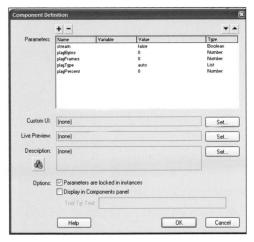

Figure 4.10
The Component Definition interface. Here is where you will add the parameters used to control the Component.

```
STREAM
PLAY_TYPE
PLAY_BYTES
PLAY_FRAMES
PLAY_PERCENT
```

The **STREAM** variable will be a `true` or `false` value and tells the **LoadInfo** movie clip whether to stop the parent movie until it is completely downloaded or stream it in. Because this variable can only ever be two possible values, in the Type column, make the **STREAM** variable a Boolean. Give it a default value of `false`.

The **PLAY_TYPE** variable tells the LoadInfo Component to start playing the movie (in the case that you selected yes for the stream variable) when either a given number of bytes, a given number of frames, or a percentage of the movie has downloaded. There is also an auto option that will tell the clip to automatically start playing the movie based on the playing time of the downloaded portion of the movie. Make this variable a List type as well, and enter **bytes**, **frames**, **percent**, and **auto** as the possible values in the List Values dialog box.

Figure 4.11
Adding list elements to the Component Parameters of an movie clip.

The **PLAY_BYTES** variable will hold the specific number of bytes that should be downloaded before the movie should start playing (in the case that **STREAM** is set to `true` and **PLAY_TYPE** is set to `bytes`). Make this variable a Number type and add `0` as the default value here.

The **PLAY_FRAMES** variable should also be Number type and have a default value of 0. It works in the same way as the **PLAY_BYTES** variable, except it defines how many frames should be downloaded before playing the parent movie. (**STREAM** would be set to `true` and **PLAY_TYPE** would be set to `frames`.)

Finally, the **PLAY_PERCENT** variable should also be a Number and default to 0. It works in the same way as the **PLAY_BYTES** and **PLAY_FRAMES** variables, except it defines the percentage of the parent movie that should be downloaded before playing it. (**STREAM** would be set to `true`, and **PLAY_TYPE** would be set to `percent`.)

These variables can now be set from the Component Parameters panel when you have the *LoadInfo* movie clip instance selected on the Stage. For the Component Parameters to have any effect on the **LoadInfo** movie clip, you need to add the necessary code to test against the **STREAM**, **PLAY_TYPE**, **PLAY_BYTES**, **PLAY_FRAMES,** and **PLAY_PERCENT** variables. Select the second frame of your **LoadInfo** movie clip and bring up the Actions window with all the code you've written so far.

On a new line, immediately after the **sizePerSecond** variable gets set (in the preceding `if` statement), add the following:

```
if (STREAM && PLAY_TYPE == "auto") {
 if ((loadedFrames / framesPerSecond) > ((totalBytes -  loadedBytes) /
➡bytesPerSecond)) {
  _parent.play();
 }
}
```

This code checks to see whether the movie is set to stream and whether the **LoadInfo** movie clip should play the movie automatically after a certain amount of the movie has downloaded. The next condition checks to see whether the time it takes to play the loaded frames (derived by dividing the frames per second into the number of frames loaded) is greater than the time remaining in the download. If these conditions are met, the parent movie is instructed to play.

Although you've added the necessary testing to let the LoadInfo Component play the movie when enough of the movie has downloaded, you should use this functionality only when you are certain that you have tuned your movie properly so that it downloads consistently in the majority of cases. If the user's connection were to slow down unexpectedly or your movie were not tuned to download consistently (you can see this in the Bandwidth Profiler), your users would be stuck waiting for something to happen and their experience will take a turn for the worse! So make sure you test that your movie downloads properly when turning on this feature of the Component.

Note

On the line after you update the ***percentageLoaded*** variable in the bottom part of the code, add these lines:

```
if (STREAM) {
    switch (PLAY_TYPE) {
        case "bytes":
            if (loadedBytes >= PLAY_BYTES) {
                if (!gPlaying) {
                    _parent.play();
                    gPlaying = true;
                }
            }
            break;
        case "frames":
            if (loadedFrames >= PLAY_FRAMES) {
                if (!gPlaying) {
                    _parent.play();
                    gPlaying = true;
                }
            }
            break;
        case "percent":
            if (fractionLoaded * 100 >= PLAY_PERCENT) {
                if (!gPlaying) {
                    _parent.play();
                    gPlaying = true;
                }
            }
            break;
    }
}
```

This code tests the value of the ***STREAM*** variable. If the movie is set to stream, it checks the ***PLAY_TYPE*** variable to see whether it should test against bytes loaded or frames loaded. If ***PLAY_TYPE*** is set to `bytes`, it compares the ***loadedBytes*** variable (which holds the number of bytes downloaded so far) and the ***PLAY_BYTES*** variable (which is set in the Component Parameters panel). If ***PLAY_TYPE*** is set to `frames`, it compares the ***loadedFrames*** variable to the ***PLAY_FRAMES*** variable, which also is set in the Component Parameters panel. If the ***PLAY_TYPE*** is `percent`, the code then compares the ***fractionLoaded*** variable (which is multiplied by 100 to make it a percentage) to the ***PLAY_PERCENT*** variable to determine whether to play the parent movie. If any of these conditions evaluate to `true`, the code checks to see that the ***gPlaying*** variable is set to `false`, which means the movie has not been told to play yet. When the parent movie is told to play, ***gPlaying*** is set to `true`, which protects the code from running into situations in which the movie is told to play over and over again.

Now add the final code to this movie clip before testing it again. Near the very bottom of your code, in the `if (isLoaded)` statement, replace the `_parent.play()` ActionScript with the following:

```
if (!STREAM) {
  _parent.play();
}
```

This code tests the **STREAM** variable to see whether it's set to not stream. In this case, the movie waits to be downloaded completely before playing. When **isLoaded** is equal to `true` (which means the movie has finished downloading), the code tells the movie to start playing again.

Save your movie now and return to the main movie timeline. With the *LoadInfo* movie clip instance selected on the Stage, open the Component Parameters panel. You should see the four variables you defined moments ago. Double-click the value for **STREAM** (which should default to `false`) and select `true`. This will tell the LoadInfo Component to stream in the movie rather than wait until the entire movie has downloaded. For the **PLAY_TYPE** parameter, set the value to `bytes`. The **PLAY_BYTES** parameter is the number of bytes that should load before playing the movie. Set this to 10,000. The movie's now ready for another test drive.

Save your work and test the movie, making sure you turn Show Streaming on. Keep an eye on your Output window, particularly the **loadedBytes** variable. When it reaches 60,000, your movie should start playing, even though it has not completely downloaded. If this does not work, check your code for errors. Syntax errors will show up in your Output window and they can help you to pinpoint the nature and location of the error. If everything works as planned, congratulations! It's now time to move on to the main movie and create a progress bar and some text fields to display some of this useful information to the user.

Progress!

Start off by creating a progress bar. Make an elongated rectangle on the main movie Stage. Make sure it is much wider than it is tall. Give it a hairline pixel stroke in the Properties panel. Then select just the interior of the rectangle (excluding the stroke), and make that rectangle into a movie clip named **LoadInfo_bar** and make sure the registration point is set to the upper-left corner. In the Properties panel, give the clip the name of **mc_progress_bar**.

Figure 4.12
Be sure to change the registration point of your movie clip to the upper-left corner in the Convert to Symbol dialog box.

Now open the Actions panel (Window>Actions) and click the body of the progress bar. Here you will enter the code for performing some fairly simple calculations to determine its size.

```
1  onClipEvent (load) {
2      var myStartWidth = this._width;
3      this._width = 0;
4  }
5
6  onClipEvent (enterFrame) {
7      this._width = myStartWidth * _parent._parent.mc_load_info.fractionLoaded;
8  }
```

Figure 4.13
Because the onClipEvent (load) *executes only once, it's good to initialize variables when it gets triggered.*

```
onClipEvent (load) {
  var myStartWidth = this._width;
  this._width = 0;
}
```

The **myStartWidth** variable holds the initial width of the progress bar and needs to be defined only once at load time. To change the width of the progress bar to match the actual progress of the download, add the following code:

```
onClipEvent (enterFrame) {
  this._width = myStartWidth * _root.mc_load_info.fractionLoaded;
}
```

In the **enterFrame** portion of this movie clip's code, the **myStartWidth** variable is multiplied by the **fractionLoaded** number provided by the *mc_load_info* movie clip instance. This sets the width of the progress bar to a percentage of its original width—the same percentage of the main movie that has been downloaded. Pretty easy, right?

Test the movie by turning on Show Streaming. The bar should update smoothly as the movie downloads. Cool, huh?

It's time to transform all these variables into usable information. Select the Text tool and click just below the progress bar on the Stage. Enter **amount downloaded:**. Click again to the right of that text, go to the Text Options panel (Window>Panels>Text Options) and make the text dynamic. This enables you to update the field with a variable value. In the Variable field, enter

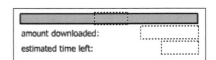

Figure 4.14
The three dynamic text boxes of information.

mc_load_info.loadedSize. This tells the field to display the value of that variable. Now, while the main movie is downloading, the **loadedSize** value will appear in this field and update automatically whenever it changes.

Next add the percentage of the download that has completed. Once again using the Text tool, click the Stage and make a dynamic text field and set its variable to ***mc_load_info.percentLoaded***. Move this text field so that it is on top of and centered along the width of the bar.

Finally, add one more dynamic text field and give it the variable name ***mc_load_ info.estimatedTimeLeft***. Add some static text to the left of it and type **estimated download time left:**. Now position these two objects just below the loaded size fields. If you didn't know already, this will show the user the estimated time left in the download.

Test your movie one last time with Show Streaming on. How do you like it? Now you have the knowledge and tools to give the user adequate feedback on the downloading movie. Take some time to add different fields or experiment with some of the other LoadInfo Component parameters.

CONCLUSION   The LoadInfo Component offers a lot of information about movies being

loaded and enables you to control the movie playback based on the amount of data loaded. Although all the information and capabilities provided by this Component can be useful, it's up to you to decide how much of this your intended user will really need. For example, should the movie download completely before playing? How transparent should this download be to Nancy? These questions are all specific to your target audience. The LoadInfo Component can help improve the user experience only after you've planned the user experience. The key is to make sure you offer your users just enough information but don't overload them with detail. Remember, your main aim is to ensure the user, Nancy, can accomplish her goals on the site.

Key Points/Don't Forget

When using the LoadInfo Component, it's good to remember the following key points, they can help you to remember the main goal here—to make your user's experience the best it can be:

- The whole purpose of this Component is to help you improve your user's experience. Don't forget to bear this in mind while you build your movie.

- If you're making a request that may take a bit of time to return, let the user know with some live feedback. Make sure time estimates are as accurate as possible.

- Don't overload the user with too much information. A lack of feedback can make her experience tedious and frustrating, but too much can overwhelm her, distracting her from her goal.

- Don't leave the user in the dark. Think about what the user will experience when coming to the web site for the first time.

- Steer clear of "indefinite feedback" that gives no indication of how long something will take. Pulsing "Loading…" text and spinning trinkets are all useless eye-candy unless the user can easily assess how long she may have to wait and, more importantly, what she is waiting for.

- Even a rough estimate is better than no estimate at all. Giving the user adequate feedback on the duration of a download could actually save the user time because she may be able to get other things done while it's happening.

- Never download your entire site to the user's computer before allowing her to decide what she needs to access on the site. Break the information up as much as possible without affecting the flow of the site. This a major usability feature, not only for the user but for the site administrator: Making changes to a site is far easier if it's been set up in a modular design.

CHAPTER 05
Scrolling Without Boundaries

Any sufficiently advanced technology is indistinguishable from magic.

—Arthur C. Clarke

The use of Flash to create information interfaces has enabled designers to develop many new devices for browsing that information. Although most of these interfaces are designed to improve the user experience, many are littered with gimmicks and controls that actually confuse the user.

Among this plethora of experimental interface elements are some that really do improve usability. One of these is the gesture-driven scrolling list.

As a Flash developer, you've no doubt seen the gesture-driven scrolling list before. Usually it is a list of image thumbnails arrayed horizontally or vertically. As the user moves his mouse over the list, it reacts by scrolling in a direction based on the mouse position or motion.

In the gesture-driven list, the speed of scrolling is dictated by the distance of the mouse cursor from its target. This dramatically reduces the amount of mouse movement required to control the scrolling. The fact that the list scrolls by merely having the user move his mouse (this is where the "gesture" part comes from) also helps by reducing the number of clicks needed to scroll through the list to...0! Gone are the smaller click areas of the scroll arrows at each end of the list, and the scrolling "thumb" in the middle of the scrollbar.

This can be a powerful interface element, but it can truly help improve web site usability only if the designer spends the time to iron out the details of how users will interact with it.

> **(mc)**
>
> When we were writing this chapter, it occurred to us that a gesture-driven scrolling list is actually pretty controversial in the world of usability. Many usability gurus recommend against using this type of control, and rightly so; it is an unfamiliar, newer type of navigational widget that many users might not be familiar with.
>
> Many of the rules of usability rely on interfaces and controls being intuitive and familiar to the user. Abiding by these rules guarantees that your users always know how to get around your interface and the site they are looking at. However, all users are different. In the case of the MODA site, the target audience was not visiting the site to get through it in the quickest possible time, but rather, users of the site wanted to spend time and enjoy the experience of looking at the images on the site. In our informal tests, we even found that users who had never used this type of scrolling list before learned to use it almost instantly and found using it to be fun and enjoyable, a key goal for the target audience of the site.
>
> Remember, the rules of usability that you will read in books or on web sites are great *guides* when designing an interface, but the one real rule to stick to is this: Know your user. In this case, our target user liked the scrolling list, and it added enjoyment to the site that a boring old scrollbar would not have.
>
> Ultimately, using standard widgets may be the safest way to ensure maximum usability of your interface, but if you don't try and develop something new and better, we could be using the same old scrollbars 10 years from now!
>
> **Author Note: Michelangelo**

In this chapter, you learn how to make your own simple, gesture-driven component that takes into consideration all the details necessary to improve Nancy's experience on the MODA site. Keep in mind the issues just discussed when you take a look at how the scrolling list works in the MODA structure.

Solutions—Making the User More Efficient

Using the gesture-driven scrolling list not only makes accessing the items in the list easier for Nancy, but it also enables you to organize the site in one simple level. This helps to make Nancy's time on the MODA site more effective by eliminating any nested areas of the site. Nancy can see all the site sections on one screen.

Cutting the amount of clicking Nancy has to do to scroll to the different exhibits also simplifies her interaction with the site and saves her time.

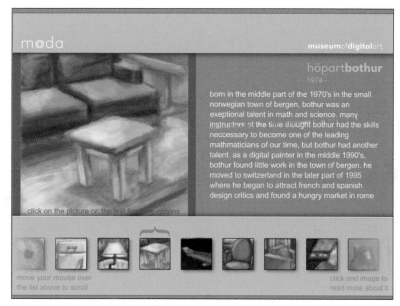

Figure 5.1
The Höpart exhibit site should focus on the artwork in the collection; the gesture-drive scrolling list helps to make this interface simple and focused.

The gesture-driven scrolling list also helps simplify the site's visual design. Without system scrollbars or similar widgets to incorporate, Nancy can focus on the artwork and the information and have a fun, enjoyable experience on the site.

To see all these benefits in action, take a look at the Höpart sample movie.

Seeing It in Action

Open the **05_scrolling_list.fla** file located in the **Projects** folder on the *Skip Intro* CD-ROM. Test the movie (Control>Test Movie) so that you can see how the gesture-driven list feels.

Notice the list has a smooth and immediate response. You also may notice

Figure 5.2
Spend some time getting the feel of the gesture-driven scrolling list. Pay attention to how it reacts to the mouse. Notice the help text on either side of the list—subtle yet helpful.

that the list scrolls quite fast when your mouse is at the extreme left or right edge of the screen, but that there's a large "slow" area in the center of the list that offers the user more control over the individual elements in the list. This is extremely important for providing user control. Although it is easier for the designer to create a list with a steady scroll rate, it would be much harder for the user to control it unless the scrolling rate were slowed down considerably.

The list contains a lot of items, so it's possible Nancy might get lost as she scrolls through the artwork. This is something you need to watch out for when using this type of list; too many elements can make it easy for the user to lose track. (The easy solution for this project was to provide a function that identified which piece of artwork Nancy was looking at.) The selected button acts as a reference point for the user as it goes by again and again; it is a simple and recognizable element.

Figure 5.3
When Show Streaming is turned on, notice how the buttons in the list fade in as the larger images finish downloading.

As the file loads, Nancy is kept informed of the download status. If you test the movie and turn on Show Streaming, you'll notice that each of the buttons in the list fades in when its corresponding full-size graphic has downloaded. This offers a visual clue as to the state of the section to which that button corresponds.

This is a classic case where not being lazy can really improve the usability of your Flash movie. With a little extra work, you can show Nancy which of the items are still downloading by initially setting each button's opacity to 25 percent and disabling its functionality. After the high-resolution image has downloaded, its corresponding thumbnail in the list returns to full opacity.

Note

Now go ahead and take some time to play around with the gesture-driven list. Get a feel for how the list speeds up and slows down. Because you have seen how the scrolling list component works, how about making your own?

IMPLEMENTATION   As with all components, this one should be flexible enough to provide Nancy with a good, usable interface element, and also accommodate different scenarios for its use in other projects. Without this flexibility, you will end up with a lot of code that might be able to do a very specific task for the MODA site but not be very reusable.

Additionally, you should be able to define the bulk of the settings for the scrolling list in the Component Parameters window. That way, the bulk of the work is already done for you when you use the clip. It's then just a matter of dragging and dropping the clip into your movie and setting a few parameters.

To have a component with the kind of power and flexibility you need, you must include a solid list of features:

■ **Adjustable speed.** The speed of the list should be easily adjustable. Smaller size movies will probably need a slower moving list so that the user doesn't lose control of it. Movies that take up bigger areas of the screen may need a faster list to help the user move quickly around the list. You'll also be able to provide different scrolling speeds for different target audiences.

- **Variable, user-controlled acceleration.** Scrolling should be fastest when the mouse is at the extreme ends of the list to offer Nancy maximum control. At the middle of the list, where most of the clicking actions will take place, scrolling should be slower so that Nancy can move her mouse without making the list speed away.

- **Adjustable orientation.** The component should enable you to choose to display the list vertically or horizontally.

- **Customizable list items.** Abstracting the code from the artwork enables you to use the code with any movie clips without having to rewrite or tweak code.

- **Adjustable activation area.** The size of the area of the scrolling list that responds to the mouse should be configurable. This is especially useful for lists with smaller items—you can create an adjustable buffer around the clip so that Nancy can easily have the list scroll when the mouse pointer is within 20 pixels of the list rather than when the mouse pointer is rolled over the list items themselves.

During the development of a very similar scrolling list several years ago, my friend Andy Scott gave me a cubic equation that turned out to be a little gem about acceleration. He pointed out that most scrolling lists use a linear equation—on a graph they look like a straight diagonal line rising from the lower left. A cubic equation looks like a gentle curve sweeping from the lower left and then reversing its curve as it arcs to the upper right. Essentially this means the scrolling timeline is less sensitive toward the center allowing for easier access to the scrolling objects, and more sensitive toward the edges allowing for greater scrolling speed. See Figure 5.4 to view what the equations look like in a graph.

Note

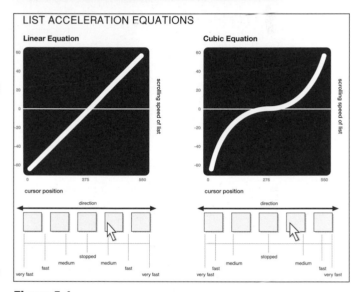

Figure 5.4
By using a cubic equation for the acceleration of the scrolling list, the user gains more control over the items in the list.

Most of these requirements point to a component that acts as a controller, sort of like a traffic cop. It's a clip that stands behind the scenes and controls other clips, moving them across the screen, adjusting their relationship to each other and the screen, and keeping aware of the mouse pointer.

Keeping watch over a developer-specified number of movie clips is not easy. The approach used here is to have the developer specify the base name of his collection of clips and the number of clips he will have on the screen. If you were to specify **mc_someClip_** as your base name, and 3 as your clip count, the scrolling list component will look for **mc_someClip_0**, **mc_someClip_1**, and **mc_someClip_2**. This will make it easy for the code to handle—and easier for the designer because he won't have to keep track of many different clip names.

As you can see, most of the features are intended to improve the user experience with the scrolling list. At the same time, several of these features make it easier for the developer to customize the component for different applications. If you can meet both these goals, you have a truly great tool.

Okay, now that you understand the requirements, you can get started on the fun part… putting it all together!

CONSTRUCTION

You've got a pretty clear objective here: to create a component that will control other clips on the Stage and enable the end users to control the movement of those clips with their mouse. This clip will not itself be visible to the user of the scrolling list, but will remain behind the scenes.

The gesture-driven component will be a movie clip made up of three frames. The first frame will handle initializing variables and defining functions for the clip. The second frame will contain the code that actually does the work—keeping the different elements in the list aligned properly, getting the mouse position, and making calculations to move the list elements on the screen. The third frame will be your loop frame; it will just tell the clip to loop back to the second frame.

Setting Up the Movie

To start building your scrolling list component in Flash, make a new movie and set its frame rate to 20 fps. Make a new layer and call it **scrolling list**. Then create a shape on the Stage (it can be anything at this point), select it, and turn it into a movie clip called **ScrollingList**. Double click the clip you just created (to edit it) and add a new layer. Name this new layer **actions**. This is where you will be adding your ActionScript. Add two more frames to the movie clip, making it a total of three frames long. Make each of these frames a keyframe. The quickest way to do this is to select all three frames in the actions layer of the timeline and convert them to key frames (Modify>Frames> Convert to Keyframes). Now you're ready to start adding the code.

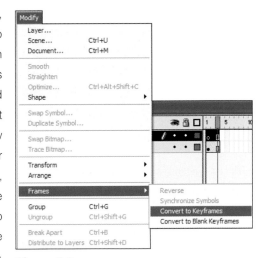

Figure 5.5

Select your three frames and convert them to keyframes (Modify>Frames>Convert to Keyframes).

Hiding the Clip

Select the first frame in the **actions** layer and open the Actions panel. Here you will hide the movie clip and define some constants that you will replace with component parameters later. Enter this code:

```
this._visible = false;

var CLIP_BASE_NAME = "mc_test_clip";
var TOTAL_CLIPS = 3;
var LIST_ORIENTATION = "vertical";
var CLIP_SPACING = 10;
var MOUSE_BUFFER = 20;
var SCROLL_SPEED = 1;
var LOOPING = true;
var SMOOTH = true;
var FRICTION = 5;
```

Remember, take the extra time to give your variables sensible names so that you and others going through your code can understand what's happening. The **MOVIE_WIDTH** and **MOVIE_HEIGHT** variables hold the width and height of your movie. If these values do not match your current movie's dimensions, change them now. **CLIP_BASE_NAME** holds the base name for the clips you'll be scrolling in the list. You will make some clips later to test the code. **TOTAL_CLIPS** is the number of clips that you will control in the list. This will be used in conjunction with the **CLIP_BASE_NAME** constant to actually find the movie clips on the Stage. The **LIST_ORIENTATION** constant will control whether your scrolling list moves from side to side or up and down. **SCROLL_SPEED** will hold a number that you will use to determine the speed at which the list should scroll. The **LOOPING** constant will hold whether the list loops around to the beginning when you reach one end of the list, or whether it stops at one end, forcing the user to scroll in the opposite direction to get to the other side. Both the **SMOOTH** and **FRICTION** constants will be used later to help add a nice little touch to the list: having it decelerate slowly when the user moves her mouse away from the list.

Public Functions

When planning your code, especially if other developers are going to use it, you should think in terms of "public or private" when organizing functions and variables. Suppose, for example, that you have a balloon movie clip that contains all the ActionScript logic necessary to float around the screen like a real balloon does. All the calculations for gravity and weight and even the size of the balloon are functions and variables that don't need any help from the outside to work properly. These could be considered private functions and variables. However, you may want to have another movie clip onscreen pop the balloon. In this case, you can provide a public `pop()` function that can safely be accessed by other code in the main movie.

The advantage to working in this manner is that you would need to explain to the other developers only about how to use the public functions to do what they want. This keeps you from having to explain to everyone using your cool balloon clip how the **material_tension** variable is handled or how your code might deal with a **gGravity** variable with a `null` value. You just provide those developers with a good public set of variables and functions so that they don't need to learn all the intricacies of your code if they don't want to.

For the scrolling list component, you may sometimes need to pause the scrolling or perhaps even reinitialize the list. Add the following public functions in the Actions panel:

```
function enableScrolling() {
 gScrollingEnabled = true;
}

function disableScrolling() {
 gScrollingEnabled = false;
}

function resetList() {
 gotoAndPlay(1);
}
```

These are very simple functions that change the value of a variable, **gScrollingEnabled**, to either `true` or `false`. The `resetList` function takes care of sending the playback head back to the first frame of the component, which will rebuild the list.

Handling the Offset

Instead of enforcing that the movie clip's registration point be in the center, for this module you will use programming. Add this code to your ActionScript panel:

```
function getClipOffset(clipObj, axis) {
 var tempOffset = 0;
 if (axis == "x") {
  tempOffset = clipObj._x - clipObj.getBounds(_parent).xMin;
 } else if (axis == "y") {
  tempOffset = clipObj._y - clipObj.getBounds(_parent).yMin;
 }
 return tempOffset;
}
```

The `getClipOffset` function takes a movie clip object and the axis of the offset you want it to return. It then finds the offset of the movie clip object by calculating the difference between the *y* position of the clip and the coordinate of the clip's left edge returned by Flash's `getBounds()` function.

Creating a Clip Array

Now you'll define the `createClipArray` function. It will use the ***CLIP_BASE_NAME*** and ***TOTAL_CLIPS*** constants to find clips on the Stage and keep them around in an array so that you can easily loop through them later. Add this code next:

```
function createClipArray(baseName, total) {
  var tempArray = new Array();
  for (var i = 0; i < total; i++) {
    if (null != _parent[baseName + i]) {
      tempArray[i] = _parent[baseName + i];
    }
  }
  return tempArray;
}

var gClipArray = createClipArray(CLIP_BASE_NAME, TOTAL_CLIPS);
```

This is one cool little function! It does some simple stuff, but makes your work much, much easier later on. The `createClipArray` function takes the base name and a total number of clips as parameters. It then loops through the same number of times as there are clips, checking to see whether a clip with the base name and a number at the end exists in the _parent movie. If it does exist (if it's not `null`), the function adds a reference to it in an array. The function then returns the newly built array to the caller of the function, the ***gClipArray*** variable. Clean, simple, and elegant.

Now make sure the `createClipArray` function works. By creating the array, you have created references to your movie clips. These references can be used to access and set properties of those movie clips, as follows:

```
arrayOfClips[0]._x = 100;
```

Here the **x** position of the clip is set, referenced by the first element of the array. This would be the same as:

```
_parent.mc_someClip0._x = 100;
```

Or:

```
_parent["mc_someClip0"]._x = 100;
```

The referencing technique provides one real advantage: If you ever want to change the path to a movie clip from _parent to, perhaps, _level233, you will only have to change it in the `createClipArray` function; you won't have to search through all your code for where you accessed the movie clip using the _parent methods. Neat, huh?

Organizing Your List Clips

First off, save your movie and then get ready to put that **gClipArray** variable to use. You are going to position all the clips on the Stage and then try to determine the scrolling list's active area based on the position of all those clips. Enter this code next in the ActionScript panel:

```
var gTopBounds = 0;
var gBottomBounds = 0;
var gLeftBounds = 0;
var gRightBounds = 0;
if (gClipArray.length > 0) {
  gTopBounds = gClipArray[0].getBounds(_parent).yMin;
  gBottomBounds = gClipArray[0].getBounds(_parent).yMax;
  gLeftBounds = gClipArray[0].getBounds(_parent).xMin;
  gRightBounds = gClipArray[0].getBounds(_parent).xMax;
}
```

These variables are being initialized and will soon hold the outer perimeter, or bounds, of the active area (the area that the mouse can roll over to activate the scrolling) of the scrolling list. Next you verify that the **gClipArray** contains something; and if it does, you set the bounds variables to the bounds of the first clip in your list.

Now add this code next:

```
var tempX = 1;
var tempY = 1;
for (var i = 0; i < gClipArray.length; i++) {

  if (LIST_ORIENTATION == "horizontal") {
   gClipArray[i]._x = tempX + getClipOffset(gClipArray[i], "x");
   tempX = gClipArray[i]._x - getClipOffset(gClipArray[i], "x") +
➥gClipArray[i]._width + CLIP_SPACING;
  } else {
   gClipArray[i]._y = tempY + getClipOffset(gClipArray[i], "y");
   tempY = gClipArray[i]._y - getClipOffset(gClipArray[i], "y") +
➥gClipArray[i]._height + CLIP_SPACING;
  }
  tempTop = gClipArray[i].getBounds(_parent).yMin;
  if (tempTop < gTopBounds) { gTopBounds = tempTop };

  tempBottom = gClipArray[i].getBounds(_parent).yMax;
  if (tempBottom > gBottomBounds) {
   gBottomBounds = tempBottom
  };

  tempLeft = gClipArray[i].getBounds(_parent).xMin;
  if (tempLeft < gLeftBounds) { gLeftBounds = tempLeft };

  tempRight = gClipArray[i].getBounds(_parent).xMax;
  if (tempRight > gRightBounds) {
   gRightBounds = tempRight
  };
}
gTopBounds -= MOUSE_BUFFER;
gBottomBounds += MOUSE_BUFFER;
gLeftBounds -= MOUSE_BUFFER;
gRightBounds += MOUSE_BUFFER;
```

This chunk of code looks like a lot but is actually pretty simple. After initializing some temporary variables, it loops through **gClipArray** and, depending on the list's orientation (horizontal or vertical), positions each clip, in order of its name, side by side separated by the distance in pixels specified in the **CLIP_ SPACING** constant. It also compensates for any clip offset that may exist. After it positions the clip, it updates the temporary variable with a new location for the next clip in the loop. Then the position of every clip is compared to the bounds' variables. The code updates them if it finds a clip that exceeds the bounds. In other words, if you have different sized clips in your list, the biggest clip is used to determine the bounds of the list. Finally, you increase the scrolling list's activation area by the amount specified in the **MOUSE_BUFFER** constant. This makes it possible for the user to activate the scrolling of the list without having to actually be positioned over the list.

Initializing Your Variables

Now it's time to initialize some more global variables:

```
var gTotalWidth = tempX;
var gTotalHeight = tempY;

var tempScaleMode = Stage.scaleMode;
Stage.scaleMode = "exactFit";
var MOVIE_WIDTH = 550;
var MOVIE_HEIGHT = 400;
Stage.scaleMode = tempScaleMode;
var gMovieCenterX = MOVIE_WIDTH / 2;
var gMovieCenterY = MOVIE_HEIGHT / 2;

var gMouseDeltaX = 0;
var gMouseDeltaY = 0;

var gOriginX = 0;
var gOriginY = 0;

var gFriction = 1 + (FRICTION / 150);

var gConstX = (Math.pow(gMovieCenterX, 3) + Math.pow(MOVIE_WIDTH, 3) +
➥Math.pow(gMovieCenterX, 2) +  Math.pow(MOVIE_WIDTH, 2)) / 4;
var gConstY = (pow(gMovieCenterY, 3) + Math.pow(MOVIE_HEIGHT, 3) +
➥Math.pow(gMovieCenterY, 2) +  Math.pow(MOVIE_HEIGHT, 2)) / 4;

var gScrollingEnabled = true;
```

The **gTotalWidth** and **gTotalHeight** variables hold the width and height of the scrolling list as a whole. These will be used later to reset the entire list position based on the width or height (cumulative) of the clips in the scrolling list.

Next you have the **gMovieCenterX** and **gMovieCenterY** variables that hold the center point on the screen for both the width (*x*) and height (*y*). These numbers will be used later to calculate the distance between the mouse cursor and the center of the screen. It uses the **gMouseDeltaX** and **gMouseDeltaY** variables to store those values.

```
100  // grab the accumulative width of all the items in the list
101  var gTotalWidth = tempX;
102  var gTotalHeight = tempY;
103
104  // find the center of the screen
105  var tempScaleMode = Stage.scaleMode;
106  Stage.scaleMode = "exactFit";
107  var MOVIE_WIDTH = 550;
108  var MOVIE_HEIGHT = 400;
109  Stage.scaleMode = tempScaleMode;
110  var gMovieCenterX = MOVIE_WIDTH / 2;
111  var gMovieCenterY = MOVIE_HEIGHT / 2;
112
113  // holds the delta betwen the mouse position and the center of the screen later
114  var gMouseDeltaX = 0;
115  var gMouseDeltaY = 0;
116
117  // the reference point from which we will determine the clip locations
118  var gOriginX = 0;
119  var gOriginY = 0;
120
121  // friction needed for falloff
122  var gFriction = 1 + (FRICTION / 150);
123
124  // these are really big numbers that we use to determine the new location of the
125  // clips. we cube that number so it becomes really big. dividing these big numbers
126  // intoit seems to solve theproblem.
127  var gConstX = (Math.pow(gMovieCenterX, 3) + Math.pow(MOVIE_WIDTH, 3) + Math.pow(gMovieCenterX, 2) + Math.pow(MOVIE_WIDTH, 2)) / 4;
128  var gConstY = (Math.pow(gMovieCenterY, 3) + Math.pow(MOVIE_HEIGHT, 3) + Math.pow(gMovieCenterY, 2) + Math.pow(MOVIE_HEIGHT, 2)) / 4;
129
130  // this will hold a boolean allowing the list to scroll or not
131  var gScrollingEnabled = true;
```

Figure 5.6
The variables being initialized.

The **gOriginX** and **gOriginY** variables will be used as a reference point from which to determine the new location of the clips on the Stage. Initialize them here to 0.

The last set of variables to initialize in this frame has to do with the smoothing effect of the component. When smoothing is set to yes, the scrolling list will slowly decelerate to a stop after the mouse cursor has left the activation area. The **gFriction** variable is set to a fraction of the **FRICTION** constant. Adding 1 to it will ensure that it is always greater than zero. This number will be used later when calculating the acceleration and deceleration of the scrolling list.

The **gConst** variables are math constants, really big ones in this case, that will also be used later to divide into another very large number and finally determine the new *x* or *y* position of the scrolling list.

Finally, you have the **gScrollingEnabled** global variable, which will be a Boolean value (true or false) that will tell the list whether to

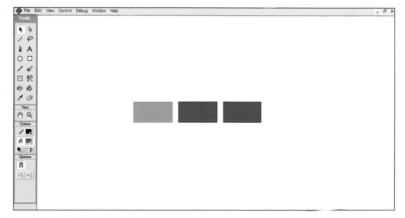

Figure 5.7
So far so good. The list elements are added to the object array and positioned properly!

scroll at all. This can be useful to temporarily stop the list from scrolling if you want to steal the user's attention for alerts or other elements. This should be changed using the enableScrolling() and disableScrolling() functions defined at the beginning of this frame.

Believe it or not, this is all the code for frame 1! Save your movie again and go to scene 1. Draw a shape on the screen and convert it into a move clip. Be sure to set the registration point of the movie to 0, 0. Now copy that movie clip and paste it in the same layer twice. Position the new clips on top of each other and give the first clip the name of **mc_test_clip0**, the second clip the instance name of **mc_test_clip1**, and the third clip the name of **mc_test_clip2**. Now test your movie. You should see that the three items have been repositioned in a vertical row. Close the test movie and change the *LIST_ORIENTATION* constant you defined at the top of the first frame to `horizontal` and then test the movie again. You should now notice that the shapes have been organized horizontally across the Stage. Great work!

Now it's time to move on to frame 2 of the gesture-driven scrolling list component. This is where you make the scrolling list actually scroll.

The Over State

The first code that you will add deals with checking the state of the mouse cursor in relation to the activation area you defined in frame 1. Make sure you have frame 2 selected and add the following code in the ActionScript panel:

```
if (LIST_ORIENTATION == "horizontal") {
 var isOver = _root._ymouse >= gTopBounds && _root._ymouse <=
gBottomBounds;
} else {
 var isOver = _root._xmouse >= gLeftBounds && _root._xmouse <=
gRightBounds;
}
```

Here, depending on what the orientation of the movie is, you test the mouse cursor position and see whether it is within the bounds of the activation area. If so, the *isOver* variable gets set to `true`. Now add this code:

```
if (isOver && gScrollingEnabled) {

} else {

}
```

This is the `if` statement that will contain the code to calculate the new position of the *gOriginX* and *gOriginY* reference points. It will evaluate to `true` as long as the *isOver* and the *gScrollingEnabled* variables are both `true`. Add this code now, inside the top portion of the `if` statement, before the `else` part:

```
var oldMouseDeltaX = gMouseDeltaX;
var oldMouseDeltaY = gMouseDeltaY;

if (SMOOTH) {
  gMouseDeltaX = oldMouseDeltaX + ((_root._xmouse - gMovieCenterX -
➡oldMouseDeltaX) / (gFriction * 2))
  gMouseDeltaY = oldMouseDeltaY + ((_root._ymouse - gMovieCenterY -
➡oldMouseDeltaY) / (gFriction * 2))
  } else {
  gMouseDeltaX = _root._xmouse - gMovieCenterX;
  gMouseDeltaY = _root._ymouse - gMovieCenterY;
  }
```

The first thing that happens here is you initialize two new variables, **oldMouseDeltaX** and **oldMouseDeltaY**, to hold the current values of the **gMouseDeltaX** and **gMouseDeltaY** variables you initialized in frame 1. Then, if the **SMOOTH** constant is set to `true`, you set the global mouse delta variables to the distance between the center of the screen and the current mouse location, subtract the previous mouse delta (**oldMouseDeltaX** and **oldMouseDeltaY**), and then divide the result by the **gFraction** variable also defined in frame 1. This results in a fraction of the delta that you add to the old delta and assign that to **gMouseDeltaX** and **gMouseDeltaY**. This code is accelerating from the last delta to the new delta. This will result in a smooth transition from a completely stopped list to a moving list. If the **SMOOTH** constant is set to `no`, you grab the delta and assign it to the **gMouseDeltaX** and **gMouseDeltaY** variables without the in-between steps of dealing with the **gFriction** variable. If you were to move your mouse to one end of the list to start it scrolling, it would start up instantaneously.

In the second part of the `if` statement (the `else`), add the following:

```
if (SMOOTH) {
  gMouseDeltaX = gMouseDeltaX / gFriction;
  gMouseDeltaY = gMouseDeltaY / gFriction;
  } else {
  gMouseDeltaX = 0;
  gMouseDeltaY = 0;
  }
```

This code gets executed if the mouse is not over the activation area. If **SMOOTH** is set to `true`, you slowly diminish the mouse delta variables by dividing them by the **gFriction** variable instead of setting them to `0` as you do if the **SMOOTH** setting is turned off.

The Heart of the System

You've now arrived at the heart of the gesture-driven scrolling list component. This is where all the code will go that actually moves the movie clips around. For starters, add this code at the very bottom of the Actions panel:

```
if (LIST_ORIENTATION == "horizontal" && gMouseDeltaX != 0) {

} else if (LIST_ORIENTATION == "vertical" && gMouseDeltaY != 0) {

}
```

```
34  if (LIST_ORIENTATION == "horizontal" && gMouseDeltaX != 0) {
35      gOriginX = gOriginX - Math.pow(gMouseDeltaX * SCROLL_SPEED, 3) / gConstX;
36      var clipOffsetX = 0;
37
38      for (var i = 0; i < gClipArray.length; i++) {
39
40          if (gOriginX < -gTotalWidth) {
41              gOriginX = gOriginX % gTotalWidth;
42          } else if (gOriginX > gTotalWidth) {
43              gOriginX = gOriginX % gTotalWidth;
44          }
45
46          if (LOOPING == "no") {
47              if (gOriginX > 1) {
48                  gOriginX = 1;
49              } else if (gOriginX < MOVIE_WIDTH - gTotalWidth + 1 + CLIP_SPACING) {
50                  gOriginX = MOVIE_WIDTH - gTotalWidth + 1 + CLIP_SPACING;
51              }
52          }
53
54          var newX = gOriginX + clipOffsetX;
55          if (newX + gClipArray[i]._width < 0) {
56              newX = gTotalWidth + newX;
57          } else if (newX > MOVIE_WIDTH) {
58              newX = newX - gTotalWidth;
59          }
60
61          gClipArray[i]._x = newX + getClipOffset(gClipArray[i], "x");
62          clipOffsetX += gClipArray[i]._width + CLIP_SPACING;
63      }
64
65  } else if (LIST_ORIENTATION == "vertical" && gMouseDeltaY != 0) {
```

Figure 5.8
The code for the horizontal setting is the same as for the vertical, except the axes are different.

This `if` statement really does all the work for the scrolling list component. First it checks what orientation was specified, and then checks whether the global mouse delta variables are anything other than `0`. The code that actually moves the clips around is contained within this `if` statement. Therefore, you can deduce that when the global mouse delta is 0 (in other words, the mouse cursor is not within the activation area bounds or the diminishing code has reached 0), the code that lies between these if statements will never get called. Although the two sections of this if statement are testing for different things, the code is identical for both—except that one deals with the *x*-axis (the horizontal one) and the other the *y*. You will address the *x*-axis version, and then replicate it for the *y* when you are through. Now, in the first if statement you just added, enter this code:

```
gOriginX = gOriginX - Math.pow(gMouseDeltaX * SCROLL_SPEED, 3) /
➥gConstX;
```

As you recall, **gOriginX** (and its y-axis sibling, **gOriginY**) act as reference points for you to use to calculate the new positions of the movie clips on the Stage. Here, you do the work of setting **gOriginX**. First, the global mouse delta (**gMouseDeltaX**) is multiplied by the **SCROLL_SPEED** constant you defined in frame 1. You then take this number and cube it, which should result in a very large number. Remember those really big math constants you defined in frame 1? Now you finally get to use them by dividing them into the resulting cubed number. So why, exactly, are you cubing a number and so on? Well, the **gOriginX** variable defines the feel of the scrolling list with speed, friction, and acceleration. If you were to use straight multiplication here, you would most likely end up with a steady acceleration that would get you the result similar to a linear equation. Instead you effectively create a larger "slow" area in the middle of the scrolling list, which will give the end user much more control over the scrolling list.

Immediately following the code you just added, enter this code:

```
var clipOffsetX = 0;
for (var i = 0; i < gClipArray.length; i++) {

}
```

clipOffsetX will be used to calculate the proper distance from the **gOriginX** position (or reference point) to the new clip position. Next you begin the for loop that will go through each of the objects in the **gClipArray** variable.

Now add the following:

```
if (gOriginX < -gTotalWidth) {
 gOriginX = gOriginX % gTotalWidth;
} else if (gOriginX > gTotalWidth) {
 gOriginX = gOriginX % gTotalWidth;
}

if (!LOOPING) {
if (gOriginX > 1) {
 gOriginX = 1;
} else if (gOriginX < MOVIE_WIDTH - gTotalWidth + 1 + CLIP_SPACING) {
 gOriginX = MOVIE_WIDTH - gTotalWidth + 1 + CLIP_SPACING;
 }
}
```

Because the **gOriginX** variable is a reference point for your movie clips in the scrolling list, you need to continuously add to it or subtract from it. This number can become quite large and unruly and will start to create more work for you when you need to offset that big value. The solution here is to limit its movements to the collective width of the movie clips. Here you test to see whether the **gOriginX** variable is larger or smaller than the total width of all the movie clips in the list. If it is, you just reposition the origin to the remainder of the origin and the total width of the movie clips.

Next the code handles the **LOOPING** constant. If the developer has selected the scrolling list not to loop, you check the position of **gOriginX** to see whether it goes past the edges of the screen. If it does, you limit it to that edge.

Now add the code that will do the actual calculation for the position of each of the movie clip elements (still inside the `for` loop):

```
var newX = gOriginX + clipOffsetX;
if (newX + gClipArray[i]._width < 0) {
 newX = gTotalWidth + newX;
} else if (newX > MOVIE_WIDTH) {
 newX = newX - gTotalWidth;
}
gClipArray[i]._x = newX + getClipOffset(gClipArray[i], "x");
clipOffsetX += gClipArray[i]._width + CLIP_SPACING;
```

First you define a new variable named **newX**, which will hold the new position for the current movie clip (**gClipArray[i]**) in the array. Then you test that new position to see whether it falls below or above the edges of the main movie. If it does, you add or subtract the total width of all the clips from the new value, essentially putting the movie clip at the very front or the very end of the list.

Next you set the **x** position of the current clip in the array (**gClipArray[i]**) to **newX** and calculate the offset for movie clips with different registration points. After that, you update the **clipOffsetX** variable to include this clip's width and spacing (**CLIP_SPACING**). And that's it! The code to handle the vertical situation is nearly identical to this except it handles the y-axis. Add that to the second part of the if statement, where **LIST_ORIENTATION** is "vertical":

```
gOriginY = gOriginY - pow(gMouseDeltaY * SCROLL_SPEED, 3) / gConstY;

var clipOffsetY = 0;
for (var i = 0; i < gClipArray.length; i++) {

 if (gOriginY < -gTotalHeight) {
  gOriginY = gOriginY % gTotalHeight;
 } else if (gOriginY > gTotalHeight) {
  gOriginY = gOriginY % gTotalHeight;
 }

 if (!LOOPING) {
  if (gOriginY > 1) {
  gOriginY = 1;
 } else if (gOriginY < MOVIE_HEIGHT - gTotalHeight + 1 + CLIP_SPACING) {
  gOriginY = MOVIE_HEIGHT - gTotalHeight + 1 + CLIP_SPACING;
 }
 }

 var newY = gOriginY + clipOffsetY;
  if (newY + gClipArray[i]._height < 0) {
  newY = gTotalHeight + newY;
  } else if (newY > MOVIE_HEIGHT) {
  newY = newY - gTotalHeight;
  }

 gClipArray[i]._y = newY + getClipOffset(gClipArray[i], "y");
 clipOffsetY += gClipArray[i]._height + CLIP_SPACING;

}
```

Test Your Work

Now that you've finished off the code for frame 2, take some time to relax—and make sure you've saved this movie! Now add one more line of code and then you can test the movie. Select the third keyframe in this movie clip and open the Actions panel. Add this line:

```
gotoAndPlay(2);
```

Now go back to the main movie (scene 1) and copy and paste your clips until you have about nine clips on the Stage. Remember to edit the **_TOTAL_CLIPS_** constant in frame 1 of this movie clip to reflect the proper number of clips. Now test the movie. Is everything working? Fiddle around with some of the other constants and keep testing the movie to see how it reacts.

The three listings that follow show all the code you should have in the three frames of your scrolling list component. Check to make sure you are in sync, and then you will move on to making a real component out of the scrolling list movie clip.

```
Listing 5.1   Frame 1 ActionScript

this._visible = false;

var CLIP_BASE_NAME = "mc_test_clip";
var TOTAL_CLIPS = 3;
var LIST_ORIENTATION = "vertical";
var MOUSE_BUFFER = 20;
var CLIP_SPACING = 10;
var SCROLL_SPEED = 1;
var LOOPING = true;
var SMOOTH = true;
var FRICTION = 5;

function getClipOffset(clipObj, axis) {
 var tempOffset = 0;
 if (axis == "x") {
  tempOffset = clipObj._x - clipObj.getBounds(_parent).xMin;
 } else if (axis == "y") {
  tempOffset = clipObj._y - clipObj.getBounds(_parent).yMin;
 }
 return tempOffset;
}
```

```
function createClipArray(baseName, total) {
 var tempArray = new Array();
 for (var i = 0; i < total; i++) {
  if (null != _parent[baseName + i]) {
   tempArray[i] = _parent[baseName + i];
  }
 }
 return tempArray;
}

var gClipArray = createClipArray(CLIP_BASE_NAME, TOTAL_CLIPS);

var gTopBounds = 0;
var gBottomBounds = 0;
var gLeftBounds = 0;
var gRightBounds = 0;
if (gClipArray.length > 0) {
 gTopBounds = gClipArray[0].getBounds(_parent).yMin;
 gBottomBounds = gClipArray[0].getBounds(_parent).yMax;
 gLeftBounds = gClipArray[0].getBounds(_parent).xMin;
 gRightBounds = gClipArray[0].getBounds(_parent).xMax;
}

var tempX = 1;
var tempY = 1;
for (var i = 0; i < gClipArray.length; i++) {

 if (LIST_ORIENTATION == "horizontal") {
  gClipArray[i]._x = tempX + getClipOffset(gClipArray[i], "x");
  tempX = gClipArray[i]._x - getClipOffset(gClipArray[i], "x") +
➥ gClipArray[i]._width + CLIP_SPACING;
 } else {
  gClipArray[i]._y = tempY + getClipOffset(gClipArray[i], "y");
  tempY = gClipArray[i]._y - getClipOffset(gClipArray[i], "y") +
➥ gClipArray[i]._height + CLIP_SPACING;
 }

 tempTop = gClipArray[i].getBounds(_parent).yMin;
 if (tempTop < yTopBounds) { gTopBounds = tempTop };

 tempBottom = gClipArray[i].getBounds(_parent).yMax;
 if (tempBottom > gBottomBounds) {
  gBottomBounds = tempBottom
 };
```

continues

Listing 5.1 Frame 1 ActionScript *continued*

```
 tempLeft = gClipArray[i].getBounds(_parent).xMin;
 if (tempLeft < gLeftBounds) { gLeftBounds = tempLeft };

 tempRight = gClipArray[i].getBounds(_parent).xMax;
 if (tempRight > gRightBounds) {
  gRightBounds = tempRight
 };
}

gTopBounds -= MOUSE_BUFFER;
gBottomBounds += MOUSE_BUFFER;
gLeftBounds -= MOUSE_BUFFER;
gRightBounds += MOUSE_BUFFER;

var gTotalWidth = tempX;
var gTotalHeight = tempY;

var tempScaleMode = Stage.scaleMode;
Stage.scaleMode = "exactFit";
var MOVIE_WIDTH = 550;
var MOVIE_HEIGHT = 400;
Stage.scaleMode = tempScaleMode;

var gMovieCenterX = MOVIE_WIDTH / 2;
var gMovieCenterY = MOVIE_HEIGHT / 2;

var gMouseDeltaX = 0;
var gMouseDeltaY = 0;

var gOriginX = 0;
var gOriginY = 0;

var gFriction = 1 + (FRICTION / 150);

var gConstX = (Math.pow(gMovieCenterX, 3) + Math.pow(MOVIE_WIDTH, 3) +
➥Math.pow(gMovieCenterX, 2) +  Math.pow(MOVIE_WIDTH, 2)) / 4;
var gConstY = (Math.pow(gMovieCenterY, 3) + Math.pow(MOVIE_HEIGHT, 3) +
➥Math.pow(gMovieCenterY, 2) +  Math.pow(MOVIE_HEIGHT, 2)) / 4;
```

Listing 5.2 Frame 2 ActionScript

```
if (LIST_ORIENTATION == "horizontal") {
 var isOver = _root._ymouse >= gTopBounds && root._ymouse <= gBottomBounds;
} else {
 var isOver = _root._xmouse >= gLeftBounds && root._xmouse <= gRightBounds;
}

if (isOver) {
 var oldMouseDeltaX = gMouseDeltaX;
 var oldMouseDeltaY = gMouseDeltaY;

 if (SMOOTH) {
  gMouseDeltaX = oldMouseDeltaX + ((_root._xmouse - gMovieCenterX -
➥oldMouseDeltaX) / (gFriction * 2))
  gMouseDeltaY = oldMouseDeltaY + ((_root._ymouse - gMovieCenterY -
➥oldMouseDeltaY) / (gFriction * 2))
 } else {
  gMouseDeltaX = _root._xmouse - gMovieCenterX;
  gMouseDeltaY = _root._ymouse - gMovieCenterY;
 }

} else {
 if (SMOOTH) {
  gMouseDeltaX = gMouseDeltaX / gFriction;
  gMouseDeltaY = gMouseDeltaY / gFriction;
 } else {
  gMouseDeltaX = 0;
  gMouseDeltaY = 0;
 }
}

if (LIST_ORIENTATION == "horizontal" && gMouseDeltaX != 0) {
 gOriginX = gOriginX - Math.pow(gMouseDeltaX * SCROLL_SPEED, 3) / gConstX;

 var clipOffsetX = 0;

 for (var i = 0; i < gClipArray.length; i++) {  if (gOriginX < -
➥gTotalWidth) {
   gOriginX = gOriginX % gTotalWidth;
  } else if (gOriginX > gTotalWidth) {
   gOriginX = gOriginX % gTotalWidth;
  }
```

continues

Listing 5.2 Frame 2 ActionScript *continued*

```
  if (!LOOPING) {
   if (gOriginX > 1) {
    gOriginX = 1;
   } else if (gOriginX < MOVIE_WIDTH - gTotalWidth + 1 + CLIP_SPACING) {
    gOriginX = MOVIE_WIDTH - gTotalWidth + 1 + CLIP_SPACING;
   }
  }

  var newX = gOriginX + clipOffsetX;
  if (newX + gClipArray[i]._width < 0) {
   newX = gTotalWidth + newX;
  } else if (newX > MOVIE_WIDTH) {
   newX = newX - gTotalWidth;
  }

  gClipArray[i]._x = newX + getClipOffset(gClipArray[i], "x");
  clipOffsetX += gClipArray[i]._width + CLIP_SPACING;
 }
} else if (LIST_ORIENTATION == "vertical" && gMouseDeltaY != 0) {
  gOriginY = gOriginY - Math.pow(gMouseDeltaY * SCROLL_SPEED, 3) /
➡gConstY;

 var clipOffsetY = 0;
 for (var i = 0; i < gClipArray.length; i++) {

  if (gOriginY < -gTotalHeight) {
    gOriginY = gOriginY % gTotalHeight;
  } else if (gOriginY > gTotalHeight) {
   gOriginY = gOriginY % gTotalHeight;
  }

  if (!LOOPING) {
   if (gOriginY > 1) {
    gOriginY = 1;
   } else if (gOriginY < MOVIE_HEIGHT - gTotalHeight + 1 + CLIP_SPACING) {
    gOriginY = MOVIE_HEIGHT - gTotalHeight + 1 + CLIP_SPACING;
   }
  }

  var newY = gOriginY + clipOffsetY;
  if (newY + gClipArray[i]._height < 0) {
   newY = gTotalHeight + newY;
```

```
    } else if (newY > MOVIE_HEIGHT) {
      newY = newY - gTotalHeight;
    }

    gClipArray[i]._y = newY + getClipOffset(gClipArray[i], "y");
    clipOffsetY += gClipArray[i]._height + CLIP_SPACING;
    }
}


Listing 5.3  Frame 3 ActionScript

gotoAndPlay(2);
```

Making the Component

Now that all the hard work of coding this clip is done, take a little extra time to make this clip into a truly reusable component. Open the library for your movie (Window>Library) and find the **ScrollingList** movie clip. Right-click (Ctrl-click on the Mac) the movie clip and select Component Definition. When the Component Definition panel comes up, use the plus sign (+) button to add new constants to the list of variables. Here is the list that you will add:

Figure 5.9
The Component Definition interface with all the constants.

- ■ **CLIP_BASE_NAME**

- ■ **TOTAL_CLIPS**

- ■ **LIST_ORIENTATION**

- ■ **MOUSE_BUFFER**

- ■ **CLIP_SPACING**

- ■ **SCROLL_SPEED**

- ■ **LOOPING**

- ■ **SMOOTH**

- ■ **FRICTION**

When adding a variable, you can double-click one of the three fields to edit the name, initial value, and type of variable it is. Make all the variables Number types for now.

Change the **CLIP_BASE_NAME** variable to the Default type.

Now change the type of field for **LIST_ORIENTATION** to a List type. Then double-click the middle column to bring up the List dialog box. Using the plus sign (+), add `"vertical"` and `"horizontal"`.

LOOPING and **SMOOTH** should be changed to Boolean types. Keep both their values at the default of `false`.

Finally, in frame 1 of your scrolling list component, remove or comment out the variables at the top of the script.

Hooray! You're done! Now you can drag and drop this component into any movie and change all the parameters without ever going into the code. What's more, you not only have a component that can really be useful for you when developing, but a tool that can help you create more usable web sites for your clients.

Figure 5.10
Be sure to comment the constants from the component.

CONCLUSION

The gesture-driven list is an interface element that really stands apart from the standard way of doing things. Zooming through large numbers of images with this type of control is far easier than the click and drag method invented years ago. With Flash, you can fine-tune this component to really go a long way in making Nancy's experience while on the MODA site better and more unique. You also have a totally generalized, flexible, and reusable control that can easily be dropped into any movie, and, with a minimum of fuss, have a gesture-driven list up and running. This is really the best kind of tool to have: one that makes the developer's *and* the users' lives easier by addressing many of the key issues in each of those segments:

- **A usable speed for any particular audience.** You can easily define different speed, friction, and orientation depending on client and user needs. This ensures that the end user will have a much more targeted experience on the site and can find that it is much easier to get to the information they want and accomplish their goals with well thought out controls.

- **Truly reusable object.** This component can be dropped into any movie and with a few clicks, poof! A gesture-driven list. This presents the kind of flexible object that can give developers the time to really think about the end users and their goals and how they can help the users accomplish these goals.

- **Improved navigation.** This tool goes beyond being a tool for browsing pictures and paintings. It can be used for any situation where a single, noncomplex organization of information needs to be given an interface.

CHAPTER 06

Less Cluttered and More Usable

*Thinking is more interesting than knowing,
but less interesting than looking.*

—Goethe

When creating a Flash interface, the designer must consider carefully all the options the potential user will need. Almost always, you must provide two sets of features:

- Those critical to user success in accomplishing their goals on the site
- Those that are not essential for the site goals to be met, but that add to the overall user experience

Often the most critical features are also global features, such as a help system. They should be accessible from anywhere and have prime real estate on the screen. The functions that enhance the user experience rather than enable it are generally not global and relate to a certain focused area of the site. To make the user experience as intuitive as possible, access to these features should be local to the area to which they relate. For example, information about a thumbnail image in the MODA site should be accessed via the thumbnail rather than through a global menu control.

To successfully design an interface that may have global and section-specific features, you should begin by organizing these different groups of features. Actions central to the user's main goals should have prime locations on the screen, whereas less critical actions can afford to be less in the limelight.

Nancy's main goals on the MODA site are as follows:

- To learn about the artist
- To view the paintings

The functionality to accomplish these goals should be given the most importance visually on the screen. Nancy's secondary goals on the site include the following:

- To find out more about each piece and how it was made
- To save a given piece to her desktop to use as wallpaper
- To print out the information she might come across on the site

To help Nancy achieve these secondary aims, you need to make sure these functions are still accessible but less dominant in the interface.

SOLUTIONS

Most of Nancy's interaction on the site will be with the scrolling list at the bottom of the screen, because that gives her access to the primary features. Some other features of the site may interest her as well but may not be part of the client's main focus or part of Nancy's goals on the site. Examples might be accessing additional information about the paintings, seeing the original sketches, printing out copies, and downloading desktop wallpaper. Because of Nancy's comfort level with computers and her obvious affinity for aesthetic value, it becomes clear that the best way to incorporate these secondary features is by storing them in the mouse under menu.

The trick when designing a user interface that incorporates a number of elements of differing importance is to keep the design simple. The main controls in the interface should be clearly distinguished from the ancillary features of the site. This is particularly important on the MODA site because its clean appearance is crucial to providing a gallery-like feel to the site. As in a gallery, here visitor attention should be drawn to the art they are seeing, not the gallery itself.

In exploring the possibilities available for providing the less critical functionality to Nancy without cluttering the interface and drawing attention away from the main controls, one mechanism offers a clear solution: the mouse under menu. This is a menu of items accessed by just clicking the target, much like the contextual (or right-click) menus in Windows, MacOS, and other operating systems. The immediate advantage that this control offers is that it is never in the way, yet always accessible. It is context-sensitive, so it will be accessible only when the item that Nancy wants to act upon is clicked.

For this control to work for Nancy, she needs to know that it is available. A straightforward way of doing this is to have a tool tip, caption, or custom mouse cursor that shows Nancy that the item under her mouse cursor is clickable.

For the MODA site, clicking a painting, for example, will bring up options to print the image, download a copy to her hard drive, or see alternative versions of the chosen image. Because Nancy must click the image to trigger the mouse under menu, she should intuitively understand the menu relates specifically to that image.

The mouse under menu adheres to Fitts's law pretty closely, too. By creating a menu system that appears at the mouse pointer, you are offering a menu that requires almost no mouse movement to access, greatly reducing the amount of time it takes the user to operate the menu.

To provide even greater usability, the mouse under menu will differ from a typical contextual menu in one key respect: It will be movable from its initial position. Contextual menus stay in the same position in which they were opened. This added control will enable Nancy to move the menu should it start to cover up a crucial part of the image or information.

> **Fitts's law** states that one of the five most accessible areas of the screen is the point where the mouse is at any given time. The other four are the top, bottom, and right and left sides of the screen. If you want more detail on Fitts's law, check out Appendix B, "Usability Resources," for books and web sites devoted to specific usability guidelines.
>
> **Note**

Seeing It in Action

Open **06_mouseMenu.fla** found in the **Projects** folder on the *Skip Intro* CD-ROM and export or test the movie. As you roll over the main picture and click, the mouse menu appears (see Figure 6.1). From here you can drag the menu wherever you want on the screen. Rolling off the menu will fade it out, so the site keeps its clean, uncluttered look.

Notice when you click that the menu appears wherever the mouse is. This is the most important characteristic of the mouse under menu. Close the test movie and open the Library panel for the sample movie. Edit the graphic symbol named Paintings and select the button on the top layer Menu button. If you look at the Actions panel, you will see how simple it is to activate the mouse under menu:

Figure 6.1
Clicking the big paintings should activate the mouse under menu.

```
on(press)
{
    mc_mouseMenu.showMenu();
}
```

The `showMenu()` function is all you have to call anywhere in the movie to show the menu. That's pretty simple.

Now click the Skip Intro Components folder in the library and open the MouseMenu folder that is inside the Skins folder. The three movie clips contained in that folder define what the mouse under menu looks like. These clips contain no code, just visual elements that can easily be changed to fit the mouse under menu to any project in which you may need it. Separating the visual parts from the code keeps other developers that may be using your components from having to dive into your code and potentially break it.

In the following section, you can take a look at how this menu was implemented to understand the power of this component.

IMPLEMENTATION

For the mouse under menu, you need to implement only a few features:

- **Mouse under.** The menu should appear directly under the mouse when Nancy clicks her mouse button.

- **Draggability.** Nancy should be able to drag the menu around the screen to avoid covering up parts of the image or text that she is viewing. The developer should, however, be able to turn off this feature.

- **Instant off.** Depending on the use of the menu, when the user clicks a selection the menu can either disappear, like contextual menus, or remain on. For Nancy and her use of the site, keeping the menu on is the better option.

Now that you have an idea of the tasks that the mouse under menu should accomplish, it's time to build it.

CONSTRUCTION

Good news! In terms of coding, the mouse under menu is not very complex, but takes advantage of some great Flash MX features that help to make this clip truly flexible.

The first step is to build the graphics for the mouse under menu. As always, even though your focus is on coding, the way you approach the visuals is just as important.

Setting Up the Movie

Make a new Flash movie and set its frame rate to 20. Create a new layer in your movie labeled **mouse menu**. Put the new layer at the very top of every layer with content in it. This will ensure the mouse under menu is on top of any other content in your movie.

On this layer, draw a rectangular shape on the Stage approximately 110 pixels wide by 30 pixels tall, and give it a black, hairline stroke and a light-gray fill. This will be the beginning of the skin movie clips for your mouse under menu.

Select the middle portion of the rectangle, 6 pixels from the top of the rectangle and about 18 pixels tall, and make it into a movie clip (F8) named **menu_middle** with its registration point to the upper-right corner.

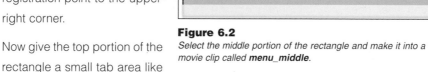

Figure 6.2
*Select the middle portion of the rectangle and make it into a movie clip called **menu_middle**.*

Now give the top portion of the rectangle a small tab area like the one illustrated in Figure 6.2. Select this whole top portion and make it into a movie clip called **menu_top**, also setting its registration point to the upper right.

Finally, select the bottom portion of the rectangle and make it into a movie clip called **menu_bottom** and set its registration point to the upper right as well. You should now have three movie clips on Stage. Double-click the middle movie clip to place it in Edit mode.

Create a new layer called **item name** and create a dynamic text field on that layer. Set the *x* coordinate of the field to 3 and the *y* coordinate to 0. Double-click to edit the text of the field and set the text to read **item Name**. Then set the variable for the field to **itemName** and make sure the field is not selectable. Click the Character button in the Properties panel for the field and also ensure that you've embedded all the characters of the font. Make this clip 10 frames long. Make frame 5 a keyframe on both layers in this clip and give the frame a frame label of **over**. On frame 6, select the light-gray section of the menu item image and change its color to a light blue. This clip will be used for every menu item in your mouse under menu.

To make these accessible from within the ActionScript you'll write later, you will have to change the linkage properties for each of the three movie clips. Start by right-clicking (in Windows) or Control-clicking (on the Macintosh) on the **menu_top** movie clip in the Library panel and selecting Linkage from the context menu. Click the Export for ActionScript check box on the Linkage Properties dialog box. Flash will automatically fill in the Identifier field with **menu_top**. Click the OK button and repeat the process for the **menu_middle** and **menu_bottom** movie clips.

Now that you've created the skins that control how your menu *looks*, now it's time to dive into the guts of this component.

Creating the Component

Make a rectangle on the **mouse menu** layer. Select the rectangle and make it a movie clip named **MouseMenu**, and then give this clip and instance name of **mc_mouseMenu**. Double-click the new movie clip symbol to open it in Edit mode.

CODE

The code for the mouse under menu will work like several of the other components in the book—it uses a frame loop. To begin, add two more frames to the movie clip and then add a new layer named **actions**. Select the three frames in the **actions** layer and convert them to keyframes (Modify>Frames>Convert to Keyframes).

Initialization

Click frame 1 of the **actions** layer, open the ActionScript editor (F2), and enter the following code:

```
var MENU_ITEMS = ["item 1", "item 2", "item 3"];
var HIDE_DELAY = 1000;
var HIDE_ON_CLICK = true;
```

These first few variables will be replaced later with component parameters. The **MENU_ITEMS** variable is an array of elements that represent your menu items. In this case, you have three menu items: item 1, item 2, and item 3.

The **HIDE_DELAY** variable holds the number of milliseconds in which the menu waits without user input before fading away.

HIDE_ON_CLICK will tell the component whether to fade away immediately after the user clicks an item in the menu.

Next you need to initialize some global variables. Add this code:

```
var gMenuShowing = false;
var gHideCalled = false;
var gTimerStarted = false;
var gStartTime = 0;

this._alpha = 50;
this.swapDepths(99999);
```

The **gMenuShowing** variable will be used later to tell different functions in the component whether the menu is currently being displayed.

The **gHideCalled** global variable is set to `true` when the `hideMenu()` function (which you will define later) gets called and is used in fading out the menu.

gTimerStarted holds the state of the timer which will hide the menu after a given number of milliseconds (defined earlier in **HIDE_DELAY**) has elapsed.

The alpha of the component is set here to 50%, but this will be changed to 0 when the component is complete. This ensures the menu is hidden from view right when the mouse menu component is loaded.

The built-in Flash `swapDepths()` function ensures the menu displays over all other items on its layer.

Building the Menu

Now it's time to start putting those skin movie clips you created earlier to good use. Start by entering this code in the Actions panel:

```
this.attachMovie("menu_top", "mc_menu_top", 1);
```

This code attaches the **menu_top** movie clip to the current movie clip. This will be the top of your menu.

Now is a good time to save your movie and test it. You should notice that the **menu_top** movie clip appears 50% transparent in the same place as the **MouseMenu** clip you created. If this is the case, you're off to a good start.

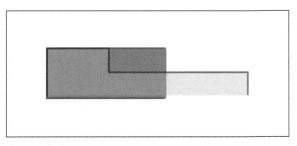

Figure 6.3
*The **menu_top** movie clip appears at the position of the **MouseMenu** movie clip you are currently defining.*

Close the test movie and return to the Actions panel for frame 1 of the **MouseMenu** movie clip. Add this code next:

```
var tempLevel = 2;
var tempOffset = this.mc_menu_top._height;
for (var i = 0; i < MENU_ITEMS.length; i++) {
    this.attachMovie("menu_middle", "mc_menu_item_" + i, tempLevel);
    this["mc_menu_item_" + i].itemName = MENU_ITEMS[i];
    this["mc_menu_item_" + i]._y = tempOffset;
    this["mc_menu_item_" + i].gotoAndStop(1);

    tempLevel++;
    tempOffset += this["mc_menu_item_" + i]._height;
}
```

This little loop is the heart of the under mouse menu component. It loops through the **MENU_ITEMS** array, attaches a new **menu_middle** movie clip for each element in the array, and then sets the itemLabel field inside that **menu_middle** movie clip to the text of that element of the array. This will enable you to add as many menu items as you need by just adding those items to the **MENU_ITEMS** array.

Now, before testing the loop, add the bottom part of the skin next by entering this code:

```
this.attachMovie("menu_bottom", "mc_menu_bottom", tempLevel);
this.mc_menu_bottom._y = tempOffset;
```

Now you're ready to test the movie again. You should notice that the whole menu appears as a whole piece. Great work so far!

As you can see, much of the real work is now done. The next several steps will deal with adding the finer details that help to make Nancy's experience the best it can be.

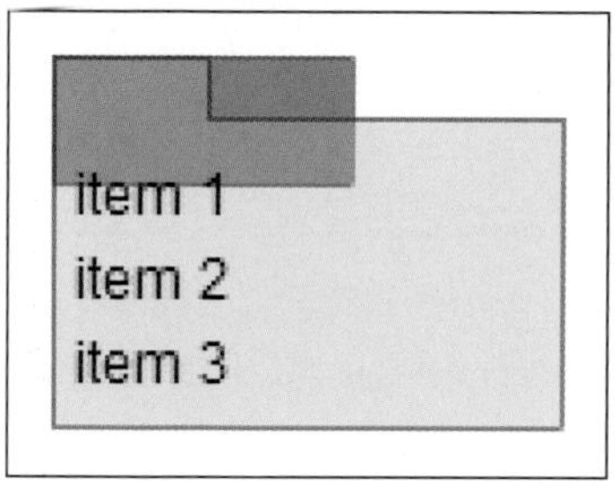

Mouse Handling

The next code you will add will handle the mouse events for the dragging of the menu. Add this code next to the Actions for frame 1:

Figure 6.4
You should see something very similar to this now, with all the items in the **MENU_ITEMS** *array showing up as items in your menu.*

```
function menuMouseDownFunc()
{
    if(this.hitTest(_root._xmouse, _root._ymouse, true)) {
        this.deltaX = _root._xmouse - this._parent._x;
        this.deltaY = _root._ymouse - this._parent._y;
        this.isDragging = true;
    }
}


function menuMouseUpFunc()
{
    this.isDragging = false;
}
```

The `menuMouseDownFunc()` function tests to determine whether the user's mouse is actually over the top of the menu. If it is, the difference between the clip's *x* and *y* coordinates and the mouse's are calculated and saved to the delta variables and the ***isDragging*** Boolean is set to `true`.

The `menuMouseUpFunc()` function sets the ***isDragging*** variable back to `false`. This will be used to tell the next function you will enter to stop moving the menu along with the mouse. Enter this code now:

```
function menuMouseMoveFunc()
{
    if(this.isDragging) {
            this._parent._x = _root._xmouse - this.deltaX;
            this._parent._y = _root._ymouse - this.deltaY;
            updateAfterEvent(mouseMove);
    }
}
```

`menuMouseMoveFunc()` checks to determine whether the ***isDragging*** variable is `true` and, if it is, updates the position of the menu and refreshes the drawing of the frame immediately to ensure the dragging is smooth.

How do these functions ever get called? These three functions will get attached to the movie clip at the top of the menu (**menu_top**), enabling the user to drag it around. Do that now. Right below the code where you attach the **menu_top** movie clip (before looping through the ***MENU_ITEMS*** array), add this ActionScript:

```
this.mc_menu_top.onMouseDown = menuMouseDownFunc;
this.mc_menu_top.onMouseUp = menuMouseUpFunc;
this.mc_menu_top.onMouseMove = menuMouseMoveFunc;
```

What this code does is attach each of the last three functions you defined to the three mouse events for the **menu_top** movie clip. It's that easy! Now before testing the movie again, go to keyframe 3 of the ***MouseMenu*** component and add this ActionScript:

```
41  this.mc_menu_top.onMouseDown = menuMouseDownFunc;
42  this.mc_menu_top.onMouseUp = menuMouseUpFunc;
43  this.mc_menu_top.onMouseMove = menuMouseMoveFunc;
```

Figure 6.5
*Attach the mouse functions to the **menu_top** movie clip to allow it to be dragged around with the mouse.*

```
gotoAndPlay(2);
```

This will ensure that the component loops over the last two frames and does not replay the frame of the clip, which would reinitialize the variables and cause the dragging to malfunction. Now save and test your movie.

You should be able to grab the top portion of the menu and easily drag it around the screen. Wow, that's smooth!

Now you will add two mouse functions to the menu items themselves. Start by going to frame 1 of the **MouseMenu** clip and adding this to its Actions:

```
function itemMouseUpFunc()
{
    if (this.hitTest( _root._xmouse, _root._ymouse, false)) {
            _root.underMenuDispatch(this.itemName);
            if (this._parent.HIDE_ON_CLICK) hideMenu();
    }
}

function itemMouseMoveFunc()
{
    if (this.hitTest( _root._xmouse, _root._ymouse, false)) {
            this.gotoAndStop("over");
    } else {
            this.gotoAndStop(1);
    }
}
```

The `itemMouseUpFunc()` function first checks to see that the mouse is released over the calling clip by using the Flash built-in function, `hitTest()`. Then it calls a dispatch function called `underMenuDispatch()` located in the root movie. A dispatch function takes in a parameter (in this case, `this.itemName`) and decides what to do with it, dispatching any other functions as a result. You will define this particular dispatch function near the end of this chapter. The `itemMouseMoveFunc()` function also checks to see whether the mouse is over the clip and, if it is, it tells the clip to go to the frame labeled **over**; otherwise the clip is told to display frame 1.

Now that you've defined these functions, it is time to attach them to the individual menu items. Inside the loop that creates each menu item, find the code that tells the newly created item to go to and stop on frame 1 (`this["mc_menu_item_" + i].gotoAndStop(1)`). Add this code immediately following:

```
this["mc_menu_item_" + i].onMouseUp = itemMouseUpFunc;
this["mc_menu_item_" + i].onMouseMove = itemMouseMoveFunc;
```

Now save your movie and test what you have so far. You should now be able to roll over each of the items in your mouse under menu and see the item highlighted. If it is not working properly, that's alright; just review the code and compare it to what's in this chapter to help you track down the problem.

You may have noticed one peculiar thing about your menu: When you drag it, the original rectangle you made at the very beginning of this chapter is still showing behind the menu and drags along with it. To fix this problem, select frame 2 of the layer that the rectangle is on and create a keyframe (F6). Now delete any items from this layer on frames 2 and 3. This will ensure that the rectangle shows up only in the first frame of the clip by removing any remnant of the rectangle from frames 2 and 3.

Open to the Public

You are now ready to add the public functions to this component. At the top of frame 1, right after you define the **_HIDE_ON_CLICK_** variable, enter this code in the Actions panel:

> The notion of public and private functions and variables is a powerful notion in the world of the C programming language; because when you declare something as private, it *is* actually private, and trying to use it will shower you with compiler warnings. In ActionScript and JavaScript, however, the notion of public and private functions and variables is purely an organizational tool and in no way changes the way Flash or your web browser interprets or manages the code.
>
> **Note**

```
function showMenu()
{
    if (gMenuShowing) {
        if (this.hitTest(_root._xmouse, _root._ymouse, true)) {
            return;
        } else {
            hideMenu();
            return;
        }
    }
    gHideCalled = false;
    gTimerStarted = false;
    gMenuShowing = true;
    this._x = _root._xmouse;
    this._y = _root._ymouse;
    this._alpha = 100;
}
```

The `showMenu()` function typically gets called as a result of a mouse click and begins by checking to see whether the menu is already showing and whether the mouse is over the menu. If the menu is showing and the mouse is not over it, the menu is hidden by calling the `hideMenu()` function (which you will define in a moment). If the menu is not already showing (**gMenuShowing** is `false`), the **gHideCalled** and **gTimerStarted** variables are set to `false`. These variables tell the clip that the `hideMenu()`

```
1  // ==================== public functions
2
3  // shows the menu at the current mouse position
4  function showMenu()
5  {
6      // if the menu is already showing...
7      if (gMenuShowing) {
8          // ...and the mouse is withing the menu, do nothing
9          if (this.hitTest(_root._xmouse, _root._ymouse, true)) {
10             return;
11         } else {
12             // otherwise, if the mouse i outside the menu, hide it
13             hideMenu();
14             return;
15         }
16     }
17     // reset the variables, position the menu, and show it
18     gHideCalled = false;
19     gMenuShowing = true;
20     gTimerStarted = false;
21     this._x = _root._xmouse;
22     this._y = _root._ymouse;
23     this._alpha = 100;
24 }
25
26 // hides the menu by setting the global variable
```

Line 130 of 130, Col 1

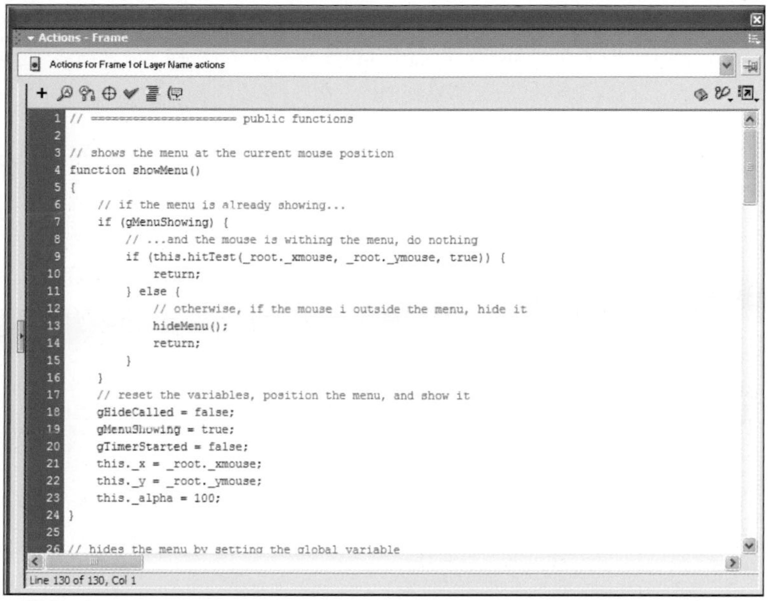

Figure 6.6
Define the clip's public functions at the top of the Actions panel. This makes it easy for other developers to spot if they open the clip and view the code.

function has been called, and that the delay timer (which hides the menu after a certain amount of inactivity) is set to `false`, respectively. The **gMenuShowing** variable is then set to `true` to tell the rest of the clip that the menu is showing. Finally, the menu is positioned at the current mouse pointer coordinates and the alpha of the clip is set to 100% opacity.

Now it is time to define the `hideMenu()` function. Enter this code:

```
function hideMenu()
{
    gMenuShowing = false;
    gHideCalled = true;
}
```

This function doesn't seem like it does very much, but it is important. After telling the rest of the movie clip that the menu is no longer showing, it sets the **gHideCalled** variable to `true`. This variable will get checked in the code you will be entering next and used to fade the menu out.

To test that the `showMenu()` function works properly, you need to hide the menu completely when it initializes. Therefore, find the line of code where you set the alpha of the clip to 50% and set the alpha to 0. Below that line of code, add this:

```
this._x = -1000;
```

This will ensure not only that the clip is invisible on the Stage (at 0 percent alpha), but also that it can no longer receive any mouse event because it will be positioned way off Stage.

As mentioned earlier, the `showMenu()` function typically gets called from a button symbol, so go to scene 1 of your movie and create a square. Select the square and make it into a button symbol (F8). Add this code to the button:

```
on(press)
{
    mc_mouseMenu.showMenu();
}
```

This very simple code calls the `showMenu()` function you created only moments ago. Now save your work and test the movie again. You should notice that the movie now begins without the menu clip showing and that clicking the button you created shows the menu at the mouse coordinates. Great! Now add the fading-out code.

Fading

Close the test movie and edit the **MouseMenu** movie clip. Select frame 2 of the Actions layer in the timeline and enter this code:

Figure 6.7
The button symbol that will activate the mouse under menu.

```
if (gHideCalled) {
    if (this._alpha <= 10) {
        this._x = -1000;
        gHideCalled = false;
    } else {
        this._alpha -= 20;
    }
}
```

Because this clip loops over frames 2 and 3, this code gets checked throughout the lifetime of the movie. If **gHideCalled** is `true` (which would be the case if the `hideMenu()` function were called), the clip begins to grow more and more transparent until it is positioned off Stage.

Test your movie and click the button you created to activate the menu. Then click outside the menu area but still in the button. You should find that the menu gently fades away when you click outside the area of the menu.

Now it is time to add the timer code, which will fade the menu out if the user's mouse pointer is outside the menu for a given amount of time. Start by adding this code right after the code you added previously:

```
if (gMenuShowing && !gHideCalled && !this.hitTest(_root._xmouse,
➥_root._ymouse, true)) {
    if (!gTimerStarted) {
        gStartTime = getTimer();
        gTimerStarted = true;
    } else {
        if (getTimer() > (gStartTime + HIDE_DELAY)) {
            hideMenu();
        }
    }
} else {
    gTimerStarted = false;
}
```

This code might look a bit daunting, but it is really pretty simple. The first `if` statement checks to see whether the menu is currently showing, that the `hideMenu()` function has not been called, and that the mouse pointer is not within the menu area. If all of those conditions are met, and if the timer has not yet been started, it is started; otherwise, the code checks to see whether the number of milliseconds defined in the **HIDE_DELAY** variable have elapsed and then calls `hideMenu()` automatically. As you recall, the **HIDE_DELAY** variable was initially set to 1000 milliseconds, or 1 second. Therefore after 1 second of the mouse pointer being outside the area of the menu, the menu should automatically fade. Save and test your movie to determine whether this works.

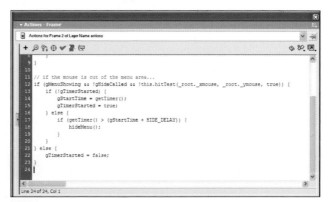

Figure 6.8
This timer code handles fading out the menu after a period of inactivity.

All that is left is to define the component parameters to make this a real, reusable component, and to add the dispatch function mentioned earlier to the root movie timeline.

From Movie Clip to Component

To begin, you will need to comment out the three variables you defined at the top of the Actions panel for frame 1 in your **MouseMenu** clip. Select frame 1 of the Actions layer in your **MouseMenu** clip, open the Actions panel for it (F2), and comment out the **MENU_ITEMS**, **HIDE_DELAY**, and **HIDE_ON_CLICK** variables.

```
1  /*
2  var MENU_ITEMS = ["item 1", "item 2", "item 3"];
3  var HIDE_DELAY = 1000;
4  var HIDE_ON_CLICK = true;
5  */
```

Figure 6.9
Don't forget to comment out the temporary variables you defined in the beginning.

Right-click (Windows) or Control-click (Mac) the **MouseMenu** clip in the Library panel and select Component Definition.

Start off by adding a **MENU_ITEMS** variable and making it an array. Then add a **HIDE_DELAY** variable of type Number with a value of 1000, and finally add a **HIDE_ON_CLICK** Boolean variable.

Click the OK button and return to your main movie timeline. Select frame 1 of the main timeline and open the Actions panel. Add the following code:

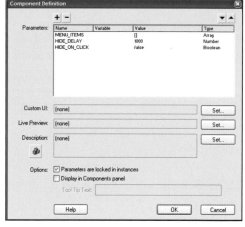

Figure 6.10
This component will have only three simple parameters.

```
function underMenuDispatch(clickedItem)
{
    switch (clickedItem) {
        case "item 1":
                trace("1 was clicked");
                break;
        case "item 2":
                trace("now 2 was");
                break;
        default:
                trace(clickedItem);
    }
}
```

This function gets called every time a menu item is clicked. It gets sent the label of the menu item and checks it against a list of cases; if a match is found, the code within that case branch is executed. Using this method, you can have the menu execute any functions you desire. In this particular case, there are cases for handling menu items named item 1, item 2, and a default case that will handle any other menu items.

To test this code, you need to adjust the parameters of your component. Select the **MouseMenu** component on the Stage and click the Parameters tab. Enter five items: **item 1**, **item 2**, **item 3**, **item 4**, and **item 5**. Notice that after adding the first one, every time you click on the plus sign (+) to add a new array element, Flash automatically adds a new item and increments the number appropriately. Now set the **HIDE_ON_CLICK** parameter to `true` and test your movie.

> The code in the sample movies included on the *Skip Intro* CD-ROM should be identical to the code discussed in the chapter except for the fact that the code on the CD-ROM is heavily commented to make it easier to go through. In some cases, however, items such as the ones listed in the menu and dispatch functions may differ from those in the sample files to make it less specific to the sample movie and more general.
>
> **Note**

```
1  function underMenuDispatch(clickedItem)
2  {
3      switch (clickedItem) {
4          case "item 1":
5              trace("1 was clicked");
6              break;
7          case "item 2":
8              trace("now 2 was");
9              break;
10         default:
11             trace(clickedItem);
12     }
13 }
14
```

Figure 6.11
The dispatch function handles the different menu item labels sent in and dispatches the appropriate functions for them.

Upon clicking any of the menu items in the mouse under menu, you should notice that the menu disappears and that the Output window displays the appropriate message for each item. That's it! You now have a complete, functional, and reusable mouse under menu component.

You need to perform one final trick for this component to be truly reusable: You need to ensure the **menu_top**, **menu_middle**, and **menu_bottom** clips tag along appropriately when you drag and drop this clip into other movies. For this to function properly, select the **MouseMenu** component in the library, Right-click (Windows) or Control-click (Mac) and select Edit. Create a new layer named **skins** and move it to the bottom of the list of layers. Now drag each of the menu skin clips (**menu_top**, **menu_middle**, and **menu_bottom**) onto the newly created layer and resize each of them so that they are about 10 pixels wide by 10 pixels tall. This effectively hides them from view. Now right-click (Windows) or Control-click (Mac) on the **skins** layer in the layer list and make it a guide layer. This further hides it completely on the Stage. Now you can drag the **MouseMenu** component to any other movie and the menu skin clips will automatically follow.

Figure 6.12
Flash automatically adds the next item in the array with an incremented number.

Figure 6.13
Making the layer a guide layer ensures that Flash will not display it.

CONCLUSION

You now have a nice little module that you can use, with minor graphic modifications, in any of your projects!

Key Points/Don't Forget

- **Mouse under menus are an excellent implementation of Fitts's Law.** There is no mouse movement on the user's part to open a mouse under menu. Just click and it opens.

- **Mouse under menus shouldn't be used as a primary navigation device.** Despite their efficiency in terms of Fitts's law, mouse under menus are hidden from the users' view until they are click. There will always be a moment's delay while the user identifies the new options presented. Ideally, mouse under menus should offer the user supplementary options. The core navigation elements of the site should be kept onscreen and easily identifiable at all times.

- **There should be some indication that mouse under menus exist.** This is extremely important. If the users don't know the menu is there, they won't use it. Informing the user—either through direct means such as instructions or through hints such as a cursor change—is essential in the use of mouse under menus.

- **Dragging has to be the single biggest UI crime in Flash design.** Yes, in some instances dragging and dropping is the perfect metaphor to use. Puzzle-type games, room planner devices, and so on all use Flash's dragging capability effectively. For the most part, however, dragging in Flash is just annoying for the user. Watch out! If you want to read more about why dragging can be a drag, check out the *Skip Intro* web site (www.skip-intro.org).

CHAPTER 07
A Point of Flexibility

On two occasions I have been asked [by members of Parliament], 'Pray, Mr. Babbage, if you put into the machine wrong figures, will the right answers come out?' I am not able rightly to apprehend the kind of confusion of ideas that could provoke such a question.

—Charles Babbage

The preceding chapter showed you how to create a user interface element called the *mouse under menu* or *contextual menu*. Despite its usefulness, if no one knows the feature exists, it is 100 percent ineffective. Remember, you want to keep your users, in this case Nancy, aware of what's happening by giving them visual clues.

This is one area where cursor feedback becomes essential in your design. Something as simple as a slight modification to the arrow cursor is enough to inform the user of some action on the part of the computer.

Flash's built-in cursor functionality is limited to calling a small set of system cursors, notably the traditional arrow, the "pointer" finger, and the text entry "I beam." For early Flash projects, these three were more than adequate. When you start to add more complex functionality, such as the mouse under or contextual menu, Nancy will need something more sophisticated to tell her that she can access additional information by clicking the mouse.

Flash MX provides a solution that allows developers to hide the system cursor and attach a movie clip. To access the watch cursor (from the Mac) or the hourglass cursor (from Windows), for example, you have to use ActionScript to hide the system cursor and then replace the cursor with a movie clip that looks like the cursor you want the user to see.

To provide the necessary cursor feedback with several different cursors, you need to build an intelligent cursor object with just the right functions to handle all of your cursor needs.

This chapter shows you how to build a powerful and flexible custom cursor component that gives you a great deal of control over the cursor. The additional cursor feedback should help improve Nancy's experience on the MODA site by discretely providing her with visual clues about how to navigate the site.

Seeing It in Action

To see a working example of the cursor object Smart Clip, open and test (Control>Test>Movie) the **07_cursor.fla** file from the **Projects** folder on the *Skip Intro* CD-ROM. If you roll over the button images, the cursor changes from the arrow to the finger. If you mouse over the larger images, the cursor will change to indicate that more information is available. If you select Show Streaming from the View menu and roll over the thumbnail images before they are finished loading, you will see the cursor change to the "wait" cursor. In this way, the module mimics the way the system cursor would behave in similar non-Flash situations.

Don't forget: Although this project explains how to create some familiar types of cursors, many other applications exist for the custom cursor. It can be used wherever a modified cursor would help the intended user understand the site.

IMPLEMENTATION

The cursor object's intended function is to alert Nancy to the presence of the contextual/mouse under menu. To do this effectively, it should incorporate the following features:

- **Action feedback.** The cursor should exhibit a visible change when rolling over an active link or button *and* when rolling off the active area to alert users that they are over a clickable item.

- **Event sensitivity.** The cursor appearance should be changeable as a result of a key or mouse button event, or both.

- **Cursor overriding.** In certain situations, such as loading large quantities of data or waiting for a network response, you may want the cursor to alert the user that something is happening and that they must wait until that process completes before continuing. The cursor needs to temporarily be immune to changes when the user rolls over a button or link, as stated earlier, so you need to effectively "hog" the cursor, not allowing it to change its appearance through action feedback or event sensitivity.

- **Cursor cleanup.** Flash cursors are active only while the system cursor is over the active Flash movie. Should the cursor leave that area, it is possible the image of the cursor will still appear in the Flash movie (giving the appearance of two cursors onscreen at the same time). Cursor cleanup determines whether the cursor has left the active area and hides the Flash cursor if this is the case.

> Taking control of a user's cursor is a touchy area. The "cursor hog" feature can be controversial, and giving the user indefinite feedback is unacceptable (see Chapter 4, "A Good Experience from the Start"). And you should never try to incorporate any feature that prevents users from exiting an event.
>
> Sometimes, however, it is unavoidable, such as in web-based applications that require the loading of lots of dynamic data or on a slow connection to the Internet. If you find a situation in which you need to hog the cursor, be sure to create some sort of relevant feedback. Either at the cursor object itself or somewhere else onscreen, you should alert users to the fact that they are waiting, why they are waiting, and, if possible, how long they will be waiting. This information will help give users such as Nancy the lowdown on the situation at hand.
>
> **CAUTION**

- **Native system awareness.** In most cases, you will want the cursors to be seamless to the user. Therefore, the cursor should notice what type of computer system the user is on and use the appropriate cursor.

CONSTRUCTION

As usual, begin by creating a new movie. Then create two layers, one labeled **cursor** and the other labeled **actions**.

In the first frame of the movie, draw an object (any color and shape will do) and convert this to a movie clip (Insert>Convert to Symbol) with a symbol name of **cursor** and an instance name of *mc_cursor*.

Double-click this icon to enter Edit mode and immediately convert the raw graphic to another movie clip. This time enter a symbol name of **cursor_graphic_CODE** and an instance name of *mc_cursorType*. You should now have two movie clips: **cursor** should be on the main stage, and **cursorType** should be inside the **cursor** movie clip. In the first movie clip, **cursor**, create two layers and label the first **actions** and the second **cursor**. Make sure your **cursorType** movie clip is on the **cursor** layer.

Figure 7.1
*The **cursor** clip can be any shape or image you want. We prefer to use specific iconography as seen in this figure to help identify the clip, especially when several clips are on the stage.*

Figure 7.2
Don't forget to add the instance names for both movie clips.

Finally, double-click the **cursorType** movie clip to enter Edit mode. Select frame 1 and insert a new keyframe (Insert>Keyframe). Making sure that you are on the second keyframe, delete the graphic you are using to represent your **cursorType** movie clip. Select frame 2 again with the cursor and open the Actions panel (F2) and insert the following code:

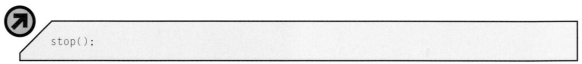

```
stop();
```

Next, select frame 1 of the movie and enter the following frame script:

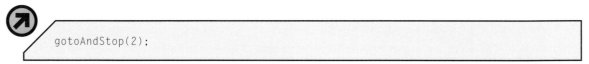

```
gotoAndStop(2);
```

The preceding alteration forces the play head of the movie clip to frame 2 immediately upon loading. This prevents the user from seeing the graphic you are using to identify the cursor object. It's purely a housekeeping issue; if you decide not to use a graphic identifier, you can skip this step.

Figure 7.3
*Setting up the **cursorType** using the `gotoAndStop(2)` action prevents users from seeing the graphic and makes development easier for you, because you won't have to search around for invisible movie clips.*

So far you've created the movie clips that will contain the majority of the code. Next you create the actual cursor libraries that hold the images of the cursor that will be used.

Building the Cursor Libraries

One of the key elements to overcome with Flash's cursor modification is its inability to apply the appropriate system cursors for Macintosh- and Windows-based systems. Luckily the problem is fairly easy to resolve, but it does require building a minimum of two almost identical cursor libraries. Start by creating a blank movie clip (Insert>New Symbol or Cmd-F8/Ctrl-F8) with an instance name of *mc_cursor_graphic_MAC*. When this movie clip is complete, you will duplicate it three times appending *WIN*, *UNIX*, and *CUSTOM* rather than *MAC*. Each of the duplicated movies will contain the cursor specific to the respective operating system.

Now right-click (Ctrl-click on the Mac) **cursor_graphic_MAC** in the symbol library and select Linkage from the contextual menu. In the dialog box that pops up, select the Export for ActionScript check box (Export in first frame will automatically be checked) and enter **MAC** in the Identifier text entry box.

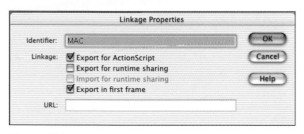

Figure 7.4
The Linkage property enables you to access a movie clip from the library via ActionScript.

You're now setting up this movie clip to take advantage of the `attachMovie();` command. This is similar to `duplicateMovie();`, but enables you to grab the movie clip from the library. This is discussed in more detail when it comes time to actually implement the code.

Double-click each movie clip you set up in the library to enter Edit mode and create four total layers labeled **actions**, **labels**, **guide**, and **cursors**.

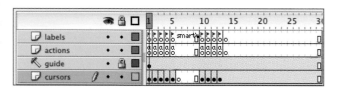

Figure 7.5
Each of the cursor libraries should have four layers.

The **guide** and **actions** layers are quite simple to set up. Each of the keyframes in the **actions** layer should have a `stop();` action attached to it, whereas the **guide** layer is there to provide a size template for designing custom cursors. Essentially the **guide** layer contains a box, 16×16 pixels for the Mac and 19×19 pixels for Windows.

Each keyframe of the **cursors** layer should contain a different cursor graphic with the **labels** layer having a corresponding label. For the MODA site, the cursor object needs only four cursor types: the arrow, the finger, a contextual menu indicator, and a busy/wait cursor. You can take the time to create these now or, if you prefer, open the project folder on the CD and drag and drop the cursor libraries into your movie. (Note that the included libraries have several more cursor options than are needed to complete this project.)

If you plan to create your own set of cursors, make sure that for each cursor you create a corresponding keyframe label. The labels used in the pre-built cursor libraries are **arrow** for the standard cursor, **finger** for the finger cursor, **wait** for the watch/hourglass, and **mouseMenu** for the mouse under menu indicator.

When you are happy with either the imported cursors or your custom-made ones, exit Edit mode and return to the main movie. It's time to start coding.

Setting Up the Events

Double-click the **cursor** movie clip to enter Edit mode. From here, the **cursorType** movie clip should already be selected; but just in case, click once on the movie clip and then open the ActionScript panel (F2). Here you're going to add all the different events to which the cursor module should respond. For this module, you'll set up all the event handlers at once. Therefore in your ActionScript panel, add the following code:

```
onClipEvent(load) {
}

onClipEvent(mouseMove) {
}
```

In total you should have two clip events set up now. These are used to make the basic cursor.

Installing the Cursor and Preparing It to Move

In the first clip event, the load event, you want to hide the system cursor and install the custom cursor created earlier. Add the following code to your onClipEvent(load) handler:

```
Mouse.hide()
this.attachMovie("MAC", "library", 1000);
```

The first line, of course, hides the mouse. This is a built-in feature of Flash. The second line uses the attachMovie() command to grab the cursor module created earlier and attach it to this, or the **cursorType** movie clip. It also gives the attached movie an instance name of *library*, so you can refer to the movie clip as _root.mc_cursor.mc_cursorType.library. Finally the cursor library gets placed on the 1000th layer.

Now it's time to move the cursor. Along with all other cursor actions, this is handled by a function one level up. So, between the `onClipEvent(mouseMove)` event add the following code:

```
_parent.moveMouse;
updateAfterEvent();
```

Pretty simple, huh? The first line calls a function stored in a frame script that will be added in just a moment. The second line is one of the most important and most overlooked lines of code in custom cursor code (see the Tip for more information). Now it's time to move on to the functions.

One of the most overlooked functions in ActionScript, `updateAfterEvent();`, is absolutely essential for custom cursors and the like. The `updateAfterEvent()` method forces Flash to redraw the screen every time the mouse moves, not just based on the movie's frame rate. This provides a much smoother, more professional looking cursor. If you fail to include this function in your code, your cursor object can look very choppy.

Tip

Making the Cursor Move

To add the functions necessary to make the cursor move, click the keyframe in the **actions** layer.

Figure 7.6
*Add the functions to the first keyframe in the **actions** layer of the **cursor** movie clip.*

The first thing to do is actually move the mouse pointer. Using the following code, this is simple:

```
function moveCursor()
{
 this._x = _root._xmouse;
 this._y = _root._ymouse;
}
```

The code sets the x and y location of the movie clip to the x and y location of the hidden cursor position, creating the illusion of a cursor.

It's time to save and test! It can be a bit difficult to see if you've got the code correct because it's meant to emulate the system cursor. To confirm things are working, you might want to make a temporary change to the cursor in the first frame of **cursor_graphic_MAC**. Make it red or add some text, anything to differentiate it from the standard cursor. If all has gone according to plan, you should see a cursor running around your your screen and that's about it. Time to move on to making the cursor change.

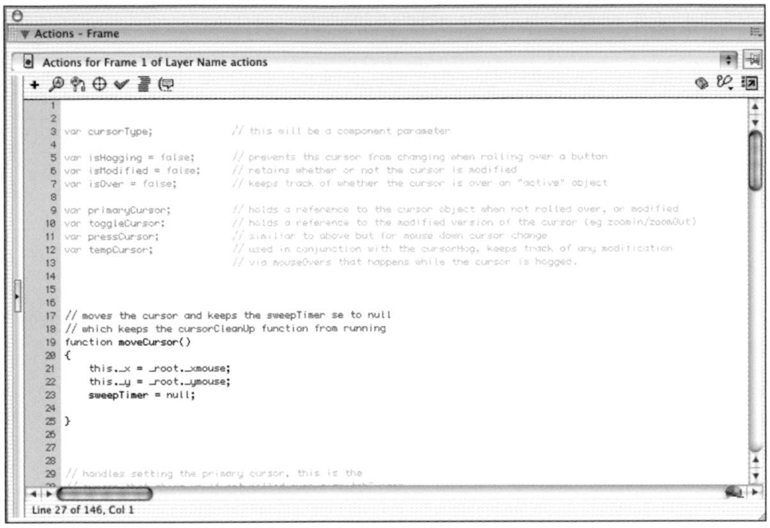

Figure 7.7
The `moveCursor` *function locks the movie clip graphic to the cursor's x and y positions.*

Handling Mouse Overs

When the cursor rolls over a button, it should switch to the finger pointer to indicate to the user there is something active there. Specifically for MODA and Nancy, when the cursor rolls over a piece of the artwork that has additional information, the mouseMenu cursor should show up. (Note: In the example movie, neither the mouse under menu nor any additional information will show up.) Switching the cursor is quite an easy task: After the `moveCursor()` function you just wrote, add the following code:

```
function switchCursor(to)
{
  this.mc_cursorType.library.gotoAndStop(to);
}
```

As you can see, the `switchCursor()` function just tells the *library* movie clip instance, which is the attached **mc_cursor_graphic_MAC** movie clip, to go to a specific frame—in this case a frame passed via the `to` parameter.

To see this work, create a standard button on the main stage and attach the following code to the button:

```
on(rollOver) {
  _root.cursor.switchCursor("finger");
}
```

That was pretty simple: On rollover, call a function and tell the function which cursor you want to see.

Save and test your movie now to see what happens. You should see your custom cursor change to the finger cursor when you roll over the button. If not, go back and check through your code for simple mistakes, such as missing quotation marks, and refer to the debugging section of Chapter 2, "Basic Training." If your cursor does change, congratulations. You should notice that the cursor doesn't switch back to the arrow key when you roll out. No problem! That's coming up next.

Handling Mouse Outs

The easiest way to switch the cursor back to the arrow, as some of you clever people may have already guessed, is to add another `switchCursor("arrow");` to the `on(rollOut)` handler. Not a bad idea, but you can go one better and set up a much more versatile and realistic cursor type.

The first step is to create a variable called **_primaryCursor_**, which should be placed at the top of the script, as follows:

```
var primaryCursor;
```

Next, in between the `moveCursor()` and `switchCursor()` functions, add a new function called `setPrimaryCursor`:

```
function setPrimaryCursor(to)
{
  primaryCursor = to;
}
```

Finally, click the **cursorType** movie clip to bring up the movie clip code. Locate the `onClipEvent(load)` handler and add the following at the end of the handler:

```
_parent.setPrimaryCursor("arrow");
```

So now you have a variable that holds what is the "primary cursor." It might seem a bit strange to do this, but it's useful for situations where you want to permanently switch the cursor—for instance, in a drawing application selecting the magnifying glass would be an instance of setting the primary cursor.

Next, click back on the first frame that contains all your current functions. After the `switchCursor()` function add this new function:

```
function restoreCursor()
{
  this.mc_cursorType.library.gotoAndStop(primaryCursor);
}
```

By using `setPrimaryCursor` and `restoreCursor`, you can make the code needed for rollouts much simpler. All you need do is call the function, as follows:

```
on(rollOut) {
  _root.mc_cursor.restoreCursor();
}
```

If you have attached the preceding code to the button on stage, save and test your movie. You should see the cursor switch to the finger and back again as you roll on and off the button. Next it's time to take a look at cleaning up the cursor when the user leaves the Flash environment.

Cursor Cleanup

Another shortcoming of Flash's cursor handling is its inability to detect when the cursor has left the Flash environment. This can cause a fair amount of confusion for users. For example, if Nancy were to notice the cursor in Flash not moving, she might well think her machine has frozen. Fortunately, there is a way around this.

Select the **cursorType** movie clip so that you can edit the movie clip code. In the `mouseMove` event handler, add the following code after the `_parent.moveCursor()` function:

```
if( (_parent._x > (_Stage.width-16))  || (_parent._x < 16) || (_parent._y >
➥(_Stage.height-16)) || (_parent._y < 16) ) {
  _parent.sweepTimer = getTimer();
} else {
  _parent.sweepTimer = null;
  _parent._visible = true;
}
```

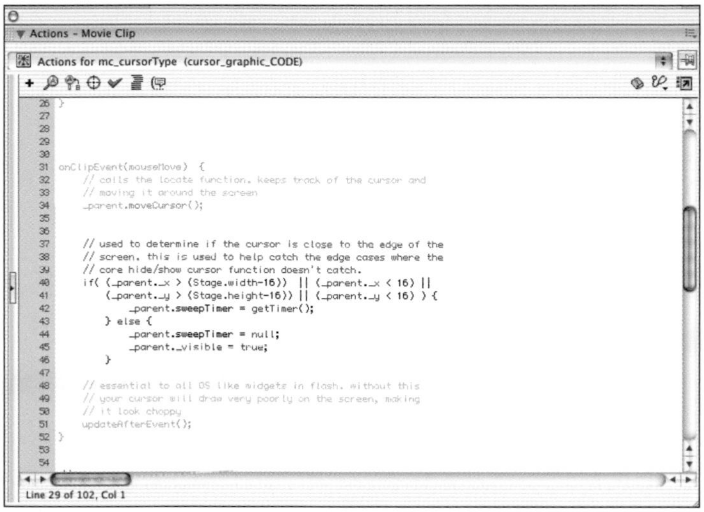

Figure 7.8
This code will remove the cursor from the Flash movie if the user's cursor leaves the active Flash movie.

This code checks to see whether the mouse is within 16 pixels of the edge of the movie and if so sets a variable ***sweepTimer*** equal to the current time. Using `Stage.width` and `Stage.height`—built in properties with Flash MX—you can easily test how close the cursor is to the edge of the movie. If the cursor extends beyond 16 pixels at any edge, then the ***sweepTimer*** variable gets set to the current time. If the cursor isn't close, then ***sweepTimer*** gets set to null. Next you need to add an `enterFrame` handler:

```
onClipEvent(enterFrame) {
  if(_parent.sweepTimer != null) {
   _parent.cursorCleanUp();
  }
}
```

The `if` statement runs only if ***sweepTimer*** has no value, or null, and ***sweepTimer*** has value only if the cursor is within 16 pixels of any edge of the movie.

After the `restoreCursor()` function, add this code:

```
function cursorCleanUp()
{
  if( (getTimer() - sweepTimer > 500) ) {
   this._visible = false;
   sweepTimer = null;
  }
}
```

```
113
114    // this unhogs the cursor allowing the cursor to
115    // change again.
116    function unHogCursor()
117    {
118        isHogging = false;
119
120        // this checks to see if the cursor has rolled over an object
121        // while it has been in cursor mode. If it has it switches the
122        // cursor. if not it restores it.
123        if(isOver) {
124            switchCursor(tempCursor);
125        } else  {
126            restoreCursor();
127        }
128    }
129
130
131    // sets the visible of the cursor to false if the
132    // cursor is close to the edge and hasn;t moved
133    // for half a second.
134    function cursorCleanUp()
135    {
136        if( (getTimer() - sweepTimer > 500) ) {
137            this._visible = false;
138            sweepTimer = null;
139        }
140    }
141    stop();
```

Line 27 of 146, Col 1

Figure 7.9
The `cursorCleanUp()` *code works in conjunction with the* `enterFrame` *event handler to determine when to hide the movie clip cursor.*

This function, called from the `enterFrame` handler, checks the current time against the time at which the cursor got within 16 pixels of the edge of the movie. If that amount of time is greater than half a second (500 milliseconds), the cursor is hidden. As long as the cursor keeps moving, **sweepTimer** is set to null and this code won't run.

Now's a good time to save and test again. To see whether all is working as it should, roll your cursor outside of the Flash movie area and you should see it disappear.

You've got quite a lot done so far. In fact, you have done enough to drop the module into the MODA web site movie if you want. The cursor object, however, can be extended for future situations. So, even though the next few sections of code aren't essential to the MODA site, they will help you create a competent cursor object.

First up is the `cursorHog()` function.

Hogging the Cursor

In some rare instances, you might need to force the cursor to retain a single icon and ignore `switchTo()` calls. This is accomplished with a new piece of code and some additions to your existing code.

Start by adding two new variables to the top of your frame script and setting them to `false`:

```
var isHogging = false;
var isOver = false;
```

And after `primaryCursor`, add the following:

```
var tempCursor;
```

Next, after the `restoreCursor()` function, add the following code:

```
function setCursorHog(to)
{
 this.mc_cursorType.library.gotoAndStop(to);
 isHogging = true;
}
```

This might look familiar because it is almost identical to the `switchCursor()` function and is called from a button in the exact same manner. The only difference is setting the **cursorHog** variable to true. You use this variable along with a conditional statement in the `switchCursor()` function to prevent the cursor changing while in Hog mode, as follows:

```
function switchCursor(to)
{
 tempCursor = to;
 isOver = true;
 if(isHogging == false)   {
  this.mc_cursorType.library.gotoAndStop(to);
 }
}
```

As for `restoreCursor()`, you don't want that running when the cursor is in Hog mode, so you must add an `if` statement to the `restoreCursor()` function as well. Your new `restoreCursor()` function should look like this:

```
function restoreCursor()
{
 if(isHogging == false)   {
  this.mc_cursorType.library.gotoAndStop(primaryCursor);
  isOver = false;
 }
}
```

To complete the cursor hog functionality, there needs to be an "unhog" function. Just after the setCursorHog() function, add this code:

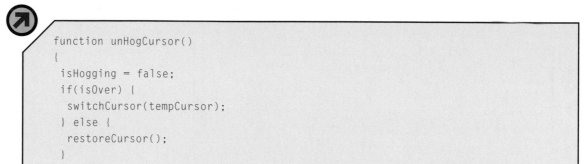

```
function unHogCursor()
{
  isHogging = false;
  if(isOver) {
    switchCursor(tempCursor);
  } else {
    restoreCursor();
  }
}
```

Save your movie before moving on to modifying the cursor.

Modifying the Cursor

With two instances, mouseDown and keyDown, the cursor might need to change, but it can't rely on the switchCursor function to change the cursor. For those circumstances, you can create a final function in your frame script. To start, however, you need to declare a few more variables. After the *isOver* declaration, add this:

```
var isModified = false;
```

Then, after tempCursor, add the following:

```
var toggleCursor;
var pressCursor;
```

Next, add the following new function code after the already existing restoreCursor() function :

```
function modifyCursor()
{
  if( (toggleCursor != null) && (isOver == false) ){
    this.mc_cursorType.library.gotoAndStop(toggleCursor);
    isModified = true;
  }
}
```

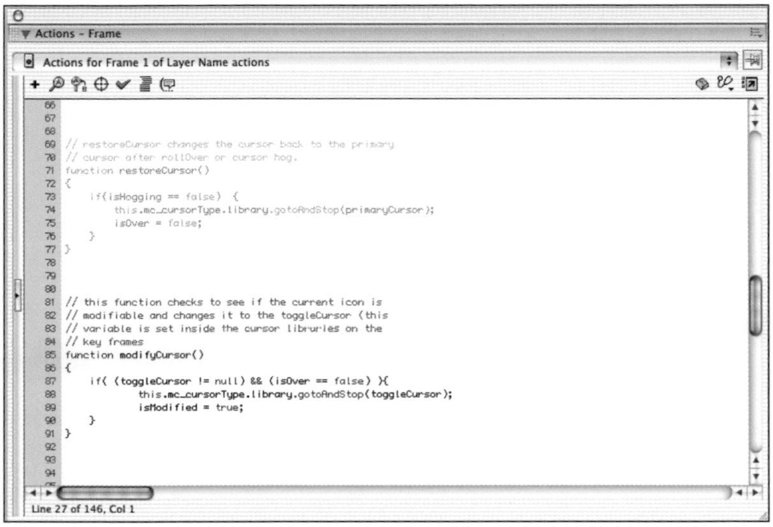

Figure 7.10

The `modifyCursor` *function is used to intercept key strokes and modify the current cursor. For example, pressing the Alt or Opt key while using a magnifying glass cursor often changes the cursor to a minus sign, indicating that a mouse click will zoom out.*

The preceding code checks two variables to see whether the cursor is over an object and makes sure that the current cursor has a toggle cursor available. If both those conditions are met, the cursor is modified and the ***isModified*** variable is set to `true`. The ***toggleCursor*** variable has to be set, of course, and the easiest place to do this is in the `setPrimaryCursor` function toward the top of the frame script. Find the already written `setPrimaryCursor` function and rewrite it to match this:

```
function setPrimaryCursor(to, toggle, via)
{
  primaryCursor = to;
  if(isOver == false)        {
    this.mc_cursorType.library.gotoAndStop(to);
  }

  if(toggle != null) {
    toggleCursor = toggle;
    toggleWith = via;
  } else {
    toggleCursor = null;
  }
}
```

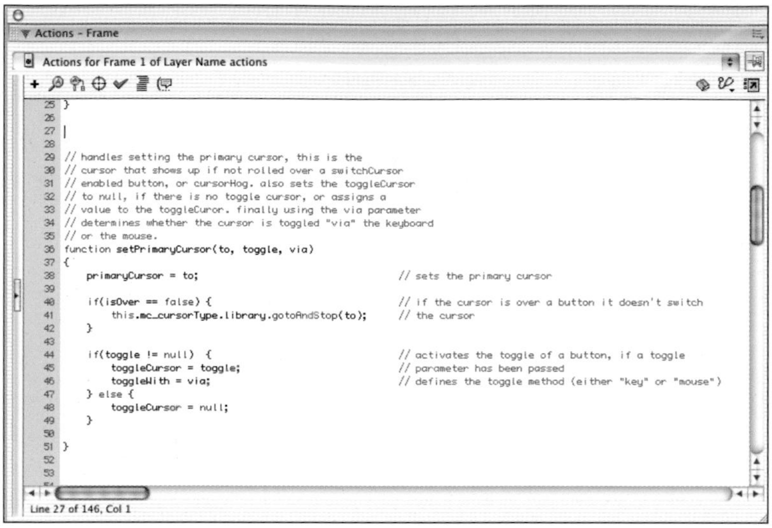

Figure 7.11

Based on the arguments, `setPrimaryCursor()` *will select which cursor image is to be the default cursor.*

The first change is the number of parameters passed to the function:

- `to`   Still holds the frame label that the cursor library should jump to when rolling over an active link/object.

- `toggle`   Holds the frame label that shows when the cursor is modified, if it is modifiable.

- `via`   A Boolean value that can be set to Key or Mouse and indicates how the current cursor should be modified.

Next is the **isOver** conditional, which prevents the cursor from changing to the primary cursor while it is still over an active link.

Finally, the code checks whether the `toggle` parameter has a value. If so, it sets two variables to hold the `toggle` and `via` parameters.

To access the `modifyCursor` function, you must explicitly state that the cursor has a toggle mode and the key to access it. Therefore when you set your primary cursor, the code should look like this:

```
setPrimaryCursor("zoomIn", "zoomOut", "key");
```

The last step in making the modifier code work is setting up the event handlers for `mouseUp`/`mouseDown` and `keyUp`/`keyDown`. Click the **cursorType** movie clip to access the clip event handlers and add the following code after the `enterFrame` handler:

If you don't plan for a given cursor to have a toggle, you can continue to call the `setPrimaryCursor()` function with a single parameter, as follows:

```
setPrimaryCursor("zoomIn");
```

Note

```
onClipEvent(mouseDown) {
  if(_parent.toggleWith == "mouse") {
    _parent.modifyCursor()
  }
}

onClipEvent(mouseUp) {
  if(_parent.toggleWith == "mouse") {
    _parent.restoreCursor()
  }
}

onClipEvent(keyDown) {
  if( (Key.isDown(Key.SHIFT)) && (_parent.toggleWith == "key")) {
    _parent.modifyCursor();
  }
}

onClipEvent(keyUp) {
if( (Key.getCode() == Key.SHIFT) && (_parent.isModified) &&
(!_parent.isOver) ) {
    _parent.restoreCursor();
  }
}
```

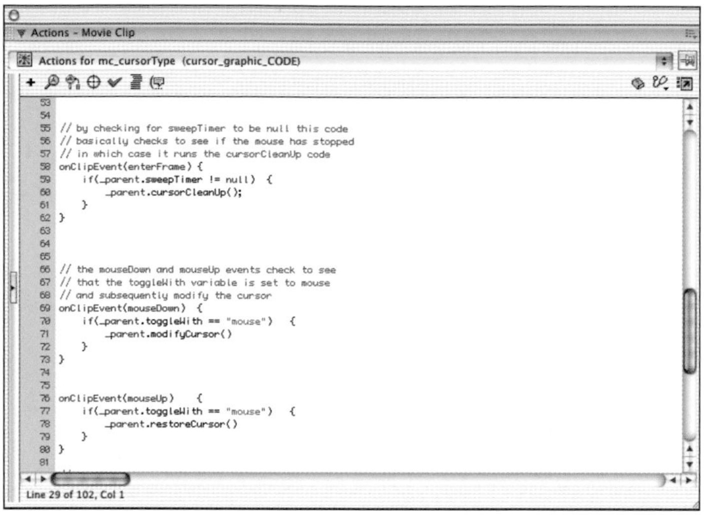

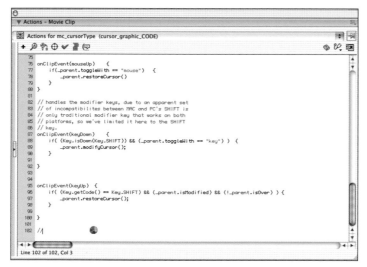

Figure 7.12
The mouse event handlers will access all the various functions you have just written and change the appearance of the cursor based on the mouse event.

Figure 7.13
The key event handlers work just like the mouse event handlers, but for key events instead.

The `mouseDown` code checks to see whether the ***toggleWith*** variable is set to mouse and if it is, executes the `modifyCursor()` function. The `mouseUp` handler does the same but calls the `restoreCursor()` function. The `keyUp` and `keyDown` handlers are also very similar: `keyDown` checks an additional conditional to make sure that a specific key is being pressed, whereas `keyUp` also makes sure the cursor `isModified` and that the cursor isn't currently over an active object.

Save your movie and test it now. If you're using the cursor libraries from the CD, there are two modifiable cursors: a magnifying glass (zoom in and zoom out) and a hand (open hand and grab hand). As far as coding the cursor itself, you are now done! All that remains is to set it up as a Smart Clip and detect what type of operating system it's on.

Components and Detection

Because you want the cursor code to be as modular as possible and easy to use, the *cursorType* variable originally set at the top of the frame script will now be set via the Inspector panel. This being the case, you can delete the variable declaration at the top of the frame script.

By now you should know how to set up a component, and if you don't, take a quick look through Chapters 4, "A Good Experience from the Start," and 5, "Scrolling Without Boundaries," which cover creating components in greater depth, or refer to the Flash MX manual. There is only one component definition for the cursor component and that's **cursorType**. The parameters for *cursorType* should be set in a list with values of AUTO, MAC, WIN, UNIX, and CUSTOM. For each of those values except AUTO, you need to create or duplicate the cursor library and apply a linkage name that corresponds to the component parameter value.

Now with those variables set, you need to add three lines of code to the movie clip itself in the onLoad event handler.

```
if( (_parent.cursorType == null) || (_parent.cursorType == "AUTO") )  {
 var version = getVersion();
 _parent.mc_cursorType = version.substring(0, 3);
}
```

This code checks the **cursorType** variable to see whether it is set to AUTO or not set at all. If either is true, the code grabs the operating system from the string that getVersion returns and sets the **cursorType** variable equal to that value.

One last step: With the **cursorType** set, modify the attachMovie line to match the following:

```
this.attachMovie(_parent.mc_cursorType, "library", 1000);
```

Go ahead and save your movie now, and then test it. If you are using a Windows-based system and haven't yet created the Windows cursor library, however, keep in mind that you won't see anything unless you set the **cursorType** clip parameter to MAC.

CONCLUSION

The cursor feedback object is extremely useful in certain circumstances. Unfortunately, in some instances on the web it has been trivialized. It's up to you as the designer to think carefully how this functionality will improve user experience on your site.

Luckily, Flash affords not only the ability to mimic the operating system cursor functionality in Mac and Windows environments, but also to extend it. For the MODA site, it was kept simple to complement the mouse under menu and enhance Nancy's experience on the site by giving her feedback when the items in the movie are loading.

Key Points/Don't Forget

- **Changing the cursor is a powerful tool.** Users are so familiar with the visual appearance and behavior of the cursor that any change will draw their attention. You must therefore be absolutely sure you need to create a custom cursor for your project.

- **Consistency is essential.** If you're creating a "serious" application or web site, it is imperative that you mimic as closely as possible the appearance and behavior of the system cursor.

- **Ensure that nonsystem cursors are beneficial.** If you plan on using a gimmick or fun cursor, ensure that its visual representation adds to the overall experience. Don't replace the cursor just because you can.

- **Don't forget the cursor is on top.** Always place your cursor on the very top level, layer, or movie clip. A cursor, no matter how informative, is of no use if it is hidden by other objects on the screen.

- **Never leave two cursors onscreen.** Don't forget to remove the "custom" cursor when the user has left the Flash movie.

SECTION II

GroceryClick.com Site Design

Experience is one thing you can't get for nothing.

—Oscar Wilde

CHAPTER 08
Overview—Convenience in a Flash

Computers make it easier to do a lot of things, but most of the things they make easier to do don't need to be done.

—Andy Rooney

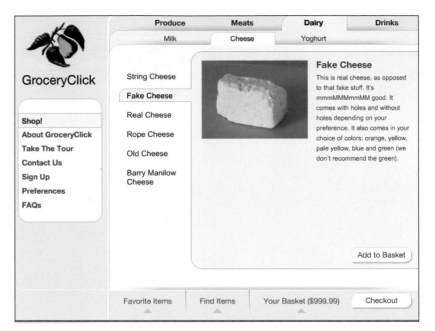

Figure 8.1
The user interface for GroceryClick.com.

One of the greatest potential conveniences of the web is e-commerce. It is also one of the most problematic. The web's short history is already littered with e-commerce projects that failed, and one of the primary reasons for this failure is that many e-commerce sites are just not usable.

Much user disenchantment with e-commerce stems from the structure of the buying process. Forcing potential customers to flip between a page where they browse for products and a separate page that contains their shopping cart leads to confusion, frustration, and abandoned carts.

To see just how inconvenient buying online can be, imagine you were forced to go through the following process in your local record shop: You browse through the racks of records, eventually deciding you want to buy a Ray Parker Junior box set. You put it in your basket, but the store requires all baskets to be at the front of the shop, so you have to march to the front of the shop and drop the CD in your basket. Before you can go back in to continue browsing a guard asks you gruffly if you want to buy the CD now or continue shopping. You have to repeat this process for *every* CD you want to buy! Not only that, but you must keep a mental note of the CDs already in your basket and if you forget you have to go back to the front of the store and get the third degree from Mr. Big again. When you decide to actually buy the CD you find your way to the cashier's desk, punch in your credit card number yourself, and type out your address, possibly twice. Without saying a word, the clerk disappears into a back room for five minutes and then returns, telling you to print out your own receipt and wait for a few days. Who in their right mind would shop at this record store?

Author Note: Duncan

Surprisingly, given that many people view it as a gimmick, Flash is an ideal tool for improving the user experience on e-commerce sites. Using Flash for the front end of an e-commerce site, designers can build a user interface that contains both the product-browsing facility and the shopping cart on the same page. The fact that it can dynamically load information without forcing the user to leave the current page gives Flash a distinct advantage over HTML in this case.

> **?** Many e-tailers blame the high incidence of customers abandoning their online shopping carts on consumer distrust of giving credit card details online. In reality, many consumers are happy to shop online but are discouraged, frustrated, and often angered by badly designed e-commerce sites.
>
> **Note**

For users it means the shopping experience will more closely resemble those with which they are familiar: shopping in a real store. They keep their shopping cart with them at all times, they can see what they've chosen and put things in and take them out at leisure, and they can easily keep track of how much they'll be spending. Overall, it's quicker, easier, and more effective—and you can do it all in Flash.

The next case study considers the issues of usability in an e-commerce setting, focusing on what can be done to make sure the client's customers have the best experience possible. Take a look at the case study to find out more about the client's goals, the user's goals, and the issues you need to resolve.

> **?** Most e-commerce sites contain two distinct areas. The front end is the part of the site that customers see and interact with. The back end is hidden from the public and includes the mechanics that drive the process—databases, catalogs, order process, fulfillment, and so on. We're interested in the front end because that's where, as designers, we can most enhance the usability and the user experience of the site. Now, this doesn't mean we want nothing to do with the back-end systems. On the contrary, the user interface and interaction we design should directly affect the design of the back-end system. This is because all aspects of a project need to take into account the user experience and design with it in mind.
>
> **Note**

CASE STUDY: GROCERYCLICK.COM

GroceryClick.com is a recent startup that aims to make online grocery shopping a truly convenient, enjoyable, and economically smart experience. GroceryClick is targeting people who might not have the time or ability to go to busy grocery stores to shop. Specifically, GroceryClick considers the following to be its target markets:

- Elderly and disabled who have trouble getting to a grocery store
- Stay-at-home parents who find it difficult to get away from tending their children to go to the grocery store
- Dual-income households where both parties work 40 or more hours per week

Mindful of the pitfalls of online retailing, GroceryClick has invested heavily in focus group studies, market research, and usability evaluations to determine what customers really want from an online grocery store.

The studies revealed the primary user complaint: difficulty keeping track of what's in the shopping cart. Users disliked having to switch repeatedly between the shopping screen and their cart to see what they had already selected. The second most common user complaint concerned the hassle involved in tracking the running total of the cost. They resented having to go to their "shopping cart" page and scroll down to the bottom of their list to update and then see the current subtotal.

GroceryClick.com's primary goal is to attract and retain customers by offering both competitive pricing and an unparalleled shopping experience. Having seen more than his fair share of bad Flash sites, GroceryClick's CEO is skeptical about a Flash-based e-commerce user interface. Fortunately, he does understand the potential benefits of the technology. He also understands

> When designing for the user, remember that just catering to the test user's complaints and feature requests is not enough to create the best user interface for your target audience. You must determine what these users *need*. You can do so with a combination of focus groups, usability evaluations, and common sense. This combination ensures you are building an experience that is good for the majority of the client's target audience, rather than the few test users you interviewed.
>
> **Note**

the absolute need for the site's development to be an iterative process—he wants to see real users determining what they really want from the site and showing how they would actually use the system.

Despite his misgivings about Flash, the client has asked you to develop and pitch a Flash-based prototype for the shopping cart/checkout module for GroceryClick.com. To do this, you need to develop the client's target user persona.

> If you haven't read the Chapter 1, "Bad Flashers Anonymous," you may want to do so now. It explains in detail what personas are and why they are used.
>
> **Note**

Character Profile

Name: Sanjeev Gupta

Age: 48

Occupation: Doctor

Sanjeev came with his wife to the United States at the age of 19 to attend medical school. After graduation and a successful internship at St. Mary of the Cross, he was offered the opportunity to stay on as a full-time surgeon. He became chief surgeon six years ago.

After his wife was diagnosed several years ago with multiple sclerosis, Sanjeev decided to move with his family to the suburbs, where he opened a small general practice in his home. Having his practice in the

Figure 8.2
Sanjeev's free time is mostly spoken for, so he's looking for a way to reduce the amount of time he devotes to shopping.

home allows him to look after his wife and keep the house in order when she is unable to. To help minimize his time on mundane tasks, Sanjeev has taken to shopping on the Internet and using home delivery. Many times Sanjeev attempts to complete these transactions between patient appointments.

Sanjeev isn't a computer newbie, having used them extensively both in school and while working as surgeon in New York. At the same time he isn't a tech-head. He treats his computer much like his car: He knows how to use it, install new applications and hardware, and reset his Internet connection, provided he has the pertinent numbers written down. In short, Sanjeev is like most frequent computer users. He wants to use it to accomplish a task; he doesn't know or need to know how or why it works.

DEFINING YOUR OWN GOALS
Sanjeev turned to the Internet for shopping because he's looking for a speedy, efficient shopping experience. He is not averse to a learning curve if the end result offers him more convenience.

With this in mind, it is clear that your role is to create on behalf of the site users an interface that is simple to use, clear, and comprehensive. Remember, however, that achieving these aims is but a small part of forging the entire shopping experience. This is a classic example of a job where Flash designers must recognize their limits and design within them.

The following four clearly identified usability features will dramatically enhance Sanjeev's shopping experience at GroceryClick.com:

> One of the most important things to note here is that Sanjeev is very bright and yet can be frustrated when shopping on the web. This is more than likely because the design or structure of the site is too complex. He also may be put off by details such as small type and bad navigation. These things can give your users an inferiority complex, making them defensive. Errors will be magnified 10 times in their eyes, and potential benefits will fade from their attention, because they feel insecure using the web site. This phenomenon is covered at length in Alan Cooper's book *The Inmates Are Taking Over the Asylum*. He calls the users apologists: They apologize because they think they did something wrong or they don't understand it, when in fact it is the interface designer who should apologize for designing a bad experience for the user.
>
> **Author Note: Michelangelo**

- **Single location.** Sanjeev might become disoriented if he's taken to an entirely new page each time he puts an item in his shopping basket. Ideally, therefore, we need to include the store catalog, Sanjeev's shopping list, a running total of the cost, and the ability to check out all on the same page. Of course with limited screen real estate, these features can't all be onscreen simultaneously. Instead, they should be easily accessible but unobtrusive while shopping and quickly hidden again when Sanjeev no longer needs them. To achieve this, we need to include a feature that works like a shopping list—easily stored in a pocket or purse and easily retrieved. By using Flash's capability to layer content and quickly hide and show it, you can create this very feature—an impossibility in HTML and very inelegant in DHTML.

- **Instant updating.** Sanjeev wants to know how much he is spending as he goes along, and he needs to know whether he has ordered all the items he needs. To minimize disruption to his shopping experience, we want to provide this updated information without disturbing any other information on the page he is on. Flash is perfect for creating this sort of application.

- **Smart scrolling.** Shopping lists can become quite large. Even using Flash's capability to create discrete interface elements, sometimes the length of the content will just exceed the limits of the screen. It is very important to allow Sanjeev access to the information, but also to let him know how much of that information is offscreen. Using proportional scroll bars is an excellent way to let Sanjeev know approximately how much more there is to his list. Creating a scroll bar that is similar to those he will have seen in his other desktop applications will comfort him by making the shopping environment more familiar.

- **Searching**. Searching is an essential feature to any e-commerce site. For many e-commerce solutions, a robust server-side search engine is a must; often these search engines are used when the user doesn't know exactly what she wants. Flash is ill-suited to compete with one of those. However, Flash can be used as a focus engine. The focus engine can assist Sanjeev when he knows what he wants but doesn't necessarily know where to find it. This works perfectly for indulgent or infrequent purchases. Suppose, for example, that Sanjeev's wife felt like having some ice cream and it wasn't an item Sanjeev usually purchased. Would he look in Frozen Foods, Dairy Desserts, or Confections? It could conceivably be in any of those. Why force Sanjeev to play a digital three-card monty when he could very easily type "Ice Cream" in a text field and be immediately transported to the Ice Cream section. The focus engine should not be used as a replacement for the more robust search engines, but should be implemented as a complementary feature.

Each of these listed features will enhance Sanjeev's experience at GroceryClick.com. The next three chapters show you how to use Flash-specific utilities to create a user experience that that includes all of these desired features.

CHAPTER 09

Tabbed Windows—Convenient Access to
Supplementary Information

*Never trust a computer you can't throw
out a window.*

—Steve Wozniak

We all know online shopping can be both confusing and time consuming. Just keeping track of what's in your shopping basket and how much you've spent usually involves jumping back and forth between different pages and, as a result, lots of waiting as those pages download.

When you're in a "real-life" shop and you want to see what products you've selected, you have only to glance down to your shopping cart. Shopping online should be just as simple. Sanjeev shouldn't have to leave the shopping environment to check his purchases or see how much he's spending.

Flash has the distinct benefit of being able to offer a "single page" metaphor. It can load and place new content dynamically, allowing the core elements of the site's navigation to remain intact on the screen. This lends a more application-like feel to the site and reduces the delay and jarring effect of making a new web page request every time you need to get more information.

Therefore, yet again, Flash can provide the solution in the form of *tabbed sliding panels*. Using sliding panels, the designer can give Sanjeev easy access to supplementary information, such as how much he's spent or what's in his shopping basket, without requiring him to "leave the store." This information can be constantly updated without reloading the page.

SOLUTIONS—GIVING SANJEEV ACCESS

To provide Sanjeev with quick access to vital information, but not interfere with his shopping activities, GroceryClick.com needs an interface element that he can call on and dismiss at any time. This will reduce the amount of time it takes Sanjeev to complete his shopping, and it will confirm he has what he wants. It simplifies the checkout process by eliminating unnecessary server requests that would otherwise force the browser to re-render separate pages for every one of these needs.

Sanjeev also will save time because he won't have to acclimate to a new page each time he updates or checks his running total or shopping basket contents. And he will no longer have to worry when flipping from the shopping page to his basket or the checkout that the system may "forget" the items he's already chosen.

By keeping all user interface elements on the screen and indicating movement, the tabbed sliding panel has significantly less chance of confusing users than its HTML counterpart, and it reduces the gap between novice and advanced users.

Finally, Flash's capability to dynamically and rapidly update textual information allows the continuous display of Sanjeev's current balance. If one-click purchasing is set up, Sanjeev can very quickly scan his total and check out without additional thought.

You can see these features in action by reviewing the **GroceryClick** sample movie, the details of which are discussed here.

Seeing It in Action

To see the tabbed sliding panels at work, locate **09_tabbedPanels.fla** in the CD-ROM's **Projects** folder. To access the sliding panels, click any of the three tabs at the bottom of the interface. Clicking those tabs causes the entire bottom of the interface to slide open revealing additional content. (The content is dummy text.) With a tab open, clicking any other tab will switch to that tab's content. Clicking the active tab will close the interface.

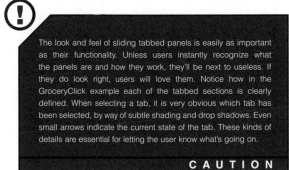

The look and feel of sliding tabbed panels is easily as important as their functionality. Unless users instantly recognize what the panels are and how they work, they'll be next to useless. If they do look right, users will love them. Notice how in the GroceryClick example each of the tabbed sections is clearly defined. When selecting a tab, it is very obvious which tab has been selected, by way of subtle shading and drop shadows. Even small arrows indicate the current state of the tab. These kinds of details are essential for letting the user know what's going on.

CAUTION

The interface will close when Sanjeev clicks a tab that is already open.

As with all the usability features in this book, attention to detail is pivotal to the success of the tabbed interface.

IMPLEMENTATION
To be effective, to be intuitive, and to enhance a site's usability, the tabbed interface must incorporate a number of features. They can be broken down into two categories: core functionality and advanced features.

The features for core functionality are as follows:

- **Click activation.** The tabbed panels should open and close to their maximum position with a single click and should do so quickly and cleanly.

- **Visual activation feedback.** The panel should "show" the user that the panels are opening. A simple appear/disappear can be confusing. If the user sees the interface sliding open, the risk of confusion is reduced.

- **Auto-hide option.** Depending on the panel's purpose, it may be appropriate for it to close automatically when the user clicks off it.

- **Multiple views/pages.** The tabbed panel should have support for multiple views or pages. Try to group logically similar sections in the same tabbed panel.

- **View location feedback.** If your design uses multiple views, the tabs should give the user very clear visual clues as to which section they are in.

The advanced features are as follows:

- **Drag open/close.** Dragging the tabbed panel should open it only as far as the user wants.

- **Force close.** When dragging it open, the tab should stay open until the user specifically closes it.

- **Clean up.** When dragging a panel closed, if the user doesn't quite close it all the way the interface should close itself.

Note that for GroceryClick.com a decision has been made *not* to include the auto-hide option or the advanced features. The steps required to program them will be covered; but because they will not improve GroceryClick's usability, they are not used.

With those points in mind, it's time to build the interface. This is a long one, so you might want to grab a Jolt Cola™.

During the initial development of this module, we designed the panels to be able to interpret the user's actions. The tabbed panels could be activated both by dragging *and* clicking. Dragging would open the tab to the user's preferred position; clicking would open and close it to its maximum and minimum height. It was cool, but possibly just too cool to be a real usability enhancement. In fact, it was a classic case where something that excites the designer might actually confuse the end user. It killed me having to take it out, because it involved some nifty coding; but in the interest of Sanjeev, it had to be done. After I agreed to take it out, Michelangelo sent me back to reread the section in Chapter 1, "Bad Flashers Anonymous," that reminds designers to keep control of their ego.

Author Note: Duncan

Why am I coding this stuff if it's not going to be used?

Excellent question! It is essential to look at the purpose of your interface widget, no matter what the circumstances. In this case there were two distinct possibilities for the tabbed interface, one is the purpose that is being used here. Sanjeev can click the tabs and get a very quick look at his shopping basket, find items, and see his favorite item list. This is the tabbed UI's core purpose: quick access to additional information. Another possibility would be to have a tabbed UI that Sanjeev would continually reference while shopping, something that would not close, but act like a panel (for example, the Internet Explorer's Explorer Bar). The panel should be editable by the users: They should be able open it to any width they want, so that the information most important to them displays in the manner that they like.

The panel-type UI works best when it's at the side of the screen and not the bottom or top. As you can see by clicking a GroceryClick tab, when it's open it expands, covering up most of the content, so Sanjeev would be unable to use both site content and his list simultaneously. Even if he were to drag it down, the content of both the list and the site would present too little information to help him use GroceryClick.

To accommodate the two distinct types of uses for this UI element, the code needs to provide for both situations. The component clip parameters take care of specifying the type of interaction required to use with the tabbed sliding panel.

If you want to see the drag version of the sliding tabbed panels, or the auto-hide features, you can open the clip's properties by selecting Properties while right-clicking the tabbed panel UI on the stage. From there you can adjust how the tabbed panels work.

Note

CONSTRUCTION

The following tutorial shows you how to create the code to insert a tabbed interface into a Flash movie. For this demonstration, you will use a three-tabbed panel.

Setting Up Your Movie

If you plan to build your tabbed interface inside an existing movie, create a new layer called **Tabbed Window** and place it toward the top of the layer stack, making sure it's above any layer that the tabbed window should appear in front of. If you are making this in a new movie, just create a new layer called **Tabbed Window**. For a new movie, the stage size is set to 640×480 with a frame rate of 20fps.

Creating the Content Window

With the new layer created, start by drawing a rectangular shape on the stage. The height and width aren't really important, but keep the overall dimensions less than those of the movie.

Convert your newly drawn rectangle to a movie clip (F8 or Insert>Convert to Symbol from the menu) and give it a symbol name of **content** and an instance name of *mc_content*. This graphic will be the base of the tabbed UI, so it should match the color of the surrounding area.

Figure 9.1
Give your content movie clip an instance name of mc_content.

Creating the Content Areas

Now you can create the tabbed views. Double-click the **content** movie clip to open it in the Edit window. To make life a bit easier, you might want to group the primitive shape (Cmd-G/Ctrl-G). Next create four new layers labeled **labels**, **actions**, **content**, and **content graphic**, with **labels** being the top layer and **content graphic** being the bottom.

Now you need to add three more keyframes on each of the first three levels. The **content graphic** layer remains the same. Click once on frame 1 of any layer, apart from **content graphic**, and press F6 or Insert>Keyframe from the main menu. Repeat this step for each layer.

Next add labels to each of the four keyframes on the **labels** layer. Click the first frame and open the Frame panel (Cmd-F/Ctrl-F, or Window>Panels>Frame from the main menu). In the Frame panel, enter **closed** for the label. Repeat this process for each subsequent frame using **favoriteItems**, **find**, and **yourBasket** for the frame labels.

If you are building this for a specific purpose, you should change these labels to match the content that will appear in your movie. For this demo, however, you will be specifically referring to **favoriteItems**, **find**, and **yourBasket**. Keep that in mind if you do change these labels because it may lead to errors in your code.

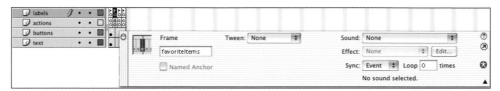

Figure 9.2
For each tab, you must create a corresponding keyframe and frame label like the one for favoriteItems shown here.

Moving on to the code layer, select frame 1 of the **actions** layer, open the Actions panel (F2), and enter a `stop();` command.

Repeat this for each keyframe in the **code** layer. This `stop();` command will prevent the playhead from leaving each frame when you skip between them.

On the **content** layer, enter some dummy content for now. In this chapter, there are just text messages identifying what the content will eventually be. It's a good idea to lock this layer now until you are ready to add the real content.

After you have each of your views completed, return to the main stage (Cmd-E/Ctrl-E).

Setting Up the tabbedWindow Movie Clip

For the remainder of this tutorial, you'll be spending your time inside the **tabbedWindow** movie clip. This will hold the recently created **content** clip and the tabs. To create the **tabbedWindow** clip, click the **content** clip to select it and press F8 (or Insert>Convert to Symbol) and give it a symbol name of **tabbedWindow**. No need for an instance name this time. This movie clip also needs several layers (nine, to be exact). You could get away with fewer, but it makes editing the file much harder. The layers in order, from bottom to top, should be **content clip**, **shadow**, **background**, **shader**, **delineators**, **text**, **buttons**, and **actions**.

Figure 9.3
Lots of layers are needed for the tabbedWindow clip.

Setting up these layers is much better explained by referring to Figure 9.4, but don't skip this part. It's just as important as the code. Fail here and the code won't matter.

The **labels**, **actions**, **delineators**, and **shader** levels all need four keyframes; the remaining layers need only the first keyframe, but should have blank frames extending to frame 4.

The **labels** layer needs labels for each of the last three frames. Click frame 2 and enter the following frame name: **favoriteItems**. For the remaining frames, enter **find** and **yourBasket**. If these names seem familiar, it is because they mimic the names of the frames in the **content** layer.

In the **actions** layer, attach a single `stop();` frame action to each frame.

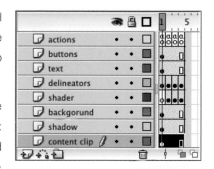

Figure 9.4

This diagram shows the intricate layering required for this movie clip to work accurately.

To the **background** layer, add a square graphic symbol that matches the width and color of the **content** movie clip. It is not important that this is an actual Flash symbol.

The **shadow** layer should contain the shadow graphics, which help separate the paneled interface from the **content** layer. This layer helps the user differentiate between elements on the finished interface.

The **shader** layer is used to darken the unselected tabs, which is why frame 1 is left blank. For each subsequent keyframe, a rectangular shape should be placed on either side of the selected tab.

The **delineators** layer is for the short vertical lines used to indicate the edges of the Flash symbols that represent each button. For added visual aid, small drop shadows are placed around the selected tab.

The **text** layer should contain the text label for each tab. Set the text to **Favorite Items**, **Find Items**, and **Your Basket ($999.99)**. The labels are separate from the buttons here to aid in providing the dynamically updated total in Your Basket.

Finally, the **buttons** layer. Because all the visual action is already handled in the layers below this, it makes sense to use a generic invisible button here. Again your projects might allow for several of these layers to be combined into a single layer. To create an invisible button, draw a rectangular shape on the stage and select the entire shape. Press F8 or Insert>Convert to Symbol and set it to Button.

Double-click the button to enter Edit mode. Click in the Hit frame and press F6 or Insert>Keyframe, and then click in the first keyframe. This part is important: Click the square shape on the stage and then press Delete. A quirk of Flash means that if you don't click the object on the stage you will end up moving the frame, not deleting it.

Exit the Edit mode. The invisible button should show up in Flash as a transparent blue square. Duplicate this button twice, for a total of three buttons, and then carefully adjust both size and scale to match the height and width of the button areas as indicated by the objects on the **background** and **delineators** layers.

After you've completed that, you're done with the graphics for this project. Before you move on, however, make sure the elements you have built give clear indications for the user. Will they know which section they are in? Is the panel visually distinct enough to be read as a separate, but integrated element? When you're happy, you can move on to the code. Don't forget to save your file.

CODE

A word of encouragement: This module contains *a lot* of code, and it's going to take a while to get through it all. Don't get discouraged, however. The end product from this lesson is just too cool not to use, so take your time and be patient.

Buttons

To begin, you'll want to add the code to the three tab buttons you just created. Click the first button, open the ActionScript Editor, and enter the following code (see Figure 9.5):

```
on(press) {
 this.mc_content.pressHandler("favoriteItems");
 }

on(release) {
 this.mc_content.releaseHandler();
}

on(releaseOutside) {
 _parent.stopDrag();
}stop();
```

Each subsequent button must change the argument, the quoted text between the parenthesis, for the pressHandler() to match the content of the button being pressed. For example, the find button should read pressHandler("find");.

The code itself is very simple, but out of context at the moment. **_mySelection_** is a variable that holds the name of this button, in this case favoriteItems. This variable hasn't been declared yet, but will be in the next section as part of the code attached to the **content** movie clip.

The next line is calling a function, again one that isn't written yet, attached to the **content** movie clip.

Then comes the code that runs whenever the mouse button is released. This code, much like the second line of code from the `pressHandler()`, is calling a function that will be written into the **content** movie clip. The text in between the parenthesis of the `releaseHandler()` function is an argument for favoriteItems. It works because `this` is a special reference to the movie clip in which the button resides. **mc_content** is a reference to the **content** movie clip, and **mySelection** is a variable.

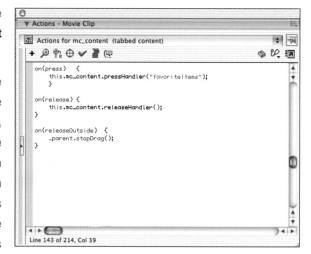

Figure 9.5
Each tab button requires this code. The most important aspect is the setting of the mySelection *variable.*

Movie Clip Code

Moving right along to the movie clip code, click the **content** movie clip and open the ActionScript panel. This **content** movie clip is where the remainder of the code will go.

The majority of the coding will be in the `onClipEvent(load)` handler. In between the {} of the `load`, it's time to declare the variable that was called from the button functions: **mySelection**.

```
onClipEvent(load) {
  var mySelection;
}
```

Now just below the **mySelection** declaration, add the function that handles the `press` and `release` event on the buttons (see Figure 9.6).

```
function pressHandler(selectedTab)
{
 mySelection = selectedTab;
}


 function releaseHandler()
 {
  this.gotoAndStop(mySelection);
 }
```

At the moment, this function is very simple. The `pressHandler()` function is receiving a string argument, `selectedTab`, from the button pushed. This argument should match one of the frame labels you already set up and gets assigned to the **mySelection** variable. When the user releases the mouse button, the `releaseHandler()` function runs. This just takes the variable **mySelection** set in the `pressHandler()` and then executes a `gotoAndStop()` command, with **mySelection** as the argument.

The reason to assign the variable on the `mouseDown` action rather than on the `mouseUp` is in anticipation of the dragging ability.

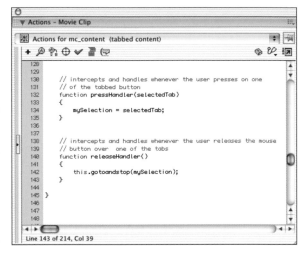

Figure 9.6
This very simple code will switch between the frame labels you set up a moment ago.

It's pretty early on, but you should now save your movie and test it (Cmd-Return/Ctrl-Enter). Clicking the tabs should switch the content. There's quite a bit of code in the next step, so you might want to take a break for a few minutes.

Making It Move

Now that the tabbed panels will switch between the various sections, it is time to add the code that will open the tabs. Start by adding the following variables to the beginning of the `onClipEvent(load)` handler (see Figure 9.7):

```
var myFriction = 2.3;
var mySelection;

var myMenuAction = "closed";

var myHidePosition = Stage.height+(this._height/2);
var myShowPosition = Stage.height-(this._height/2);
var myPos = "_y";
```

- **myFriction.** Used as the "drag coefficient." It's the amount of friction that will affect the window when opening. Instead of just flicking open, the sliding panel will glide to a stop, so you need a degree of friction to slow the window down.

- **mySelection.** The same as used in the `release` and `press` handlers. It's just good form to declare your variables before using them.

- **MyMenuAction.** Holds the action of the tabbed panel. Possible actions are `open`, `close`, `opened`, and `closed`. Because the menu should always start in the `closed` position, give **myMenuAction** an initial value of `closed`.

- **myHidePosition** and **myShowPosition.** Hold the coordinates to which the panels should open and close. Instead of your having to enter the numbers manually,

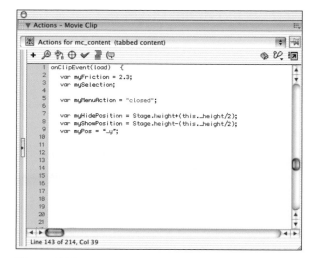

Figure 9.7

Setting up some of the variables to be used throughout the movie.

the code will dynamically create the values by using the known information. If you did well in Algebra I in high school, the next bit should be a piece of cake. We didn't, so check out the following tip for how this stuff works.

- **myPos = "_y";.** Tells the code how the tabbed panel is oriented (horizontal or vertical). This anticipates the conversion of the movie clip to a component clip later in the chapter.

In one sense, algebra can be seen as finding *x*, or the missing value, when other values are known. In this instance, the unknown values are the open and closed position of the tabbed window. The known values are the height of the movie, the height of the movie clips (using the `height` property), and the location of the movie clips (_y). The _y property is set to dead center of the movie clip. With all this information, determining the open position is simple.

The goal here is to get the tabbed panels to sit flush with the bottom of the movie. The bottom of the movie is 640 pixels from the top, as held in the `Stage.height` property. If you were to set the _y position of the movie clip to 640, that would be a start, but because the movie clip's registration point is at the center of the movie clip, the tabbed panels will appear only halfway closed.

Therefore you need to "move the clip down" a bit further. Figuring out how much is easy. Think about it; if the movie clip is halfway down and it needs to be all the way down, what do you need to add to 640? Take a moment to really think about this. If you're not great with math, sketch the problem out in real physical space; it really helps us in these situations.

Did you come up with half the height of the movie clip? Good job, you're totally right! By taking half of the movie clip's height, you can move the clip down just the right amount so that it sits flush with the bottom of the movie. Therefore the correct formula for getting the **myHidePosition** is `Stage.height + (this._height/2)`.

Because the `height property` *is* being grabbed from the **content** movie clip and not the whole tabbed UI, the tabs aren't taken into account. This means you can make them as tall or as short as you want and they will still position themselves perfectly along the bottom of the interface!

See, math *can* be useful.

Tip

Now that you have all these variables set up, it's time to put them to use.

Setting the Initial Position

After you have the formula working, use the answer to set the _y position of the tabbed panels:

```
_parent._y = myHidePosition;
```

Great job! The panels start out in the closed position now. Save your movie and, if you want, test it before moving on.

Open the Tab Function, Getting It Ready to Move

Next comes the bulk of the code for opening the tab. It looks pretty intimidating, but take it easy and it should make sense. Add the following:

```
function openTab()
{
 if(Math.abs(_parent[myPos]-(myShowPosition)) > 1)     {
  curPos = _parent[myPos];
  difPos = myShowPosition - curPos;
  setPos = difPos / myFriction;
  _parent[myPos] = _parent[myPos] + setPos;
 } else {
  myMenuAction = "opened";
  _parent[myPos] = myShowPosition;
 }
}
```

The openTab() function is going to employ some pseudo-physics, to allow the tabs to slide open (see Figure 9.8). It's a much more visually pleasing, less jarring way to activate the tabs. The trick is finding the right amount of "friction" to keep the process from taking too long.

What's all this square bracket stuff? Well, in simple English it allows the dynamic creation of variables, properties, and so on. It's used here to generate positional properties. For example, parent[myPos] is actually read by the computer as _parent._y, because myPos was set to _y at the top of the script.

Note

Starting with the top line, the code is asking whether the distance between the tabbed panels, _parent[myPos], and its fully extended position, myShowPosition, is greater than 1. If so, the next set of three variables—**curPos**, **difPos**, and **setPos**—are used to simulate friction working on the tab, slowing it down. You also can think of it as "easing out" in animation terms. Anyway, **curPos** is the current position of the tabbed UI. **difPos** is the difference between the current position of the tabs and their end position. **setPos** divides **difPos** by the constant variable **myFriction**, which was set at the top of the code a few pages ago. The last step is moving the tabs, which is done by adding the number created by **setPos** to the value of the tab's current position, `_parent[myPos]`.

The `else` statement takes care of the times when there is a difference between the tab's current position and its fully extended position. When that happens, the code forces the tabbed panels to their maximum extended position and sets the **myMenuAction** variable to `open`. These two steps prevent the `openTab()` function from executing even though the tab is open.

Figure 9.8

*A simple execution of pseudo-physics to open that tab. This can be turned off by setting the **myFriction** variable to 1.*

This function by itself won't do anything. You have to set some variables that enable you to access this feature.

Accessing the Move Function

There are two parts to opening the tabbed panels. First there must be an event that tells the panels to open, and then there must be an event to tell the `openTab();` function to keep executing while the tabs aren't open. Unfortunately, this can't be done in one event or action. Instead, the initialization action has to be in the `releaseHandler()` function, setting a variable that will allow the execution code to run. In the `releaseHandler()` section, add the following code to the end of the function:

```
myMenuAction = "open";
```

With the `releaseHandler` setting the **myMenuAction** variable, the code can be executed from an `onClipEvent(enterFrame)` handler. Add this code after the `onClipEvent(load)` event :

```
onClipEvent(enterFrame) {
  if(myMenuAction == "open") {
   openTab();
  }
 }
```

This code says (on `enterFrame`) if `myMenuAction` is `open`, call the `openTab()` function.

Still with us? It's been a lot of work up to this point and we do have a lot more to go, but you've reached a milestone. Congratulations! Save your movie and give it a whirl.

Closing the Tab

Good news: Adding the code to close the tab is really easy. In fact, it's almost identical to the code used to open the tab.

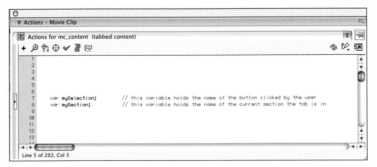

Figure 9.9
Using the `enterFrame` handler to open the window.

The only slightly tricky bit is determining whether the user is switching between tabs or asking the tabbed panels to close. Basically you can interpret the user's actions this way: If the user clicks the already selected tab, the window should close; if the user clicks another tab, the interface should switch tabs. Tweaking the `releaseHandler()` function will take care of this.

To accomplish this, add a new variable at the top of the `onClipEvent(load)` handler. Just after the already created **mySelection,** add another called **mySection**:

```
var mySection;
```

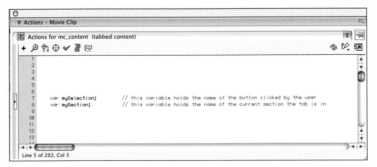

Figure 9.10
*These two variables keep track of the current section the tabbed window is in and the last button clicked. **mySection** is used to help check whether to close the tabbed window or switch between tabs.*

Just like opening the tab has a function, `openTab()`, the closing action needs one. For legibility it makes sense to place this code after the `openTab()` function:

```
function closeTab()
{
 if(Math.abs(_parent[myPos]-(myHidePosition )) > 1) {
  curPos = _parent[myPos];
  difPos = (myHidePosition - curPos);
  setPos = (difPos / myFriction);
  _parent[myPos] = (_parent[myPos] + setPos);
 } else {
  myMenuAction = "closed";
  _parent[myPos] = myHidePosition;
  mySelection = "closed";
  _parent.gotoAndStop(mySelection);
 }
}
```

If it looks familiar, it should. There are only four differences between this and the `openTab()` function. Instead of using **myShowPos**, the code is looking at **myHidePos**; and instead of setting **myMenuAction** to "open", it sets to "closed". Finally, **mySelection** is set to "closed" and the movie clip itself is told to `gotoAndStop` at the frame held inside the **mySelection** variable. This resets the visual appearance of the tabs when they close.

Now you need to modify the release handler so that it acts properly (see Figure 9.12). The code for the release handler needs to be able to deal with both drag and click activation methods. (Remember, however, for GroceryClick only click activation is required.)

Figure 9.11
The code is almost identical to the `openTab()` *function, only this closes the tab.*

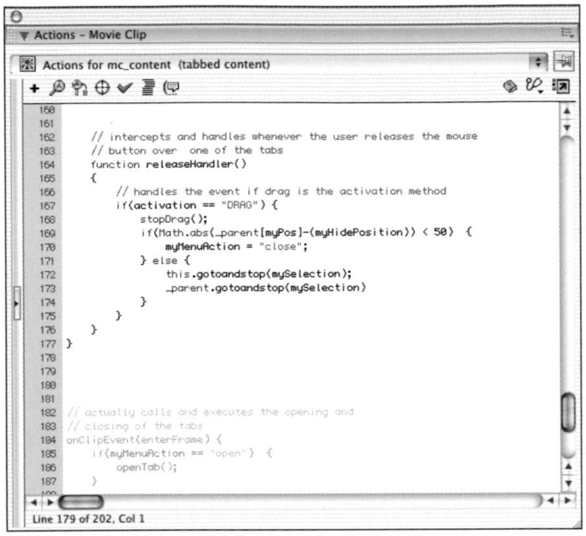

Figure 9.12
The release handler gets a major overhaul.

```
function releaseHandler()
{
 if(activation == "DRAG") {
  stopDrag();
  if(Math.abs(_parent[myPos]-(myHidePosition)) < 50) {
   myMenuAction = "close";
  } else {
   this.gotoAndStop(mySelection);
   _parent.gotoAndStop(mySelection);
  }
```

There's a bit more to come, but start with this chunk of code that handles dragging. Notice that the variable **activation** is being checked for its value. This variable can either be "DRAG" or "CLICK" and is declared at the top of the load movie, which hasn't been done yet.

Next, because this bit of code is handling a dragging event, the stopDrag() function needs to be called; When the user releases the mouse, the UI should stop dragging.

Following that, there's another if statement. This is actually pretty cool: It checks to see whether the tabbed panels are within 20 pixels of the bottom and if so sets **myMenuAction** to "close", thus closing the menu. This is basically a cleanup feature, mentioned in the key features list, which activates if the user doesn't quite get the tabs closed.

Okay, if the tabbed panels are not within 20 pixels, both this movie clip (which contains the images of the tabs) and the content movie clip (which contains the content) get sent to a frame with the same label as the **mySelection** variable.

Moving right along, it's time to see how the code deals with the click activation method. It's a tad more complex because it needs to understand what state it's in and apply the correct action based on that state. So right after the preceding code, add the following:

```
} else if(activation == "CLICK") {
  this.gotoAndStop(mySelection);
  _parent.gotoAndStop (mySelection);
  if((mySection == mySelection) && (myMenuAction == "opened")) {
   myMenuAction = "close";
  } else if(myMenuAction == "closed")    {
   mySection = mySelection;
   myMenuAction = "open";
   } else if((mySection != mySelection) && (myMenuAction ==  "opened"))
{
    mySection = mySelection;
   }
  }
```

Just as the dragging code starts out by checking the activation method, this code checks for `"CLICK"` activation. The next two lines, `this.gotoAndStop(mySelection);` and `_parent.gotoAndStop(mySelection);`, are just like they were in the drag part of this code. They tell their respective movie clips to go to the correct frame.

The rest of the code might look unwieldy, but it's asking only three sets of questions. The first question, or the first `if` statement, asks whether the currently selected tab is the same tab that the user just clicked. If so, is the menu open? If the answer to both questions is yes, the menu is closed by setting the **myMenuAction** variable to `"close"`. If one or both of those is no, the code asks another question: Is the menu closed? If so, the current section, or **mySection**, is set to **mySelection** and the menu is opened by setting **myMenuAction** to `"open"`. Finally the code asks one last set of questions. Is the button just selected by the user *not* the same as the currently selected tab view? If so, is the menu open? If both of those are true, the tab view is switched and **mySection** is set to **mySelection**. This is done so that the next time the release handler is called it will check to see whether the two are equal and will close the tab.

Now you need to add one more variable to the top of the `onClipEvent(load)` event handler:

```
var activation = "CLICK"
```

Remember, because this is for GroceryClick, activation should be set to `"CLICK"`. Later on **activation** will be turned into a component parameter allowing for it to be set dynamically.

It's also time to tweak the press handler to handle both `"CLICK"` and `"DRAG"` activation methods. Just below where you set the **mySelection** variable add an `if` statement. Your code should look like this after you have finished:

```
function pressHandler(selectedTab)
{
  mySelection = selectedTab;
  if(activation == "DRAG") {
    _parent.startDrag(false, myLeft, myTop, myRight, myBottom);
  }
}
```

Looks much nicer than the release handler, eh? Here the variable **mySelection** is being set to **selectedTab**, which is a parameter that is passed from the tab buttons. (If you go way back to the beginning of the code, you can see that the name of the tab is between the parenthesis.)

The only other thing that happens here is the code checks to see whether the **activation** type is set to `"DRAG"`. If the type is `"DRAG"`, the code tells the `_parent` object—the entire tabbed UI—to start dragging, but to lock to the **myLeft**, **myTop**, **myRight**, and **myBottom** variables, none of which have been set yet. (Because this is for GroceryClick.com, the drag function isn't enabled.)

Figure 9.13
The code to handle mouseDown *events passed from the tab buttons.*

150

Adding the Auto-Hide Feature

The auto-hide feature is really quite simple to implement. It's about time for some instant gratification, anyway.

At the top of the code, add another variable just after the **myFricition** variable:

```
var autoHide = 1;
```

The auto-hide feature looks for mouse clicks that occur outside of the active tabbed panel interface, which means using the onClipEvent(mouseDown) event, as follows:

```
onClipEvent(mouseDown) {
  if((_parent.hitTest(_root._xmouse, _root._ymouse) != true) && (autoHide ==
➡1)){
    myMenuAction = "close";
  }
```

The mouseDown code looks for two things: Is the mouse clicking outside the tabbed interface, and is the autoHide feature true? If both these are true, **myMenuAction** is set to true and the tabbed panels will close.

In the previous code, true is replaced by 1; and if you wanted to set **autoHide** to false, you would substitute 0. Although it's easier to read true and false, when the time comes to make this into a component clip, true and false can't be passed via the Clip Parameters panel. It's just easier to use 1 and 0 now rather than go back and alter it later.

![Actions panel showing the auto-hide code for mc_content (tabbed content).]

Figure 9.14
The auto-hide code is relatively simple.

Speaking of making this into a component clip, that's coming up next and there's quite a bit of work to do. Save what you've got and get ready.

Making Your Code Portable

This next bit of code is really more for you as the developer/designer than it is for the end user. You could skip this section and the user wouldn't see any difference in the way the tabbed window works. You would have to alter the `startDrag()` method to constrain the dragging. But what happens when, a month from now, you decide to change the location of the tabbed window from the right side to the left, or even change its orientation? There would be quite a bit of code to rework and that's never any fun. Wouldn't it be nice if you never had to touch this code again, but could change the shape, location, and orientation at will? Well you can; it's just going to take some work.

To start with, you want to convert as many variables as you can to component clip parameters so that you can adjust as many features via the Clip Parameters panel as possible.

Adding the Clip Parameter Variables

Replace the values assigned to **myFriction** and **autoHide** to `_parent.myFriction` and `_parent.autoHide`, as follows:

```
var myFriction = _parent.myFriction;
var autoHide = _parent.autoHide;
```

In addition to changing existing variables to parameters, create two new variables that will have values assigned via the Clip Parameters panel.

```
var myLoc = _parent.myLoc;
var myAlign = _parent.myAlign;
```

myLoc will hold a value that will determine the location of the tabbed window. Possible values are `TOP`, `BOTTOM`, `LEFT`, and `RIGHT`. **myAlign** will determine where the window will be aligned, either left, right, or center.

Adding the Last of Top Variables

There are two new variables, **myPin** and **myPinPosition**. You also want to remove the values that had originally been assigned to three of the top variables: **myPos**, **myHidePos**, and **myShowPos**. These will now have dynamically generated values created in a new function called `initialize()`.

```
var myPos;
var myPin;
var myHidePosition;
var myShowPosition;
var myPinPosition;
```

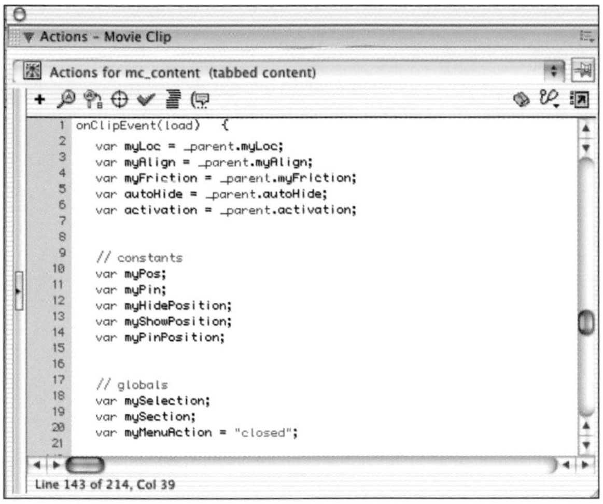

```
 1  onClipEvent(load)   {
 2      var myLoc = _parent.myLoc;
 3      var myAlign = _parent.myAlign;
 4      var myFriction = _parent.myFriction;
 5      var autoHide = _parent.autoHide;
 6      var activation = _parent.activation;
 7
 8
 9      // constants
10      var myPos;
11      var myPin;
12      var myHidePosition;
13      var myShowPosition;
14      var myPinPosition;
15
16
17      // globals
18      var mySelection;
19      var mySection;
20      var myMenuAction = "closed";
21
```

Line 143 of 214, Col 39

Figure 9.15
Here are all the variables at the top of the movie clip code, reorganized and grouped in a logical manner.

The Initialize Function

The initialize() function will use the ***myLoc*** and ***myAlign*** variables to dynamically set the location of the tabbed window. Start by creating a new function called initialize() just after the last declared variable, ***myPinPosition***:

```
initialize()
{

}
```

Inside the body of the `initialize()` function, add the code that follows:

```
if(myLoc == "BOTTOM")     {
myHidePosition = Stage.height + ((this._height/2));
myShowPosition = Stage.height - (this._height/2);
myPos = "_y";
myPin = "_x";

myLeft = getPinPosition(Stage.width);
myRight = getPinPosition(Stage.width);
myTop = myShowPosition;
myBottom = myHidePosition;
}
```

This code fragment looks at the **myLoc** variable, set in the Clip Parameters panel. In this particular instance, if `myLoc="BOTTOM"`, it will execute the code between the next set of {}. Remember, the **myLoc** variable will be set in the Clip Parameters panel and only have possible values of `TOP`, `BOTTOM`, `LEFT`, and `RIGHT`.

Figure 9.16
The `initialize()` *code used to set the tabbed window's location.*

Examining each line, you can see what's happening:

```
myHidePosition = Stage.height + ((this._height/2));
myShowPosition = Stage.height - (this._height/2);
```

These two lines are actually identical to the lines of code previously used to determine the show and hide position for the tabbed window.

```
myPos = "_y";
myPin = "_x";
```

myPos and **myPin** hold a string value of either "_x" or "_y".

```
myLeft = getPinPosition(Stage.height);
myRight = getPinPosition(Stage.width);
myTop = myShowPosition;
myBottom = myHidePosition;
```

These four variables are used to constrain the drag action of the tabbed window. The `startDrag()` function currently doesn't constrain the tabbed window at all. Because the tabbed window can be placed against any edge of the screen (top, bottom, left, and right), the values for the constraint need to change based on that location. In this instance, **myTop** and **myBottom** are just set to the already generated **myShowPosition** and **myHidePosition** variables.

The values for **myLeft** and **myRight** are somewhat complicated to come up with and require you to make another function to calculate the values. The new function, which will be called `getPinPosition()`, will take the argument passed to it and run a series of calculations. The result of those calculations will then be returned as a number to the `initialize()` function.

```
if(myLoc == "TOP") {
 _parent._rotation = 180;
 myHidePosition = 0 - ((this._height/2));
 myShowPosition = 0 + (this._height/2);
 myPos = "_y";
 myPin = "_x";

 myLeft = getPinPosition(Stage.width);
 myRight = getPinPosition(Stage.width);
 myTop = myHidePosition;
 myBottom = myShowPosition;
}

if(myLoc == "LEFT")          {
 _parent._rotation = 90;
 myHidePosition = 0 - ((this._height/2));
 myShowPosition = 0 + (this._height/2);
 myPos = "_x";
 myPin = "_y";

 myLeft = myHidePosition
 myRight = myShowPosition;
 myTop = getPinPosition(Stage.height);
 myBottom = getPinPosition(Stage.height);
}

if(myLoc == "RIGHT")         {
 _parent._rotation = 270;
 myHidePosition = Stage.width + ((this._height/2));
 myShowPosition = Stage.width - (this._height/2);
 myMyPos = "_x";
 myMyPin = "_y";

 myLeft = myShowPosition;
 myRight = myHidePosition;
 myTop = getPinPosition(Stage.height);
 myBottom = getPinPosition(Stage.height);
}
```

As you can see, the difference in code is very slight, so you need to pay careful attention as you copy the code.

Finally, the `initialize()` function needs to set the initial position of the tabbed window interface based on the values just generated.

```
_parent[myPos] = myHidePosition;
_parent[myPin] = myPinPosition;
```

The final piece of code is a function whose sole purpose is to return a value for the two remaining values for the constraint of the tabbed window.

```
function getPinPosition(orientation)
{
  if(myAlign == "START") {
   myPinPosition = this._width/2;
  }

  if(myAlign == "MIDDLE")        {
   myPinPosition = orientation/2;
  }

  if(myAlign == "END")   {
   myPinPosition = orientation - (this._width/2);
  }

  return myPinPosition;
}
```

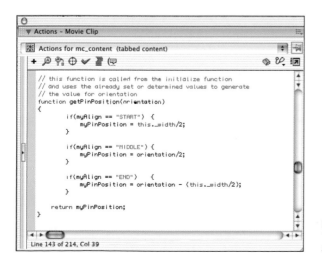

Figure 9.17
This code allows the tabbed window UI to dynamically set its alignment via the Properties panel.

Start by writing the normal function code:

```
function getPinPosition(orientation)
{

}
```

The `getPinPosition` function will set the location of the tabbed panels against whichever side of the screen they are attached. For the code to know which property (*x* or *y* location) to adjust, the function needs to be passed a parameter, *orientation*, which informs the code the value it will be dealing with when determining where to position the tab.

```
if(myAlign == "START") {
 myPinPosition = this._width/2;
}
if(myAlign == "MIDDLE")   {
 myPinPosition = orientation/2;
}
if(myAlign == "END")      {
 myPinPosition = orientation - (this._width/2);
}
```

Here the ***myAlign*** variable is checked in order to assign orientation—either left, center, or right of the screen. The equation changes based on the selected orientation.

How does it actually work? Assume that the tabbed panels are set to the bottom of the screen. The movie is 600 pixels wide and the panels are each 300 pixels wide. Therefore, from that ***orientation*** would be set to `Stage.height`, or `600`. For `START`, the equation is pretty easy; half the width of panels is 150. The *x* location of the tabbed panels is set to `150`. Because the registration point of the movie is dead center, the panel will appear aligned to the left. For `MIDDLE`, you take half the width of ***orientation***, which would be 300, so the *x* location for `MIDDLE` is `300`. Finally for `END` you take half the width of the panels, 150, and subtract that from ***orientation***, or 600, which leaves you with a value of 450, so the *x* location of for `END` is 450. It's algebra again. Figure out *x* when you have only three elements to deal with. I bet you wish you hadn't been drawing Batman comics in math class now... oh wait, that was me.

```
return myPinPosition;
```

After the value for **myPinPosition** has been set, the `return` command is used to return the value of **myPinPosition** back to the `initialize()` function.

Last Step of Code

Finally, all this code won't work unless ActionScript is specifically told to activate it. Therefore, just before the very last } on the `onClipEvent(load)` handler, enter the following line of code:

```
initialize();
```

Wow, that was a lot of work. You wrote almost 150 lines of code! Great job. All that's left is setting up the component clip.

Setting Up a Component Clip

In the Library panel (Cmd-L/Ctrl-L), select the tabbedWindow and right-click (Ctrl-click) the small icon next to tabbedWindow. Select Component Definition.

Click the plus sign (+) to create new variable. Double-click the Name field and enter **myLoc**. Then double-click the Type field and select List from the drop-down menu. Now double-click the Value field. Yet another window appears with the plus and minus sign. Click the plus sign and enter **BOTTOM**, where defaultValue appears. Repeat this step for **TOP, LEFT**, and **RIGHT**. After you have all four of your values for the myLoc component paramater set, click OK.

Back in Define Clip Parameters, press the plus sign again and enter **myAlign** for the variable name. Set the type to List and double-click the Value field. In the pop-up window, click the plus sign and enter **START**. Repeat this step for **MIDDLE** and **END**. After you have finished setting the variables, click the OK button.

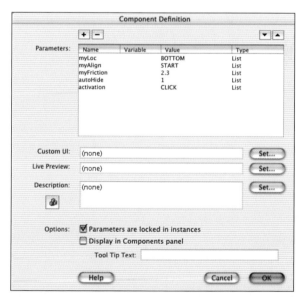

Figure 9.18

Defining the clip parameters for this component clip.

CONCLUSION

Another one down, and a good one at that. The tabbed interface is an extremely important weapon in your arsenal of interface elements. Not only is it a great usability feature, it's also great from a design perspective. Parking all those ugly pages at one edge of the screen reduces visual clutter.

Key Points/Don't Forget

- **It's the design, dummy!** After all that work on code, it may seem strange to focus on the design. If the users don't visually understand where they are and what's happening, all the code in the world won't help them.

- **Sliding panels are *not* good primary navigation devices.** Don't hide your main interface behind one of these panels; it takes too much time for the user to open the tab and then click. This device is intended for supplementary information or secondary navigation.

- **Use your space wisely.** Tabbed sliding panels enable you to create some valuable extra space on the interface. Make sure you use this space for *useful* extra content. It's not just about more; it's about better!

- **Focus on simplicity.** Tabbed sliding panels are intended to simplify the user's interaction with the interface by minimizing the navigation they need to go through. When adding panels to your movie, make sure they achieve this aim.

- **This is one cool usability element!** Now and then it's okay to note just how superior to HTML Flash can be. This is one of those times. Just try creating something like this in HTML and you'll see what we mean.

CHAPTER 10
Needles and Haystacks—Site Searches

The 'silly question' is the first intimation of some totally new development.

—Alfred North Whitehead

Sometimes you have to present your user with lots of information; there is just no way around it. Unfortunately, large amounts of information are not very productive for a user who is looking only for a small piece of information; it's the proverbial needle in a haystack situation. HTML-based web sites offer two ways to search through a given haystack of information:

- **Server-side CGI.** This scours and returns relevant pages based on the user's search request (theoretically). These searches are usually for pages outside of the current page and require an active Internet connection.
- **Client-side "Find in Page" feature.** The browser usually handles this type of search itself, looking for text contained on the currently shown page. If the page is displayed, the Find in Page search will work regardless of Internet connection.

This book focuses on the second type of search, the Find in Page search. Specifically relating to Sanjeev and the GroceryClick.com site, there are going to be instances where Sanjeev has a long list of items. This could be a long list of "favorite items" or a list of items currently in his basket. In either case, enabling Sanjeev to enter a search term and be instantly transported to that selection is a far better experience than making Sanjeev scroll through a list, no matter how well organized or categorized.

Seeing It in Action

Open the **10_find.fla** found in the **Projects** folder on the *Skip Intro* CD-ROM and export or test the movie. Note that to make life a bit easier, this find code has been moved out into its own movie; in the real world, it would be integrated in the previously created GroceryClick.com code. Because it can be difficult to continually navigate through multiple levels of movie clips, for ease of use the code here is in its own movie.

To initiate a search, enter a search term in the text entry field and click the Find button or press the Return/Enter key. If the search term is matched, its appearance will change: The matching text will be boldface, underlined, and set to the site's orange accent color. Clicking or pressing the Return/Enter key will find the next instance of the term. Should there be no matches, an alert message appears letting the user know.

To see how fast the new Flash MX text handling is, enter **kwyjibo** as the search term (kwyjibo is the very last word of the text field). The search should take almost no time at all, despite the search string being several hundred words long.

If you're ready, it's time to make this magic happen.

IMPLEMENTATION
Flash MX offers a quantum leap in terms of its handling of text searching and manipulation. What took dozens and dozens of lines of code in Flash 5, and didn't work too well, can now be done in a third of time and is immeasurably faster than previous attempts at heavy text manipulation. Take a look at the following requirements for an effective Find on Page search engine.

- **Search.** This is the obvious one; the code should be able to look through text and locate a match for the search term Sanjeev enters.

- **Indication.** After the search term has been found, the code needs to somehow indicate to the user that success, as well as where the search term is. You can use several methods. For this chapter, however, you will create a smart clip that can have any number of settings to allow for multiple visual indications of a found search term.

- **Clearing the marked text.** When the user moves on to a new search or wants the next appearance of a search term, it's very important that you get rid of the last found term. Leaving more than the currently "found" text highlighted will lead to confusion on the part of the user.

- **No matches.** To keep a smooth user experience, there needs to be a clear indication when a search term has no matches.

- **Find all matches.** Just because the code finds and indicates the first found search item doesn't necessarily mean that is the term the user was looking for; therefore, the code should automatically continue to search for the next available match every time the user clicks the Find button or presses the Enter key.

- **Search term change.** If the user changes the search term in the middle of another search, the code needs to be smart enough to start back at the very letter of the text field.

Now that you have an idea of the goals of the Find menu, it is time to build it.

CONSTRUCTION
The physical setup of the movie is quite simple. Like the example movie of the GroceryClick.com model, it might be easier for you to start in a new Flash movie because it can be a pain having to open the Find tab every time you want to test the code.

Creating the Search Field
Start by creating a text field on the stage. Make this text field fairly large because you will want to fill this up with a lot of text. This text field should be set to a dynamic text field with a variable name of **searchField**. Before moving on to the search clip, paste a decent amount of text inside this field.

Creating the Clip

The movie clip itself is comprised of four elements:

- Input text field
- Find button
- Code logic
- "No matches" user feedback

Start by creating a new text field somewhere on the Stage; the field should be a single line high and long enough to enter search terms in. This text box will represent the area for Sanjeev to enter the search term, so be sure to set the text box type to `input` text. Also give the text field a variable name of ***input***. With the text box set correctly, convert the text box to a movie clip by pressing F8.

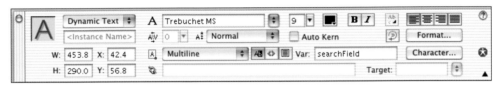

Figure 10.1
The text boxes should all be set to dynamic text, with HTML as an option.

Because the remainder of the code takes place inside of this movie clip, open the movie clip in Edit mode.

To make life easier, name the current, and only, layer **input field**. Then create three additional layers: **actions**, **buttons**, and **error message**.

On the **buttons** layer, add a button that will act as the button to initiate the find. Nothing very special required about this button; it should just be very simple, but the aesthetics are up to you. For the button, click once and open the Actions panel (F2) and enter the following code:

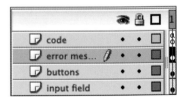

Figure 10.2
Don't forget to use layers while developing. It makes life much easier.

```
on (release, keyPress "<Enter>") {
  if (input != null) {
    find();
  }
}
```

Whenever the user clicks this button, or presses the Enter/Return key, this code checks to see whether the input text field that you created earlier is empty. If it isn't, the code calls the `find()` function.

CODE

The `find()` function itself resides on the **actions** frame, so click once on that frame and make sure you still have the Actions panel still open.

Your first step is to declare a variable called ***gLastFoundIndex***. This variable will keep track of the character position of the last found occurrence of the search term.

```
var gLastFoundIndex = 0;
```

The next step is to convert the field that you are searching to all lowercase. Not only will you convert the searchable field to lowercase, but also the search term. What this enables you to do is give your user the flexibility to enter search terms without concern to case sensitivity. To convert a string to lowercase, you can use the `.toLowerCase()` string object, as follows:

```
var searchableField = _parent.searchField.toLowerCase();
```

Now on to the find itself. Start by creating a new function called `find()`.

```
function find()
{

}
```

Then convert the search term, or the term that the user enters in to the dynamic text field named input, to all lowercase. Again this is done so that there are no issues with case sensitivity.

```
var searchString = input.toLowerCase();
```

With both your search term and searchable text field set, it's time to do the actual searching. You are in a tremendous amount of luck, because it takes only two small lines of code to accomplish this. (Technically you could get away with one, but the second line will actually save you some time later on.) Basically you create two new variables and assign them a value held by `indexOf` and `lastIndexOf` respectively.

```
nextInsctance = searchableField.indexOf(searchString, gLastFoundIndex);
lastInstance = searchableField.lastIndexOf(input);
```

So how does this work? Well `indexOf()` and `lastIndexOf()` both work the same way: They take a string (in this case your searchable field, the one converted to all lowercase and stored in the **searchableField** variable) and look for a match of the search term—in this case, the string held in the **searchString** variable. If there is a match, both `indexOf()` and `lastIndexOf()` return a number that represents the first character's found location. In other words, if you were to search for the word *is* in the sentence "Flash is cool," and were to use `indexOf()`, it would return the number 6, because there is a match of *is* and that match starts at the sixth position in the "Flash is cool" string.

The big difference between `indexOf()` and `lastIndexOf()` is that `lastIndexOf()` occurrence looks only for the very last occurrence of the search term. `IndexOf` on the other hand looks for a match starting from the second argument passed to it. If you look closely at the code, you can see it does indeed have two arguments. The first **searchString** is obviously the string that `indexOf` is looking for; the second represents where to start looking, or which character to start looking at. Currently **gLastFoundIndex** is set to 0, so the search will start at the very beginning of the search field.

If there are no matches, the number returned by both `indexOf` and `lastIndexOf` is −1.

Using these two Flash functions is a bit like casting a fishing net: You're never quite sure what you've caught until you reel in the net, which is the next step in your code. Enter the following `if` statement:

```
if(nextInstance != -1) {
```

This looks at the **nextInstance** variable to see whether anything was found, or more precisely to see that **nextInstance** didn't return a value of −1. Therefore, with something found you now have to indicate to the user where the match has occurred:

```
Selection.setFocus("_parent.searchField");
Selection.setSelection(nextInstance, (nextInstance + input.length));
```

The first line of code focuses Flash on the text field that you are searching. This is important, otherwise the next line of code won't work.

What the next line does is use the `setSelection()` method to select the found text. `setSelection()` accepts two arguments: the character to start the selection at, and the character to end the selection at. The first argument is really easy to come up with, because you already have it. The value returned by the `indexOf` method and stored in the **nextInstance** variable is always the first character of the selection. The last character of the selection is only slightly more difficult to get, but it's still rather simple in comparison to some of the other code you've done in the book. By getting the length of the input or search term using `input.length` and adding that value to the value of **nextInstance**, you have both your start and end values for the `setSelection()` method.

That really brings to a close the guts of the Find on Page. It's really now about tweaking the code to really help the users and provide them with a better experience. Now start, or continue, by enabling the user to search for multiple occurrences of a given term.

Selection or selected text might sound fancy, but you're very used to seeing it. Whenever you select text in a word processor or web browser, it highlights—usually inverting the typical black text on a white background to black background with white text. That's the same thing you're doing with the `setSelection()` method.

Note

Directly after the `setSelection()` code, enter another `if` statement:

```
if(nextInstance != lastInstance) {
  gLastFoundIndex = nextInstance + input.length;
} else {
  gLastFoundIndex = 0;
}
```

Here's where it starts to make sense why you used both `indexOf()` and `lastIndexOf()`. This statement looks to make sure that the current occurrence isn't also the last occurrence of a search term. If it isn't, the **gLastFoundIndex** is increased. Remember that the `indexOf` starts looking for matches after that second parameter. By increasing that number it will look for the next search term, not the current one. The amount that it's increased by is also of note. You could very easily increase **gLastFoundIndex** by 1 and the code would work just fine locating the next occurrence. But think about this sentence: "There are three occurrences of the word there, aren't there?" If you were to search for the word *there*, `indexOf()` would return a value of 0 for the first run through. You also know though that the search term is 5 characters long, so the next 4 characters in the sentence, 1–4, couldn't very well be a match because they are all part of the first match. Therefore you can increase the next character to search by 5, or the length of the word for which you are searching. Although not a huge time saver in Flash MX, it does save time in Flash 5.

If, on the other hand, **nextInstance** and **lastInstance** do match, **gLastFoundIndex** is reset to 0 and the search continues from the top again.

It's time to move on to the very last two lines of code. You need to close the very first `if` statement, as follows:

```
} else {
  this.mc_errorMessage._visible = true;
}
```

This code is the `else` statement that handles when `indexOf()` does return a –1 or cannot find a match for the user's search term. Although there are infinite possibilities as to what to do when no matches are found, this example shows a very simple movie clip's visibility property to be set to `true`.

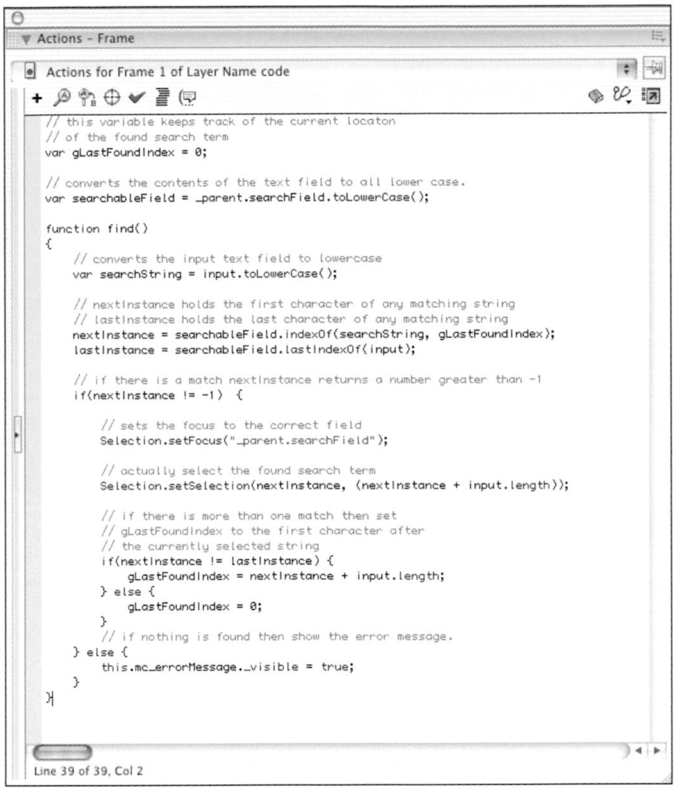

Figure 10.3
The entire `find()` logic code. Really small for something so powerful, eh?

Now you're at the last step, which is to create the "No Matches Found" error message.

Use the **error message** layer to create your error message. (See the following note for Jef Raskin's idea about error messages.) The error message used in this example is a simple one that requires no user interaction. A click of the mouse or a press of the button will get rid of the error message and start the searching. The error message should be converted to a movie clip (F8) and have the following code attached to it:

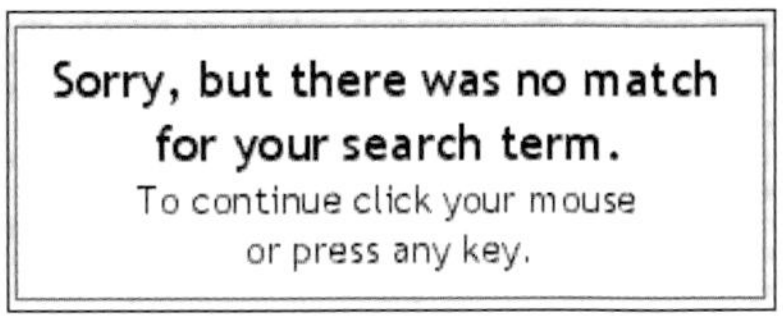

Figure 10.4
It's important to let your users know when no matches exist.

```
onClipEvent(load) {
  this._visible = false;
}


onClipEvent(mouseDown) {
  if(this._visible == true) {
    this._visible = false;
  }
}

onClipEvent(keyDown) {
  if(this._visible == true) {
    this._visible = false;
  }
}
```

The code attached to the movie clip makes sure that when it first loads up, it is not visible to the user, but when it is visible to the user, it can be quickly banished from the screen.

As stated previously, this is a very simple example of an error message designed only to alert the user that the search was not found. With a little more ingenuity and elbow grease, smarter error messages are possible.

Thanks to Flash MX, this search feature, not to mention tons of other possibilities, are just beginning to present themselves. Think of this as just the beginning.

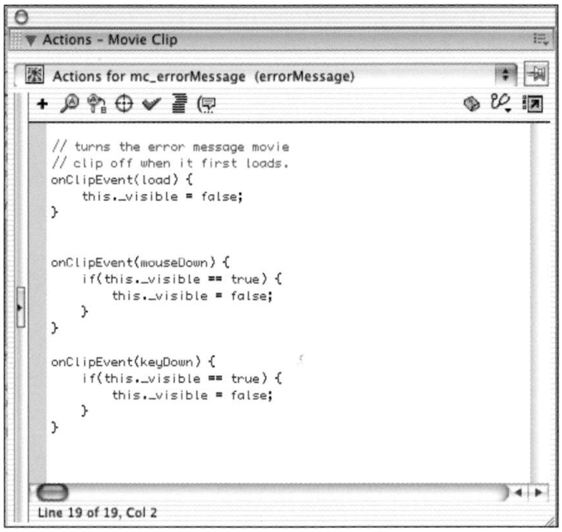

Figure 10.5
The code to attach for a simple error message.

One interesting idea that Jef Raskin proposed in *The Humane Interface* is that of the transparent error message. Although it poses some conflicting problems with overlaid text, and the example shown in his book has been precisely laid out to avoid the overlap, there is still a great deal of merit in the idea of a transparent error. Specifically, it enables the user to see the error that might have otherwise been covered up.

Note

CONCLUSION

You've got a nice portable Find on Page search object, but this code is only the tip of the iceberg. (In fact, this chapter and its code was rewritten five or six times, including a few times in Flash 5.) You can do so many great things with this type of engine. Replacing the `Selection.setSelection` with string splicing and HTML markup gave a much brighter and more permanent indication of the text. Unfortunately HTML markup requires you to not embed the fonts that wouldn't work with GroceryClick.com due to the masking involved. There is also a version that dynamically sorts through every single text field in a given movie clip. A search and replace is only a few lines of code away. All very cool solutions and, given a different project, all very useful.

Key Points/Don't Forget

- **Search the page not the site.** As mentioned in Chapter 1, "Bad Flashers Anonymous," it's important to know your tools, know when to use Flash, and known when not to use Flash. Well, the Find on Page is a great use of Flash, but a site search engine built in to Flash isn't such a great idea. Flash can't match the speed and power of a backend solution.

- **Focus the user's attention.** This object is all about drawing attention to a piece of information for which the user is looking. Make sure that you are bringing it to the user's attention and that the markup tags you select pop out from the rest of the text.

- **Give the user control.** Flash 5 can't deal with strings as effectively as it should. Enable the user to see that progress is happening and to cancel the search.

SECTION III

Wind-Automata Developer Site

Beautiful snowflakes they fall nowhere else.

—Zen Proverb

CHAPTER 11
Overview—A Familiar Setting

Things are entirely what they appear to be and behind them…there is nothing.

—Jean-Paul Sartre

So far, you have seen some pretty cool things (a little physics, some gesture-based interaction). We've been borrowing from our grab bag of Flash tricks to improve usability for users like Nancy and Sanjeev. Sometimes, however, the target audience for a specific project demands something familiar, something intuitive. In these situations, you really have to keep your ego in tight check and watch out that you don't cut corners. Drop-down menus, radio buttons, tool tips, and scrollbars—even the most casual computer users are familiar with these elements. Because most people use these hundreds of times a day, you must pay close attention to the details, bearing in mind how existing implementations of the elements are handled in consumer applications and operating systems. Just as importantly, observe how they don't work in those systems. A poorly implemented scrollbar or drop-down menu is worse than having nothing at all.

This next case study addresses a set of users who need a no-nonsense interface to the data they seek online. Take a look now at the client and its particular needs in this project.

CASE STUDY: WIND-AUTOMATA KNOWLEDGE BASE

Figure 11.1
The Wind-Automata developer site.

Wind-Automata, Inc. is an established software development firm in southern California that focuses on developing factory automation systems for industrial engineering firms. At the beginning of last year, Wind-Automata hired a marketing agency to help increase the brand awareness of its existing product line, Wind Central. The marketing firm spent months developing a new, more "high-tech" look for the company's identity and rebranded the entire software suite with new nomenclature and brand identity. Both Wind-Automata and the marketing firm are quite pleased with the new strategy for the software products but are concerned about the comfort level of existing customers transitioning to the new names and features.

Wind-Automata's marketing firm has approached you to create a web site. It must incorporate the new branding but maintain the focus on existing customers, keeping this audience content by ensuring a good user experience for them. The new developer's site will be accessible only to existing Wind-Automata customers, so it is doubly important that these site users be given an experience on par or better than their current one. With the help of its marketing agency, Wind-Automata found that to meet its customers' needs it would need to provide them with some value-added features, which should be available through its new web site. Combined with the existing site's offerings, the new site needs the following features:

- Tech notes

- Software updates

- Help forums

- Articles

- Online versions of the software manuals

- Access to a network of other customers via a message board

- A searchable knowledge base of information about the product

Wind-Automata hopes that this will not only add value for customers, but also ease the workload on the technical support phone center by providing users with access to the latest information via the web.

Wind-Automata has three key concerns regarding the site:

- **The new site has to be organized and accessible but without a clutter of buttons or links.** Users of the preceding site complained that too many things were crammed onto the screen at once.

- **The new site should have an efficient mechanism with which the user can get back to the top of a section hierarchy with minimal clicks.** Due to the vast amounts of information on the site, Wind-Automata is concerned that users could easily become disoriented. The new design should provide an efficient escape route that doesn't rely on site visitors using the Back button to dig their way out.

- **Users should be assisted in the transition from the old product names to the new product names.** Wind-Automata doesn't want users to click links blindly; it wants users to feel confident in navigating the new site.

With Wind-Automata's goals in mind, take a look at the persona developed for this project. Remember personas help you tailor an experience for the target audience. Personas are discussed in more detail in Chapter 1, "Bad Flashers Anonymous," and in Alan Cooper's *The Inmates Are Running the Asylum*.

> When you are looking at a Flash movie, the web browser's Back button does not respond the same way as it does on a regular web page. Users may not know, or need to know, that the site they are looking at is using the Flash plug-in, so the Back button will not work as expected. Robert Penner has an excellent solution for the Back button dilemma in Flash that can be seen at his web site (www.robertpenner.com). Although a fantastic and clever way to tackle the problem, it unfortunately does not work on Internet Explorer on the Macintosh. For this reason, it is not used in this book.
>
> **Note**

Character Profile

Name: Judy Wong

Age: 23

Occupation: Industrial Engineer

Judy is fresh out of college with a masters degree in industrial engineering and is currently working for Jameson Engineering Group. Being on the tail end of Generation X, Judy grew up with computers, both in her household and at school and is very comfortable with them. Not only is she very at home using computers, she is also on the Internet a lot and visits several sites on a daily basis. As an industrial engineer and child of the computer generation, Judy is very critical of inefficient web sites. She has little time or patience for those sites that are either unable or unwilling to get her the information she wants quickly, and without a lot of learning. She likes web sites that are simple and easy-to-use.

Figure 11.2
Judy is responsible for maintaining the automation software and development tools.

One of Judy's responsibilities at work is to maintain the automation software and develop tools and utilities for department coworkers as needed. One of the main software packages Jameson Engineering Group uses is the suite of Wind-Automata software, which handles all the automation tasks the company needs. Judy spends most of her day using at least one of the tools in this suite and if she has problems she visits the Wind-Automata web site or calls the developer support hotline.

Judy would prefer not having to use the phone for developer support, where she will have to wade through several phone menus, and finds that it is sometimes quicker to search the web until she finds an answer to her development question. She has been anticipating the Wind-Automata developer knowledge base site ever since it was announced in the Wind-Automata developer's newsletter, and she cannot wait until the web site is finally available.

Now that you know a bit about Judy and Wind-Automata's goal for the site, you can begin to create a set of goals, incorporating Judy's usability issues, that should be used as the target for developing the web site.

DEFINING YOUR OWN GOALS   Judy is going to be tough to satisfy.

Being an engineer, she has high-quality standards and does not settle for inefficient and overly complex things. You know she will pick up on mistakes or poorly designed controls; she pays attention to the details, which means you should too. Judy needs a site that helps her to work more efficiently. Flash enables you to give Judy a much more targeted experience by building features in to the Wind-Automata site that go a long way in improving the usability of the site and making her experience a better one.

Take a look at some of the features of the Wind-Automata site that will help to improve the site's usability and Judy's experience there:

- **Hierarchical menus.** Wind-Automata has lots of information, categorized into a number of sections and subsections. A good solution for quickly navigating this nesting tree of information is the hierarchical menu. These have been used many times on many sites all over the web, but rarely implement the subtle details that make this tool really work. Judy will be very comfortable with the concept and use of these familiar menus as long as they are designed correctly.

- **History (a breadcrumb trail).** Judy can quickly get lost, scavenging through so much information. Because the information on the Wind-Automata site is deep and nested, and you want to offer Judy a better alternative than the Back button to get herself out of the section she might be in, you need to provide a quick and easy way to jump around previously visited pages. A breadcrumb trail offers a great usability improvement in this case and will enable Judy to instantly return to the top level of the knowledge base from anywhere within it. The breadcrumb trail provides a mechanism of navigation that is familiar to Judy because it is the most logical.

- **Tool tips.** The new Wind-Automata web site will be significantly different from the site that Judy visited before. This means that you need to provide her with an unobtrusive and convenient help system to aid her through the transition from the old nomenclature to the new. Tool tips provide an effective tool when you have a clear navigation menu, but need to offer expanded information about the destination of each menu item. The tool tip can help to clarify what sections contain the information that Judy needs. Because this is used as a transitional tool, it must be developed in a manner that it easily accessible for Judy when she first starts to use the new Wind-Automata knowledge base, but must remain unobtrusive and invisible as she becomes more familiar with the system.

With your goals lined up and a good understanding of the client and user issues for this project, it's time to start putting these elements together in Flash.

CHAPTER 12
A Simple Hierarchy

"To Start Press Any Key." Where's the ANY key? I see Esk ["ESC"], Catarl ["CTRL"], and Pig-Up ["PGUP"]. There doesn't seem to be any ANY key. Woo! All this computer hacking is making me thirsty. I think I'll order a TAB.

—Homer Simpson

Keep it simple. This is not only an important concept in the world of web design, but also an important rule for design in general. In terms of user interface design, simplification helps focus the goals of the interface and can ultimately benefit the user by presenting them with only the most important options. But sometimes the information for a web site is inherently complex and no level of simplification can remove the layers of data a user must navigate to get to his goal.

Now you know that even the simplest design approach can yield a multilevel, information-rich site that requires the user to dig into the site through clicking and more clicking. This isn't necessarily a bad thing. A user might go to a company's "About Us" page, go to "Investor Relations", and then, under "Investor Relations", go to "Stockholder Meetings". This logical organization makes sense, and because the target user for the site might not need to find out about stockholder meetings every time they visit the site, the fact that the page is buried under several clicks of the mouse is tolerable. Now, if the user of the site needs to get to the information much more often (say, every time he visits the web site), this deep-digging to get to the information might not be as tolerable by the user and it becomes a hindrance to his goal on the site. This might not mean the structure and organization of the site is wrong, it might mean that you need to find a way for the user to reach his target quicker.

For the Wind Automata site, users like Judy will be coming back again and again to get to data that is nested a layer or more beneath the top level of the site. The first priority for you in designing the site is to organize it so that the information is structured in a logical manner. This will make it easy for Judy to find the information she wants on the site. When studying Judy's persona, you realize that she will be making use of the developer's Tech Topics on a nearly daily basis. Your next priority becomes designing a way for her to quickly move past the levels of organization in the site so she can get to the data she wants quickly.

Judy's needs require a control that will let her get to any deeply nested piece of information in as little as one click. This looks like a job for the hierarchical drop-down list. This widget works very much like the drop-down menus you might be familiar with in Windows or Macintosh operating systems. Because of the close similarity, the controls should work as much like the classic drop-down menus as possible so that Judy doesn't have to think about how to use the menus. She just needs to think about what she wants to do with them.

The hierarchical menu is one of those controls that is actually extremely simple to use, but takes a lot of planning to get it done right. Take a look at the following section to see how the hierarchical menu should work for Judy.

Seeing It in Action

The Wind Automata Tech Topics section is organized into several levels of information. You can see the way the hierarchical menu makes navigation easy for Judy by clicking the Tech Topics link in the main navigation bar in the sample movie (see Figure 12.1). To see the sample movie, open the **12_hierMenu.fla** file found in the **Projects** folder on the *Skip Intro* CD-ROM. Test the movie and try out the different menu items. Pay close attention to the cascading menu items such as News and Tech Topics.

The first thing you should notice is that the menus appear instantly when a menu item is clicked and fade away when you click outside the boundaries of the menu. The fading away offers a nice effect to the menus, but doesn't hinder Judy's experience because the menus are immediately available when she selects one. This is a good example of the kind of compromises that should be made when designing with your target user in mind. You don't have to completely eliminate entertaining visuals in place of usability, you just need to find the right balance.

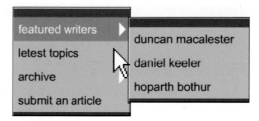

Figure 12.1
Notice that when the menu cascades, it offers a bigger "hit" area in which you can move your mouse to choose from a submenu.

Also notice that when a menu item cascades, the "hit" area for the menu changes so it will be more comfortable for Judy when she moves her mouse to choose an item in the submenu. Many cascading menu systems overlook this safety feature and create frustration for users because users might overshoot the menu item when moving their mouse over the submenu. Try this feature out: Click on the Tech Topics menu item and move your mouse down the archive option. Now, keeping your mouse near the right-most side of the menu (next to the cascading choices), slowly move your mouse below or above the archive option in the menu while moving to the right, towards the Nov 2001 option. You should notice that you have a lot of flexibility to miss the archive menu item all together yet it remains selected. These types of hidden features are what give users a better experience, even if they can't place their finger on exactly what it is that makes it better.

Another thing you should notice is that the menus respond the same way you would expect them to respond—the same way the menus in your desktop operating system and applications you use everyday respond. This ensures that Judy can quickly use the menu and get to her destination on the site rather than spending even a fraction of her valuable time trying to learn how to wrangle the cascading menus to get to where she wants to go.

These are a couple of the features in the hierarchical menu component that you will notice right off the bat. There are several more subtle features that you will use in your implementation that will help Judy's experience be the best it can be.

IMPLEMENTATION

The hierarchical menu component builds off many of the coding practices covered in Chapter 6, "Less Cluttered and More Usable," for the mouse under menu. The code is slightly more complex, but in the end it all works together to make the final component flexible, reusable, and most of all, usable.

The hierarchical menu component, while contained neatly in a small, easily drag-and-droppable package, relies on several other pieces for it to function properly. In the end, what you will see is a menu button, which, when clicked, will reveal the menu itself, which is made up of individual menu items. A menu item can also have a submenu associated with it, which is also made up of other menu items.

Now take a look at the other features of this component:

- **Click to show and hide**. The menu component should act as much like your operating system's menus as possible to make it easier for Judy to use it quickly. One thing this means is that the user should be able to show the menu with one click and hide it with one click. Clicking anywhere outside the menu should also hide the menu.

- **Submenus.** For the hierarchical menu to really be useful to Judy, it needs to show her the different levels she might want to go to on the site. The menu component should display nesting submenus.

- **Safety features.** One of the problems with some menu implementations is that they are very sensitive. When a user rolls over a submenu, for example, there is a very small margin of error for the user to keep the mouse rolled over the proper submenu item. If the user's mouse ventures too far from the menu item, bam! The submenu items disappear. This jarring effect can be minimized with some thoughtful design up front. This component will make the rollover area bigger for submenu items when the mouse is rolled over it. This will give the user a little extra room to move her mouse over to the submenu items without having the items disappear. We call this the "invisible triangle".

- **Dynamic.** These submenus should be dynamically defined so that a site like Wind-Automata can have menus that update along with the site. The component will read its menu values from a set of arrays that should be defined when the movie starts and can be dynamically updated if needed.

- **Customizable**. The hierarchical menu component should allow you to customize the appearance of the menu items and submenu items so you can tailor the menu to your particular project.

When you drop the hierarchical menu component into a new project, all you should have to do to get it up and running is define the arrays that will hold the menu item names and structure, and change the look of the menu items.

This component has clear benefits for Judy. It not only gives her one-click access to the sections she visits frequently on the Wind-Automata site, but it also gives you, the developer, a great reusable tool that you can use in other projects if usability is needed. This next section shows you how to construct this clip.

CONSTRUCTION

As stated earlier, the hierarchical menu component is built much like the mouse under menu component in that it uses some simple "skin" movie clips that contain no ActionScript, so they can easily be edited to fit the feel of any project you are working on. You will also need a main menu movie clip button and an array of menu items for each of these. Let's walk through the specific structure of the clip.

Here is how you will use the hierarchical menu component in your movie: First, you will drag the component into your movie. In the main movie for a project, preferably in the first few frames, you might define an array, like this:

```
var homeMenu = ["test item", ["item 1", ["item 2", "item 3"]], "another item"];
```

The name of this variable will be passed on to the component by way of the main menu movie clip button. Then, when the user clicks on the main menu button, the menu component reads through the array and dynamically generates the menu. You will notice that the example array here is actually several nested arrays. This is how you will create cascading or hierarchical menus. Based on the example array above, the first menu you will see when you click on the main menu movie clip is:

- test item
- item 1
- another item

If the user was to roll over the "item 1" menu item, a submenu containing "item 2" and "item 3" would appear. It might sound complicated but it's quite flexible. Another way of defining the example array is to split up the different nested arrays into other variables, like this:

```
var homeSubMenu = ["item 1", ["item 2", "item 3"]];
var homeMenu = ["test item", homeSubMenu, "another item"];
```

This works exactly the same way as before, with the exception that it might be a bit more readable in your ActionScript, especially if you have many items or submenus.

The main component is made up of several chunks of code. The first handles building the menu on screen from the menu array variables, the second handles mouse events for the menu items, and the third handles the fading out effect when the menus disappear.

Each menu item in the hierarchical menu is an attached movie clip. This menu item clip is very similar to the menu item clip from Chapter 6—the mouse under menu component. Each item is a movie clip with a normal state and an "over" state for when the user rolls over the item. Submenu items use a movie clip that is nearly identical to the regular menu item clip, with the exception of the arrow graphic, which shows the user that the menu has subitems, and the invisible triangle, which helps the user gain more control over the submenus.

If the movie clips used for the items contain any code, it is simply "assigned" in ActionScript when the menu is dynamically generated. This keeps the code in one place and the artwork in another without having to maintain any fragile ties between them.

Okay, now that you have a rough idea of how the component is put together, it's time to start building it.

Setting Up the Movie

Make a new Flash movie and set its frame rate to 20 fps. Name the first layer in the movie **actions**. Select the first frame on that layer, and open the Actions panel for that frame (F2). Enter the following code:

```
var homeMenu = ["test item", ["item 1", ["item2", "item 3"]], "item 4"];

stop();
```

This will define the menu that the component will build dynamically. The menu will initially appear with the items "test item", "item 1", and "item 4". "item 1" will contain a submenu with two more items— "item 2" and "item 3".

Skinning the Menu

Next, create a layer underneath the actions layer and name it **menu**. Create a rectangle on that layer about 130 pixels wide by 60 pixels tall. Give the rectangle a light gray fill with a black hairline stroke. Select the middle portion of the rectangle, about 15 pixels from the top of the rectangle and about 30 pixels tall, and make it into a movie clip called **h_menu_middle**, and be sure to place its registration point to the upper left. Select the remaining top portion of the rectangle and make it into a movie clip called **h_menu_top**, retaining the registration point setting you used earlier. Select the bottom portion of the rectangle that is left and make it into a movie clip called **h_menu_bottom**, and ensure that its registration point is set to the upper left, as well.

Now edit the **h_menu_middle** movie clip. Add a new layer to the clip and name it **text**. Now add a text field to the layer, placing it within the bounds of the gray rectangle and over the left.

Make sure the field is set to be Dynamic and give it a variable name of **itemName**. Also make sure the field is not selectable and embed all characters of the font in the field for the time being. Lastly, type **item name** into the field so you have something to see while you position the field.

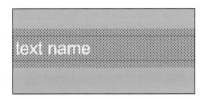

Figure 12.2
Select the middle portion of the rectangle, about 30 pixels tall.

Now add about nine frames to this clip's timeline and add a keyframe at frame 5 on the layer with the rectangle on it. Label that frame **over**. Select the gray rectangle sprite in frames 5 through 10 and give it a fill color of blue.

This clip will be used for every item in your menu except for items with a submenu. Lets make that clip next.

Figure 12.3
Add a text field to the movie clip and position it like so.

Open your Library panel (Ctrl-L/Cmd-L), right-click (Ctrl-click) on the h_menu_middle symbol, and select Duplicate. Name your new movie clip **h_menu_middle_sub** and edit it.

Add a new layer to the movie clip and name it **arrow**. Now draw a small white arrow pointing to the right, and position it to the far right of the menu item.

Figure 12.4
*The **h_menu_middle_sub** movie clip with the white arrow indicating that there are submenu items to the right.*

Now it's time to add the invisible triangle. During development you can leave this triangle slightly opaque, making it much easier to adjust. Start by adding a new layer to your movie clip and calling it **invisible triangle**. Make frame 5 of this layer a keyframe and, on that frame, draw a small red square on that layer, select the red square, and while holding down the Shift key, rotate the square 45 degrees to the right so that it resembles a diamond. Now select the right half of the diamond shape and delete it. Select the shape's fill and make the color 30% alpha with the color mixer. Group the entire triangle and move it so its right side lines up with the menu items. Lastly, stretch the triangle toward the left. You can now begin to imagine how that triangle benefits your submenu items.

Now open the Library panel for your movie and right-click (Ctrl-click) on the **h_menu_bottom** movie clip and select Linkage.... In the Linkage Properties dialog box, select Export for ActionScript and click the OK button. You'll notice that Flash automatically fills in the Identifier name for you. Repeat this process for the three remaining skin elements.

Figure 12.5
The invisible triangle! It's been left opaque so you can see how it interacts later in development.

That rounds out the defining of the skin elements of the menu. Now it's time to create the main menu movie clip button that will display the hierarchical menu when clicked.

Return to the main movie timeline and create a small gray rectangle about 20 pixels tall and 60 pixels wide. Place a static text field on top of the gray rectangle and, for nostalgia's sake, enter **File** in the field. Select them both and create a movie clip called **menuButtonHolder** and set its registration point to the upper-left corner.

Figure 12.6
In homage to our desktop ancestors, we create the File menu button.

Select the movie clip on stage and open the Actions panel. Enter the following code:

```
onClipEvent(load)

{

    var menuName = "home";
    var menuArray = _parent.homeMenu;
}


onClipEvent(mouseDown)
{

    _parent.mc_hierMenu.clickMenu(menuName, menuArray, this);
}


onClipEvent(mouseMove)
{

    _parent.mc_hierMenu.moveMenu(menuName, menuArray, this);
}
```

This is the code that displays the menu when the item is clicked. If another menu item is already displaying its menu, rolling over this clip will automatically display its menu, as well.

The first portion of this code initializes two variables, ***menuName*** and ***menuArray***. The ***menuName*** variable holds the name of the menu that you will be looking for in the dispatch code you will write later in this chapter. Each menu name should be unique.

The ***menuArray*** variable can either be the array of items you wish to have in the menu or it can point to a variable containing those items. In this case, this variable just points to the **homeMenu** array you defined earlier.

The two different clip events for mouse down and mouse move call two different functions in the component. These functions expect to receive the name of the menu, the array of elements for the menu, and a reference to the actual main menu button itself so the menu can be properly positioned in relation to it.

Now that you have taken care of all the details that support the hierarchical menu component, it's time to dive into the component itself.

Building the Component

Start by adding one final rectangle to the stage. Select it, make it into a movie clip called **HierarchicalMenu**, and give it an instance name of **mc_hierMenu**. Double-click to edit this clip.

Add a new layer to the clip and call the layer **actions**. Make the layer three frames and make each frame a keyframe. Select the first frame on the **actions** layer, open the Actions panel, and add the following code:

```
this._x = 0;
this._y = 0;

this.mainMenuClip = this;
gFadeClipArray = [];
```

This basic code sets the x and y coordinates of the component to the upper-left corner of the stage. This is crucial as the component relies on this so it can position the menus and submenus accurately on the stage.

Next, assign the ***mainMenuClip*** variable—***this***. Yes, it looks strange, but basically you are setting up a reference to the component. This will be used later by nested menu item and submenu item movie clips, so it will be much clearer then.

The ***gFadeClipArray*** variable gets initialized to an empty array. This variable will hold any group of menu items or group of submenu items that will need to fade off screen.

Start defining the main function that will handle the drawing of the menu. Add the following code:

```
function drawMenu(menuName, menuArray, menuX, menuY)
{
    removeFromFadeList(this["mc_menu_box"]);

}
```

Drawing the Menu The `drawMenu()` function takes four parameters: the name of the menu, the array of menu items, and the x and y location where the menu should appear. The first line in this function calls another function, which will be covered in more detail later. Essentially, the call removes the current menu group from the **gFaderArray** so they don't fade out unexpectedly when you are trying to use them. To start filling out this function, add the following code within the `drawMenu()` function:

```
this.createEmptyMovieClip("mc_menu_box", 1);
this["mc_menu_box"]._alpha = 100;
this["mc_menu_box"]._x = menuX;
this["mc_menu_box"]._y = menuY;
```

The first thing the `drawMenu()` function does is create a new, empty movie clip named **mc_menu_box**. This empty box will hold all of the menu items for a given menu. Putting it in one movie clip like this makes it easy to control a menu and manage removing the menu items from the screen when necessary. Once the empty box is created, its alpha is set to 100% and its coordinates are set to those passed into the `drawMenu()` function.

Next, add the following code to the `drawMenu()` function:

```
this["mc_menu_box"].attachMovie("h_menu_top", "mc_menu_top", 1);

var tempLevel = 2;
var tempOffset = this["mc_menu_box"].mc_menu_top._height;
```

Here you are attaching the **h_menu_top** skin movie clip to your empty movie clip. Next you prepare some variables that will be used in the loop that churns out the actual menu items. Enter the following code:

```
for (var i = 0; i < menuArray.length; i++) {
    var menuItemName = "mc_menu_item_" + i;

    tempLevel++;
}
```

This code is the beginning of the loop that will cycle through the array of menu items and generate the right movie clip for both regular menu items and cascading submenu items.

Next, add the following code under the line where you initialize the **menuItemName** variable, inside the loop:

```
    if (typeof(menuArray[i]) == "object") {
        this["mc_menu_box"].attachMovie("h_menu_middle_sub", menuItemName,
➡tempLevel);

    } else {
        this["mc_menu_box"].attachMovie("h_menu_middle", menuItemName,
➡tempLevel);

    }
```

Here you check the type of array element using the built-in `typeof()` function. If the element is another array, signifying a submenu, `typeof()` will return the string "object", which is checked against here. In the case of a submenu, the **h_menu_middle_sub** movie clip is attached to the container movie clip. If it is just a standard menu item, the **h_menu_middle** movie clip gets attached.

Now, just above the `else` in the top portion of the `if` statement, add the following code:

```
        this["mc_menu_box"][menuItemName].itemName = menuArray[i][0];
        this["mc_menu_box"][menuItemName].menuArray = menuArray[i][1];
        this["mc_menu_box"][menuItemName].menuX =
➡this["mc_menu_box"][menuItemName]._width - 8;
        this["mc_menu_box"][menuItemName].menuY = 0;
        this["mc_menu_box"][menuItemName].drawMenu = drawMenu;
```

This is more code that gets called if the menu item is a submenu. The array is broken out and assigned to the menuArray property of the menu item's movie clip. Also notice that the `drawMenu()` function (that is being defined right now) gets added to the clip, as well. This is so the clip can parse its own array of menu items (the submenu) when requested by the user.

Now, add the following code just under the line where the **h_menu_middle** movie clip gets attached, in the bottom part of the `if` statement:

```
    this["mc_menu_box"][menuItemName].itemName = menuArray[i];
    this["mc_menu_box"][menuItemName].onMouseUp = menuItemMouseUpFunc;
```

In this segment of code the `menuItemMouseUpFunc()` function (which will be defined a little later) gets assigned to the `onMouseUp` event for the standard menu item movie clip.

Next, add the following code to Actions panel, just above the line that increments the `tempLevel` variable (`tempLevel++`):

```
    this["mc_menu_box"][menuItemName].mainMenuClip = this.mainMenuClip;
    this["mc_menu_box"][menuItemName].fullItemName = menuName + ":" +
➡this["mc_menu_box"][menuItemName].itemName;
    this["mc_menu_box"][menuItemName].onMouseMove = menuItemMouseMoveFunc;
    this["mc_menu_box"][menuItemName]._y = tempOffset;
    this["mc_menu_box"][menuItemName].gotoAndStop(1);

    tempOffset += this["mc_menu_box"][menuItemName]._height;
```

Here the `onMouseMove` function is attached with the `menuItemMouseMoveFunc()` function and will get called whenever a `mouseMove` event happens to that menu item. Both types of menu items are finished by adding a reference to the parent component clip, the name of the item (concatenated with a "path" of names so it is easy for developers to read), and their y positions and frames are properly set.

Now that wasn't so hard, was it? Complete the `drawMenu()` function by adding the following code to the end:

```
    this["mc_menu_box"].attachMovie("h_menu_bottom", "mc_menu_bottom",
➡tempLevel);
    this["mc_menu_box"].mc_menu_bottom._y = tempOffset;
    this.menuShowing = true;
    }
```

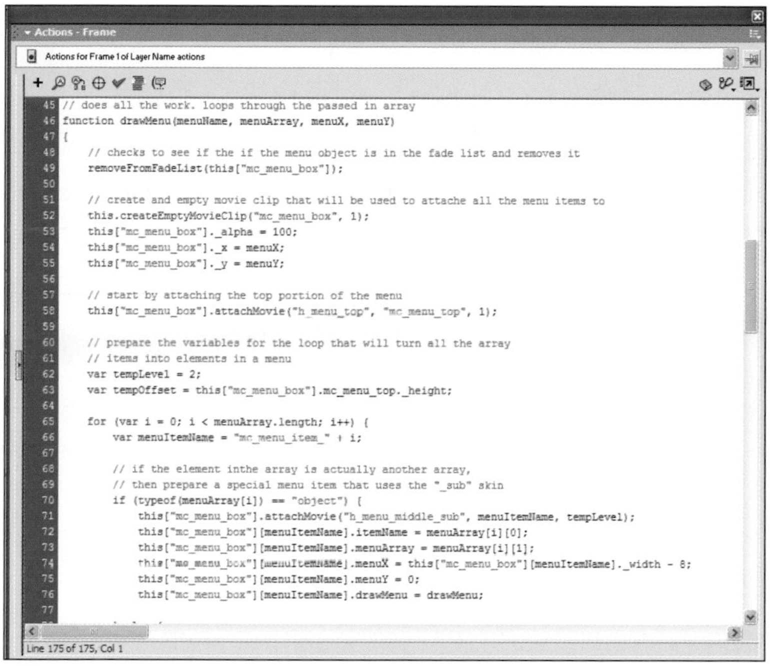

Figure 12.7
For code-heavy components like this one, be sure and comment your code adequately.

This code adds the bottom portion of the menu. Now it's time to start adding the other smaller functions of the component. Add the following code:

```
function eraseMenu()
{
    if (!this.hitTest( _root._xmouse, _root._ymouse, true) &&
➡this.menuShowing) {
        gFadeClipArray.push(this["mc_menu_box"]);
        this.menuShowing = false;
    }
}
```

The `eraseMenu()` function does just what it sounds like it does, it erases a menu from the screen. This function is specifically used by the top-most movie clip to get rid of a menu and all its potential submenus in one swipe. Part of the process is to add each group of menu items (held together in an `mc_menu_box` instance) to the **gFadeArray**, which you'll deal with later.

Mouse Handling Now, add the following code to deal with the mouse movements for the menu and submenu items:

```
function menuItemMouseMoveFunc()
{
    if (this.hitTest( _root._xmouse, _root._ymouse, true)
        && this._parent.activeMenu != this
        && !this._parent.activeMenu.hitTest( _root._xmouse,_root._ymouse,
➡true)) {

        if (null != this._parent.activeMenu["mc_menu_box"]) {
            gFadeClipArray.push(this._parent.activeMenu["mc_menu_box"]);
            this._parent.activeMenu.menuShowing = false;
        }
        this._parent.activeMenu.rolledOver = false;
        this._parent.activeMenu.gotoAndStop(1);

        if (null != this.menuArray) {
            removeFromFadeList(this["mc_menu_box"]);
            this.swapDepths(99999);
            this.drawMenu(this.fullItemName, this.menuArray, this.menuX,
➡this.menuY);
        }
        this._parent.activeMenu = this;
        this.gotoAndStop("over");
        this.rolledOver = true;
    }
}
```

```
// attach  the functions that check for rollover and such
this["mc_menu_box"][menuItemName].onMouseMove = menuItemMouseMoveFunc;
```

Figure 12.8
The menuItemMouseMoveFunc() *gets attached to clips in the* drawMenu() *loop.*

The menuItemMouseMoveFunc() function gets attached in the drawMenu() loop to each menu item and submenu item movie clip. This function takes care of all the mouse rollover events that occur and updates the clips accordingly. It begins by checking to see if the user is rolled over a particular item, the item is not currently the active item, and the user is not also rolled over the active item. If all these conditions are met, a new activeMenu is selected and the menus are drawn if available.

When the submenus are drawn, the menu group is set to a big depth to ensure that the menus are always above all the items on its layer and ultimately the rest of the movie. You'll also notice that the menu group is removed from the fader list so it doesn't continue to fade out, even when its just been activated. Lastly, this function sends the **h_menu_middle** skin clips to each of their rollover states in their own timelines. This further enforces the desire to keep all the code (or as much as possible) inside the component itself and keep the skin clips relatively code free.

Now, enter the following code into the Actions panel:

```
function menuItemMouseUpFunc()
{
    if (this.hitTest( _root._xmouse, _root._ymouse, true)) {
            _root.hierMenuDispatch(this.fullItemName);
            gFadeClipArray.push(this.mainMenuClip["mc_menu_box"]);
    }
}
```

This is another function that gets attached to menu items in the `drawMenu()` loop. In this case, if a user clicks within the boundaries of a menu item, a message is sent to the dispatch function (which you will define later) located at the _root level timeline. The menu item group is then added to the list of clips to fade out in the *gFadeClipArray*.

Now, you've entered a lot of code, and because this component relies heavily on all the pieces being there, it would be a good idea to save your movie before continuing on to the next batch of code.

Add the following code to the Actions for this frame:

```
function removeFromFadeList(menuObj)
{
    for (var i = 0; i < gFadeClipArray.length; i++) {
        if (gFadeClipArray[i] == menuObj) {
            var tempIndex = i;
            break;
        }
    }

    if (null != tempIndex) {
        gFadeClipArray[tempIndex].removeMovieClip();
        gFadeClipArray.splice(tempIndex, 1);
    }
}
```

Remember this function? It is called from a couple of places in the code. What it does is simple: given a movie clip, it searches through all the clips currently slated for fading, and if it finds this particular clip, it removes it from the list. This helps you control the fading and ensures that only menu items that need to fade, fade!

Test Run!   Now, only one function needs to be added before testing can finally start. This function is the public function called by the movie clips on the main timeline that you defined earlier in the chapter.

Add the function at the top of your Actions for frame 1, just below where you first initialize *gFadeClipArray*:

```
function clickMenu(menuName, menuArray, clipObj)
{
    if (clipObj.hitTest( _root._xmouse, _root._ymouse, true)) {
        if (this.clickedObj == clipObj) {
            this.clickedObj = null;
            eraseMenu();
        } else {
            this.clickedObj = clipObj;
            drawMenu(menuName, menuArray, clipObj._x, clipObj._y +
➥clipObj._height);
        }
    } else {
        if (this.clickedObj == clipObj) {
            this.clickedObj = null;
            eraseMenu();
        }
    }
}
```

This function gets called whenever the mouse is clicked. It checks to see if the user's mouse cursor was in the bounds of the calling movie clip, and if it was, it checks to see if the menu for that movie clip object was already visible. If the menu is visible, it is told to disappear; otherwise, drawMenu() is called and passed the caller movie clip's coordinates with which to position the menu items. If no clip was clicked, the clip currently showing a menu is told to erase that menu.

One last thing before any testing begins: Go to frame 3 in the **HierarchicalMenu** movie clip and add the following code in the Actions panel:

```
gotoAndPlay(2);
```

As usual, this ensures that the movie clip loops over the last two frames and doesn't attempt to reinitialize any variables and such.

Figure 12.9
Remember to add the looping code to your 3-frame segment.

Now that you have the code that detects the mouse clicks ready, save your movie and test it! Keep in mind, however, the menu will appear when you click on the File menu button you placed on the stage, but will not yet disappear. Don't worry, though, it is working properly.

Take some time to notice how the invisible triangle works, too. It's a really useful feature that, if attempted, is heavily code-driven. Here you've been able to extend the use of the Flash timeline to get the same effect.

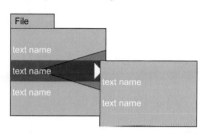

Figure 12.10
Play around a bit with the invisible triangle to get the feel of the menus.

Great work so far! It's definitely a lot harder to code when you can't test as often, but it's nice to see the results nonetheless. Now, return to your movie and add the following function to frame 1 of the **HierarchicalMenu** clip, just below the last function you entered:

The invisible triangle safety feature is a hidden feature that was made visible just for testing. Few operating systems, let alone web-based cascading menus, make use of this type of feature, even though its been proven to improve the usability of cascading menus. This is one of the areas where developers can get lazy and not take that extra step to solve the problems a user might face.

Note

```
function moveMenu(menuName, menuArray, clipObj)
{
    if (clipObj.hitTest( _root._xmouse, _root._ymouse, true)) {
        if (this.clickedObj != clipObj && this.menuShowing) {
            this.clickedObj = clipObj;
            drawMenu(menuName, menuArray, clipObj._x, clipObj._y +
➥clipObj._height);
        }
    }
}
```

This code is also called by the button movie clip on the stage. In this case, if a menu is showing for one menu button clip, then simply rolling over the other menu button clips will activate their respective menus. This keeps the menu component functioning as much as possible, like the menus you are familiar with in everyday desktop applications.

Fading Away Now its time to wrap this puppy up! The last bit of code you need write is the code that fades the menus when they are dismissed by the user. Select frame 2 of the **actions** layer in the timeline of the **HierarchicalMenu** movie clip and open the Actions panel. Add the following code:

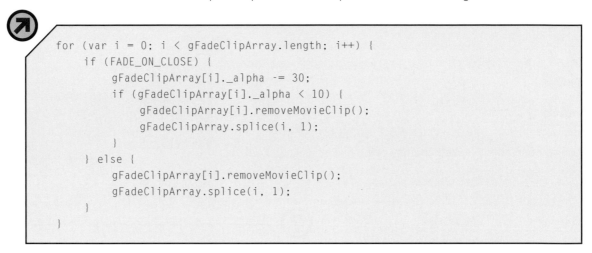

```
for (var i = 0; i < gFadeClipArray.length; i++) {
    if (FADE_ON_CLOSE) {
        gFadeClipArray[i]._alpha -= 30;
        if (gFadeClipArray[i]._alpha < 10) {
            gFadeClipArray[i].removeMovieClip();
            gFadeClipArray.splice(i, 1);
        }
    } else {
        gFadeClipArray[i].removeMovieClip();
        gFadeClipArray.splice(i, 1);
    }
}
```

As the component is already looping on frame 2, a `for` loop is added there to fade all the menu items that have been placed in the **_gFadeClipArray_**, and when a clip's lowest opacity is reached, they are removed.

That's almost all the code! Now it's time to add the one component parameter that you can change—whether or not the clip will fade when it disappears. Open your library, right-click (Ctrl-click) on the **HierarchicalMenu** movie clip and select the Component Parameters. Add Boolean type variable to the list and give it a name of **FADE_ON_CLOSE**. Now you have a truly portable, usable component!

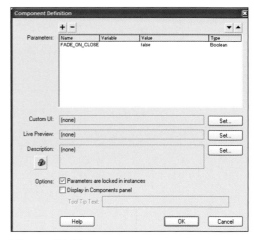

Figure 12.11
Adding the only parameter to the define components dialog.

Dispatching Menu Clicks   Now whenever an item in the menu is clicked, a message is sent to a function that should be made available at the root of the movie. Return to the main timeline of your movie and select the first frame. Open the Actions panel and add the following code just above the `stop()` statement:

```
function hierMenuDispatch(clickedItem)
{
    switch (clickedItem) {
        case "test item":
            trace("the first item was clicked in the menu");
            break;
        case "item 1":
            trace("item 1 was clicked");
            break;
        default:
            trace(clickedItem);
    }
}
```

This is the dispatch function that is called when any of the menu items in a hierarchical menu are clicked. You can replace the `trace()` statements with functions of your own to take full advantage of the capabilities of the component.

Packaging   Because you want to have maximum portability of your component, you should take a few extra measures to ensure that pieces don't get lost when you're dragging and dropping the component into different projects. Right now, if you were to drag the hierarchical menu component into another movie, you would still have to drag each of the skin elements for the movie in, as well. One easy trick is to combine them so that if you drag the component into another movie, it automatically brings along the skin components. Edit your hierarchical menu component and add a new layer called **skins** and place it at the bottom of all the other layers. Now drag the four skin components (**h_menu_top**, **h_menu_ middle**, **h_menu_middle_sub**, **h_menu_bottom**) onto the **skins** layer and shrink them so they are well hidden behind the original square shape. Now, right-click (Ctrl-click) on the **skins** layer in the layer list and select Guide. Now the skins elements are completely hidden from view, yet they are always connected with the component.

CONCLUSION

As this smart clip exercise demonstrates, if you want to make sure a user's experience is consistent and familiar, you need to spend the time required to cover every detail. A clip like this does not get built if you are lazy about the finishing touches.

Key Points/Don't Forget

- **The clip's invisible triangle really makes this an easy to use, cascading menu system.** Because the arrow is implemented as a standard Flash shape as opposed to a series of code-calculated points, it is easy to fine-tune the shape and size to fit your target audience.

- **Building the menus from a series of arrays means that you can easily change the menu items without ever touching the clip again.** In fact, because the menu items are looped through every time a menu is shown, you could build a user interface where the menus are updated in real time if the site structure is changed frequently—for example, in a discussion board.

- **Although you or another designer will have to go into the clip to do the visual design, it only needs to be done once.** All the menus and menu items will follow suit in standard Flash style and the skin elements have no code in which to get stuck in.

- **Paying close attention to detail will help this menu work like the user expects.** Especially when this type of control is so common on the desktop, you need to make sure your version stays up to par or improves the user's experience.

CHAPTER 13

Tool Tips—Know Before You Go

None of these usability problems are inherent in Flash. You can design usable multimedia objects that comply with the guidelines and are easy to use. The problem is simply that current Flash design tends to encourage abuse.

—Jakob Nielsen ("Flash is 99% Bad")

OVERVIEW

Tool tips, like any good user interface element, are almost invisible in their implementation, and yet almost every application has some sort of tool tip help. Everyone knows that if he gets stuck trying to figure out exactly what that "paint brush" icon does, he can hold the cursor over the button for a moment and one of those ubiquitous little yellow notes will pop up to explain. Tool tips are the digital equivalent of Post-It notes, placed there thoughtfully by the developer.

Tool tips are an excellent tool, particularly for people just starting out with an application or site. But even experienced users of complex or feature-rich applications will probably appreciate the help that tool tips can provide.

We are used to these little helpers when using an application or computer operating system, but what about on a web site? On an HTML document, thoughtful designers may include helpful `<alt>` tags to aid navigation. Flash movies, however, all too often present users with an interface that has none of these helpful features.

With some simple additional coding, the Flash designer can help. In this chapter, you learn how to build a tool tip engine for Flash that experienced and inexperienced users alike will intuitively understand

SOLUTIONS

The Wind-Automata site needs a solution that eases existing users into the new naming and branding conventions. Because this is a transition event and one that will have different start and end times for different users, the solution needs to enable users to access it when they need it and to ignore it when they don't.

Tool tips provide access to help that depends on users and their level of experience. Should Judy find herself six months down the road faced with a new set of products, there is no need for her to turn on a special help feature, or click aimlessly around. Instead, the tool tip, without asking, will appear when she needs it.

Seeing It in Action

Insert the CD-ROM that accompanies this book and locate the **13_toolTips_build.fla** file in the **Projects** folder. Open the movie and test it (Control>Test Movie). To see tool tips working, roll over any of the software boxes and hold your cursor still for just a moment.

The first and most obvious thing you should notice is that tool tips don't show up immediately. Instead a slight delay occurs, enabling experienced users to zip through an interface without having to see the tool tips, whereas novice users pausing for a fraction of a second will see the tip.

You also should notice that once a tool tip appears, if you roll straight over another tool tip-enabled item there should be no delay. This detail is important because it keeps the user from having to wait repeatedly through the delay to find the purpose of every button in a toolbar, for example.

In the Wind-Automata site, the tool tips have been set to lock to the mouse cursor while they are visible. This feature enables the user to move the tip should it obscure the button it's describing.

Now having experienced the different features of the tool tip smart clip, take a look at features of the clip broken down into a set of specific tasks that the tool tip module must perform.

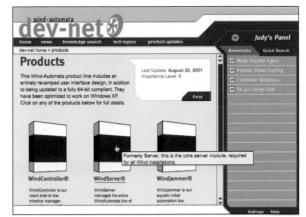

Figure 13.1
A view of the tool tip in action.

IMPLEMENTATION   Based on the observations of tool tip behavior, the following

six features must be implemented to create a truly functional and usable tool tip:

- **Time-delayed initialization.** Tips won't show up until after Judy has kept the cursor over a tool tip-enabled button for a specified amount of time.

- **Instant off.** Tips should disappear instantly when Judy rolls the cursor off the button or clicks the button.

- **State maintenance.** Tips will show up instantly if the cursor rolls over another button within a specific amount of time. This helps in instances where Judy might be presented with several similar elements and needs to find the correct one. Instead of having to wait for the delay time for each button, Judy can see the tips immediately if she rolls within a certain period of time over other tool tip elements.

- **Placement.** Tips should never cover up the button they are describing, nor should they ever appear off the edge of the screen.

- **Message dependent.** Tip size should be variable and be able to contain multiple lines of text.

- **Mouse follow.** The tool tip should have the option to follow the cursor. This enables Judy to move the tip should it be obstructing some other element.

Okay, that's enough theory. It's time to apply these features in Flash.

> One feature that's not included here, but that would be really great, would be a "smart" tool tip. A "smart" tool tip differs from current tool tips in that it begins to adapt to the individual user in its delay time. If the user is spending lots of time waiting for tool tips, the delay time could dynamically decrease. There isn't the space to go in to this here, but there might be a few surprises at the book's web site, www.skip-intro.org. Check it out!
>
> **Author Note: Michelangelo**

CONSTRUCTION

The following tutorial shows you how to create the code to insert tool tips into a Flash movie. You will initially create the graphic and text boxes in which all the tool tips will appear and then you will input the code that provides the necessary functionality. After you have created the tool tips code, you will be able to add relevant tool tips to any element of your movie.

Setting Up the Movie

You might find it easier to build the tool tip clip in a new movie instead of trying to build it in an existing movie. Either way your first step is to create a new layer in your movie labeled **tool tips**. If it isn't already at the top of the layer stack, go ahead and drag it to the top now (but keep it below any layers that you have set aside for code or frame labels). The **tool tips** layer must be on top of all your other layers or the tips won't appear on top of your elements.

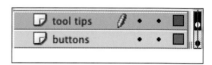

Figure 13.2
Make sure your tool tip movie clip is in the top layer of your movie.

Drawing the Tool Tip Graphic

Because you're going to be using ActionScript to effect the tool tip graphic, you have to take a few extra steps when creating the graphic itself. First, select the Fill panel and choose a fairly light color—it doesn't have to be yellow. Next select the Stroke panel and choose Hairline from the drop-down list of line types. Selecting the hairline style enables

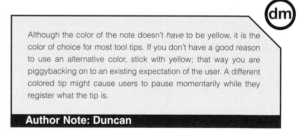

Although the color of the note doesn't *have* to be yellow, it is the color of choice for most tool tips. If you don't have a good reason to use an alternative color, stick with yellow; that way you are piggybacking on to an existing expectation of the user. A different colored tip might cause users to pause momentarily while they register what the tip is.

Author Note: Duncan

you to dynamically change the size of the tool tip without altering the stroke weight of the line. After you've selected your stroke and fill, click once in the **tool tips** layer and draw a rectangle approximately 320 pixels wide by 240 pixels high.

Converting to a Movie Clip

Select the rectangle you have just drawn on the stage and convert it to a movie clip. Give it a symbol name of **toolTip_graphic**. In the Instance Properties panel, enter the instance name *mc_toolTipGraphic*.

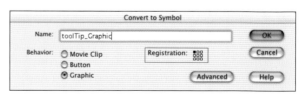

Figure 13.3
With Flash MX you can easily set the registration point when creating the movie clip.

Because you'll be controlling the movie clip with ActionScript, you want to change the registration of the movie clip from the center to the upper left. A movie clip's registration is indicated by the plus symbol (+). It's best to set the registration point of a movie clip when creating the clip itself. If you can't do that, open the movie clip in Edit mode and drag the clip so that the plus symbol is in the upper-right hand corner. You can also select the object while in Edit mode and enter 0.0 for both the x and y coordinates in the Info panel.

Create the Text Field

So, you have the graphic, but now you need the ability to dynamically display different messages. From the toolbar, select the Text tool and, using the Text Options panel, set the text to Dynamic, change Single Line to Multiline, and make sure that Wrap is the only option selected. With these settings, draw a text box approximately the same height as the graphic element and approximately 20 pixels narrower than the graphic itself. For the font, select Courier 12 point. Now, in the Text Options panel, enter the variable name **toolTipText**.

Figure 13.4
The text field should be a few pixels smaller than the tool tip graphic itself.

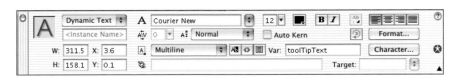

Figure 13.5
Don't forget to set your text box options.

Convert It to Another Movie Clip

Select both the text box and the **toolTip_graphic** and convert both to a single movie clip called **toolTip**. In the Instance Properties panel, enter an instance name of *mc_toolTip*. Notice that the registration point of the newly created movie clip is back at the center. Remember, every time you create a new movie clip, its default registration is center. Use Modify>Transform>Edit Center to place the center point in the upper-left corner. When you're done, exit Edit mode to the main movie (Cmd-E/Ctrl-E) by clicking the **Scene 1** link in the upper-left corner of the Flash window.

That's it for drawing. Before moving on, make sure you've got all the elements you need. On the stage you should have a movie clip with an instance name of *mc_toolTip*. This movie clip contains two items: a dynamic text box with a variable name of **toolTipText** and a movie clip with an instance name of *mc_toolTipGraphic*. If you have all three, it's time to code!

CODE
As usual, there's a fair amount of code to go through here.

Buttons

If you're building this file from scratch, you need to create a button. (Go ahead and do that now.) If you're using an existing Flash movie, select any button you want. Click the button once, open the ActionScript editor (make sure it's in Expert mode), and add the following code:

```
on(rollOver) {
  _level0.mc_toolTip.showTip("Enter text here");
}
on(rollOut) {
  _level0.mc_toolTip.hideTip();
}
on(press) {
  _level0.mc_toolTip.hideTip();
}
```

This part is quite simple. You're calling two functions: On rollover you call the `showTip()` function; and on rollout or press, the `hideTip()` function is called. You haven't created either function yet, so nothing will happen if you test the movie now.

Because the functions, when you write them, will be attached to the movie clip with the instance name of *mc_toolTipGraphic*, which is inside the movie clip with an instance name of *mc_toolTip*, and because you want to be able to access the code from anywhere in the Flash movie (from other levels or from loaded movies, for example), you need to set an absolute reference to the code: `level0.mc_toolTip.showTip()`. You also need to tell Flash that you want this tool tip text to display between the `()` of the `showTip()` function. When you write the tool tip code for the buttons, make sure your message is enclosed within a pair of quotation marks (" ").

Figure 13.6
This code shows and hides the tool tip, also passing the message to display to the showTip() *function.*

The great thing is, now that you have this code you never need to open the button again unless you want to change the message the tool tip displays. With the button code complete, you can move on to the bulk of the code that actually makes the tool tip work.

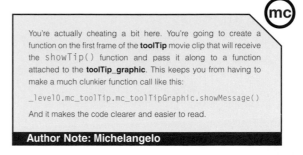

You're actually cheating a bit here. You're going to create a function on the first frame of the **toolTip** movie clip that will receive the `showTip()` function and pass it along to a function attached to the **toolTip_graphic**. This keeps you from having to make a much clunkier function call like this:

`_level0.mc_toolTip.mc_toolTipGraphic.showMessage()`

And it makes the code clearer and easier to read.

Author Note: Michelangelo

Passing the Function

You now need to create a "function bridge." You create this function bridge by initializing a new function on the first frame of the **toolTip** movie clip. To do this, double-click the **toolTip** graphic on the stage, and with the clip in Edit mode, create a new layer called **tool tip code**. Clicking once on the first frame of the new layer, enter this code:

```
function showTip(messageText) {
  mc_toolTipGraphic.initMessage(messageText);
}

function hideTip() {
  mc_toolTipGraphic.hideMessage();
}
```

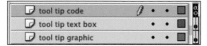

Figure 13.7
The "function bridge" should be placed on a frame in its own layer.

This code just intercepts the function call from the buttons, transforming the text message the button is sending into a parameter called **messageText**. It also calls another function contained in the **toolTipGraphic** movie clip. With the function bridge complete, you can really move on to the meat of the code.

Figure 13.8
As you can see, the code is merely calling another function.

Hide and Seek

Make sure you are still in the Edit mode for the **toolTip** graphic. (You can tell by looking in the upper-left corner of the window. If you see something that says **toolTip** you're all set.) Click the **toolTipGraphic** movie clip once. (This is where having the **toolTipGraphic** on one layer and the text box on another comes in handy. You might want to lock the text layer now to avoid selecting the wrong thing.) With **toolTipGraphic** selected, open the ActionScript editor and enter the following code:

```
onClipEvent(load) {

}
```

Almost all the code is going to go between the first and last {} you just created. It's easy to forget that last one after inputting lots of code, so you always put it in when you create the handler or function.

Now between the {}, enter this code:

```
function initMessage(text)
{
 _parent.toolTipText = text;
}

function showMessage()
{
 _parent._visible = true;
}

function hideMessage()
{
 _parent._visible = false;
}
```

Close the ActionScript window. You can now test your movie to see the results (Cmd-Return/Ctrl-Enter).

Really easy, right? All that's happening on `initMessage();` is text is being dynamically set to the content held by the **text** parameter. The **text** parameter holds the text set when creating the

If I am creating a function and find that it ends up being called more than once to do different things, I know I need to separate that code into two simpler functions that can each focus on a specific task. Then I can name the functions much more appropriately so that the code is easer to read through. In the case of `showMessage()` and `initMessage()`, it isn't very obvious yet, but later in the code you'll see the importance of having two separate functions.

Author Note: Michelangelo

206

button. Then set the **visible** property of the movie clip to `true`. Even easier on `hideMessage()`—it's nothing more than setting the **visible** property of this clip to `false`.

Now it's time to tackle setting the width and height of the tool tips.

Setting the Height and Width

Because the code you are writing is becoming more complex, it will be much easier if it's "modularized," or broken into separate functions. Start by creating a new function called `setMessageWidth()` and moving some of the code from the `showMessage` and `initMessage()` functions. Place the following code after the `hideMessage()` function:

```
function setMessageWidth()
{
   _parent.toolTipText = gText;
   _parent._visible = true;
}
```

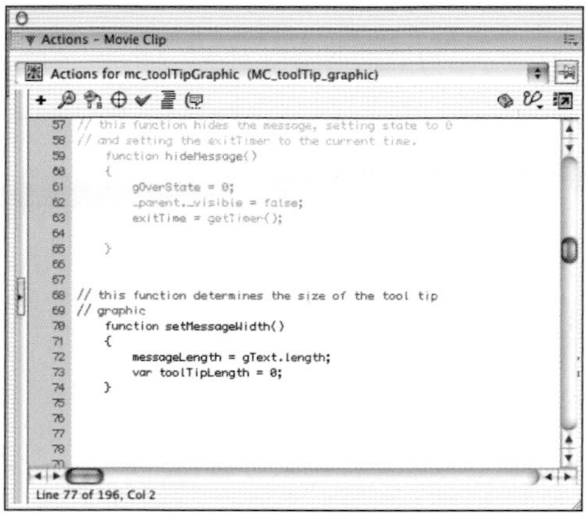

Figure 13.09
Insert the `setMessageWidth()` *function after the* `hideMessage()` *function.*

Now rewrite the `initMessage()` and `showMessage()` functions as follows:

```
function initMessage(text)
{
   gText = text;
   showMessage();
}

function showMessage()
{
   setMessageWidth();
}
```

With the `initMessage()` function, the contents of the **text** parameter have been transferred into the global variable **gText** and the `showMessage()` function called. The `showMessage()` function calls the newly created `setMessageWidth()` function.

It might seem like creating more work than needed by separating things into three functions, but as you'll see in the upcoming step where the width of the tool tip graphic is set, it makes life a lot easier.

To accurately set the width of the tool tip, you need to know a few things, such as the length and width of the message being shown, how wide the fonts are, and how many letters there are on one line. Luckily some of this can be done automatically. Some of it has to be hard coded, however.

Start by declaring some new constant variables (*constant* meaning they won't change their value once they've been set). Enter the following code at the top of your `onClipEvent(load)` handler, right after the {:

```
var CHAR_WIDTH = 7;
var CHAR_HEIGHT = 17;
var TIP_MAX = _parent._width;
var TIP_MIN = 21;
var MAX_CHAR = Math.floor((TIP_MAX-(CHAR_WIDTH*3));

var gText;
```

Each of these variables contains specific information about the physical dimensions of the Arial 9pt font. If you change your font, you will almost certainly need to adjust these numbers.

- **TIP_MAX** sets the maximum width of any tool tip to the current width plus a small extra space. If this isn't set, the tool tip graphic would appear as one long line.

- **TIP_MIN** handles cases where there is very little tool type text—fewer than three characters in length.

- **MAX_CHAR** determines the maximum number of characters allowed per line by dividing the maximum tool tip width set in **TIP_MAX** by the width of a single character, **CHAR_WIDTH**.

Figure 13.10
These constants will be used to help determine the physical size of the tool tip.

In this particular case, there are 42 allowable characters per line. The reason for the `CHAR_WIDTH*3` line is that it approximates out to 21 pixels, which is the buffer you created when drawing the tool tip text.

- **gText** is the variable used to hold the text of the message.

With the variables set, you can input the code that will use them. Immediately after the (of the setMessageWidth() function, enter the following code:

```
messageLength = gText.length;
var toolTipLength = 0;
```

This will calculate how long the message is. **gText** is the variable holding the text message, **length** will return how many characters there are in the message, and **toolTipLength** will be used to hold the length of the movie clip.

Now you want to make sure your message is under a certain length, (in this case, 150 characters). If it's over that limit, everything beyond the first 150 characters is cut via the substring function.

```
if(messageLength > 150) {
 messageLength = 150;
 gText = gText.substring(0, 150);
}
```

Next the **toolTipLength** variable gets assigned the value of the total number of characters in the message, **messageLength**, multiplied by the width of an individual character, **CHAR_WIDTH**; this gives you the total width in pixels that the message text would be if it were all placed on one line.

```
toolTipLength = (messageLenth * CHAR_WIDTH);
```

With a raw value for **toolTipLength**, you want to check it against the constant variables, **TIP_MAX** and **TIP_MIN**, to make sure that the tool tip isn't bigger or smaller than it can handle. If it's either bigger or smaller, **toolTipLength** gets set to **TIP_MAX** or **TIP_MIN** respectively. If **toolTipLength** is neither bigger nor smaller than the preset limits, add 8 pixels to **toolTipLength**. This will give the tool tip graphic a few pixels to the left and right of the text.

```
if(toolTipLength>TIP_MAX) {
toolTipLength = TIP_MAX;
} else if(toollipLength < TIP_MIN) {
 toolTipLength = TIP_MIN;
} else {
 toolTipLength += (CHAR_WIDTH*2);
}
```

Now that you have the width, you need to determine the height of the tool tips. This is actually very simple: Divide the **messageLength** variable by the maximum number of characters per line, **MAX_CHAR**. This calculation will return a relatively small number, somewhere in the neighborhood of 0 and 6 depending on your message length. The number returned is the number of lines of text your message is going to make up. If that number is less than 1.1, it's rounded to 1; otherwise, that number in the second line of the equation is rounded up to the next whole number and multiplied by **CHAR_HEIGHT**, and this determines the pixel height of the tool tip.

```
toolTipHeight = (messageLength / MAX_CHAR);
if(toolTipHeight < 1.1) {
 toolTipHeight = 1;
}
toolTipHeight = (Math.ceil(toolTipHeight) * CHAR_HEIGHT);
```

Now apply the values of **toolTipLength** and **toolTipHeight** to the height and width properties of the **toolTip** movie clip.

```
this._width = toolTipLength;
this._height = toolTipHeight;
```

If you haven't already done so, save your movie now, and then go ahead and take it for a test drive! If you set up multiple buttons with different messages in them, your tool tip graphic should resize to match the amount of text contained within the message.

If it works, great job. You've done a lot of work and there isn't too much more to go. Now you just need to focus on getting your tool tips to pop up in the right place. If it doesn't work yet, don't fret—go over the code again looking for obvious errors and look at the "Common Mistakes" section of Chapter 2, "Basic Training," to help you isolate the problem.

Setting the Placement of Your Tool Tip

Now you're going to make the tool tips appear right beside the object the cursor is pointing at. To do this, you need to add a few more variables to the top of the onClipEvent(load) event handler, right after the first {:

```
var X_POSITION = "BOTTOM";
var Y_POSITION = "RIGHT";
var MOUSELOCK = 1;

var OFFSET = 15;
```

- **X_POSITION** and **Y_POSITION** are used to set the default location of tool tip. The most common location for tool tips is to the bottom-right of the cursor, so use those values for now. Set up the code to handle up to six locations: TOP, CENTER, BOTTOM, RIGHT, CENTER, and LEFT.

- **OFFSET** is the distance in pixels that the tool tip should be offset from the cursor.

- **MOUSELOCK** is a Boolean variable that will be used later on to tell the tool tip to move with the cursor or stay in its initial position. Setting **MOUSELOCK** to 1 now means the tool tip will move, and setting it to 0 will keep it stationary.

Now you're going to create another function called setMessagePlace(). It doesn't really matter where this goes, but for legibility place it directly after the setMessageWidth() function.

Figure 13.11
These constants are used in determining how the tool tip behaves.

Figure.13.12
This code calculates the location of the tool tip.

```
function setMessagePlace()
{

}
```

Next in the `showMessage()` function you need to call the `setMessagePlace()` function. When you're done it should look like this:

```
function showMessage(text)
{
 setMessageWidth();
 setMessagePlace();
}
```

Now you need to set the placement of the tool tip based on the **X_POSITION** and **Y_POSITION** variables that were set a few moments ago. Take a look at the code to set the vertical location of the tip:

```
if(X_POSITION == "LEFT") {
 tipX = _root._xmouse - (this._width + OFFSET);
} else if(X_POSITION == "CENTER") {
 tipX = _root._xmouse - (this._width / 2);
 } else if(X_POSITION == "RIGHT") {
 tipX = _root._xmouse + OFFSET;
}
```

Basically there is a series of three `if` statements, each of which is checking to see whether the variable **X_POSITION** is set to `LEFT`, `RIGHT`, or `CENTER`. Starting with `LEFT`, if **X_POSITION** was set to `LEFT`, the preceding code runs, setting a variable called **tipX**. Because you want the tool tip to appear to the left of the cursor, subtract the entire width of the tool tip and the **OFFSET** amount from the current vertical location of the cursor.

If **X_POSITION** was set to `CENTER`, subtract one half of the width of the tool tip from the current vertical cursor location.

Finally, if **X_POSTION** was set to `RIGHT`, the code just says whether **tipX** is equal to the current vertical location of the cursor plus the **OFFSET** amount.

The same principle applies to determining the y or horizontal location of the tool tip.

```
if(Y_POSITION == "TOP") {
 tipY = _root._ymouse - (this._height + OFFSET);
} else if(Y_POSITION == "CENTER") {
 tipY = _root._ymouse-(this._height / 2);
 } else if(Y_POSITION == "BOTTOM") {
 tipY = _root._ymouse + OFFSET;
}
```

All you've done up to this point is assign some values to the two variables **tipX** and **tipY**. You need to actually set the **_property** value of the tool tip movie clip to these variables:

```
_parent._x = tipX;
_parent._y = tipY;
```

Take a second to save your work now. You also should be able to test what you have; and now, your tool tips also will show up. If things haven't worked out, take a look at the "Common Mistakes" section in Chapter 2. If you're all set, you can move on to boundary awareness.

This is one of the most important and often overlooked features of tool tips, even from industry giants (not mentioning any names). The basic concept behind boundary awareness is checking the height and width of the tool tip, and the starting x and y locations that were just set. Based on the calculation, if the tool tip is going to show up offstage, pop it to the opposite side of the cursor. The code for this calculation looks like this and should be placed *before* setting `_parent._x = tipX` and `_parent._y = tipY`; otherwise the tool tip won't take in to account the boundary checking:

```
if(tipX > Stage.width - (this._width)) {
  tipX = _root._xmouse - (this._width + _root._xmouse - Stage.width);
} else if(tipX < 0) {
  tipX = 0;
}

if(tipY > Stage.height - (this._height)) {
  tipY = _root._ymouse - (this._height + _root._ymouse - Stage.height);
} else if(tipY < 0) {
  tipY = 0;
}
```

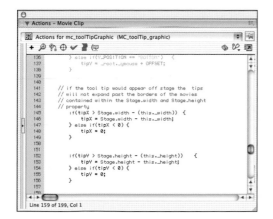

Figure 13.13
The boundary awareness code, preventing the tool tip from appearing offscreen.

You're probably an old hand at all these calculations by now, but it's still important to consider the logic behind the vertical boundaries.

That logic says: If *tipX* is going to be greater than the edge of the movie, then lock its horizontal position so that the right side of the tool tip never extends past that movie boundary.

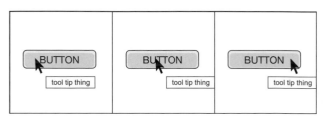

Figure 13.14
The boundary awareness feature works as shown in this figure. As soon as the tip hits the edge of the screen, it stops following the mouse.

You really are almost done now. There's just one more really important feature of the tool tips to create: the delay mechanism to prevent tool tips from showing up immediately on rollover. It involves some hefty code, so you might want to save and take a break.

Timed Tips

It gets a bit tricky again here. You need to have the tool tips appear only after a period of time has passed, and hide instantly on rollout. Making things more complex, if you roll over another button within a specified amount of time, the tool tips should appear instantly, without the initial delay. It's tough, but not too tough.

Begin by adding yet more variables to the top of the `onClipEvent(load)` handler, just above the function `initMessage(text)`.

```
var DELAY = 1000;

var gTimeIn = false;
var gOverState = 0;
```

- *DELAY* is the amount of time the user should hold her cursor over a button before the tool tips show up. The time is in milliseconds: for every 1 second, you must enter 1000.

- *gTimeIn* keeps track of whether the *DELAY* has passed. If set to `false` as it is now, the *DELAY* has not passed.

- *gOverState* is a variable that will be used to keep track of what state the tool tips are in. There are two possible states: 0 means the cursor is not over a button, and 1 means the cursor is over a button.

Now you need tweak the `initMessage` function, as follows:

```
function initMessage(text)
{
 gOverState = 1;
 gText = text;
  if(gTimeIn == true) {
   showMessage();
  } else {
   initTime = getTimer();
  }
}
```

The first thing that should happen when the user's cursor rolls over the button is that the code should be informed what's happened. By adding the preceding line of code, everything is already written; it's explicitly stating that the cursor is over a tool tip–enabled object.

Figure 13.15
Adding the timer/state check to `initMessage()`.

```
gOverState = 1;
```

`gText=text;` is fine. You can leave that as is. After that line, add the following:

```
if(gTimeIn == true)        {
 setMessageWidth();
 setMessagePlace();
}
```

This says if **gTimeIn** is true, show the tool tip. The actual timer hasn't been written yet, so **gTimeIn** is false and this code will not execute.

If the code hasn't executed, that means the timer has not started, so the next line starts the timer.

Figure 13.16
Adding the timer/state check to hideMessage().

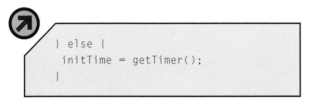

```
} else {
  initTime = getTimer();
}
```

initTime will hold on to the exact millisecond the cursor entered a button, and will be checked against this later.

You also need to rewrite the hideMessage() function. You want the tool tips to disappear on rollout or press, but you also want them to show up instantly again if Judy rolls over another button within a certain amount of time.

```
function hideMessage()
{
  gOverState = 0;
  _parent._visible = false;
  exitTime = getTimer();
}
```

As with showMessage() the first thing to do is tell Flash that the cursor has left a button, by setting the **gOverState** variable.

```
gOverState = 0;
```

_parent._visible = false; is fine, you can leave that just as it is.

```
exitTime = getTimer();
```

The last thing to do is set **exitTime** to the exact time that the cursor leaves the buttons. You'll use this later to test against the current movie time.

Now to create your timer function, which is going to be called `checkTipState()`, use the following code:

```
function checkTipState()
{
 if((gOverState == 1) && (getTimer() >= initTime + DELAY) && (gTimeIn ==
 false))  {
  gTimeIn = true;
  showMessage(gText);
 }

 if((gOverState == 0) && (getTimer() >= exitTime + DELAY) && (gTimeIn ==
 true)) {
  gTimeIn = false;
 }
}
```

It looks messy, but it's quite simple. The first `if` statement asks if all the following conditions are true: Does `gOverState == 1` (is the cursor over a button)? Is the current time greater than the sum of the time the cursor first entered the button and the delay time: Is `getTimer() >= initTime + DELAY`? Finally it asks whether the time is already up. This keeps the code from continually executing by saying after the first time through, don't run this again until **gTimeIn** is reset to `false`.

Figure 13.17
The `checkTipState()` code is what actually keeps track of the time and the tool tip's state.

If all those conditions are true, the code sets `gTimeIn = true`, allowing the tool tips to show up without any further delay and preventing this code from running again. It then calls the `showMessage()` function and, because **gTimeIn** is true, it will execute the `setMessageWidth()` and `setMessagePlace()` functions.

The second `if` statement handles the mouse-out event. It looks to see whether `gOverState == 0;` (that the mouse is no longer over a button) or whether the current time is greater than the sum of the time since the cursor left the button and the delay time. Finally it looks to see whether **gTimeIn** is true, which as before keeps this code from running more than once before **gTimeIn** is reset.

If all those conditions are true, **gTimeIn** is set to false, meaning the user would have to hold the cursor over a button for the delay time again to trigger the tool tip.

Finishing Up!

Here is the very final piece of code to be contained within the onClipEvent(load) handler, immediately before the final }:

```
hideMessage();
```

You don't want the tool tips showing when the movie loads up, so just as the load event is finishing, call the hideMessage() function, which will set the visible of the clip to false. Nice, huh?

You're not quite done yet. You need to add two more small pieces of code, for two different movie events. These can both be added right after the onClipEvent(load) handler.

The first event is the enterFrame event, onClipEvent(enterFrame). Whereas the first bits of code will run only once, or when specifically called, the enterFrame handler runs every time the Flash playhead hits a new frame, or in the event of a single frame movie, it will run however many times a second that the movie's frames per second is set at.

```
onClipEvent(enterFrame) {
  checkTipState();
}
```

This code calls the checkTipState() function. Basically the movie is constantly checking for the conditions to be true that will trigger the tool tips to jump into action.

Now's a good time to save your movie again, and to test it. Your code is almost complete and should dynamically set the size of the tool tip graphic, set its placement relative to the movie boundaries, and be on the delay setting.

Great job! This has been a lot of work, but it's well worth it.

If you want the tool tips to follow the cursor movement, you have just one more nugget of code to write.

```
onClipEvent(mouseMove) {
  if((gOverState == 1) && (MOUSELOCK == 1)) {
    setMessagePlace();
    updateAfterEvent();
  }
}
```

This code allows the tool tip to follow the mouse while it's still over the button. Conveniently, the code to set the placement of the tool tip is already done! You wrote it a while back and put it in the setMessagePlace() function. All you have to do now is check whether the cursor is over a button, gOverState == 1 and **MOUSELOCK** is true. If it is, just call the setMessagePlace() function. How cool is that? For this you also add one extra line called updateAfterEvent(). This will force Flash to redraw the tool tip every time you call the setMessagePlace() function, giving a much smoother appearance to the tool tip's movement.

Figure 13.18
*If **MOUSELOCK** is true, this code will allow the tool tip to follow the mouse while it's over a button.*

And with that you are done with the core code of the tool tip. You could stop here and have a very functional clip, but one that would work for only one movie at a time. With a little more code you can make the tool tip a smart clip that can be dragged and dropped into *any* movie.

Components

You've read ad nauseam about the modularity of code. Now take one final step to make the code so portable that you need never open the ActionScript window to modify your tool tips. If you return to the very top of your onClipEvent(load) handler, you can change these variables from this:

```
var DELAY = 1000;
var MOUSELOCK = true;
var X_POSITION = "BOTTOM";
var Y_POSITION = "RIGHT";stop();
```

To:

```
var DELAY = _parent.DELAY;
var MOUSELOCK = _parent.MOUSELOCK;
var X_POSITION = _parent. X_POSITION;
var Y_POSITION = _parent. Y_POSITION;
DELAY*=1000;
```

All that's happening here is assigning **DELAY** to a variable, which can be set via the Component Definition panel. You need only to make the movie clip a smart clip now. You also are adding one small line, `DELAY*=1000;`. This will take the value that you place in the smart clip and multiply it by 1000 to give you the time in milliseconds. You need the time in milliseconds because the `getTimer()` function works in milliseconds.

In the Library panel, right-click (Ctrl-click on the Macintosh) your **toolTip** movie clip and select Component Definitions from the contextual menu. Click the plus symbol (+) to add a new variable. In the Name column, enter **DELAY** and give it a value of **1**.

For **MOUSELOCK**, **X_POSITION**, and **Y_POSITION**, you need also to create variables using the plus symbol, but for each of these variables you need to double-click the Type column and select List from the drop-down menu. Then double click in the Value column to bring up the list editor. For both **X_POSITION** and **Y_POSITION**, you need to create three new entries (click the plus symbol three times) and replace default value with **RIGHT**, **CENTER**, and **LEFT** for **X_POSITION**. Repeat the process for **Y_POSITION** using **BOTTOM**, **CENTER**, and **TOP** for the values.

Because **MOUSELOCK** is a Boolean, you want to force the user to choose either a true or false, or a 1 or 0. For brevity's sake, and because smart clips don't understand true or false as being Boolean values, you will use a 1 and 0. Repeat the preceding process for adding values to the list, entering only two values this time. Replace the default value with **1** and **0** respectively.

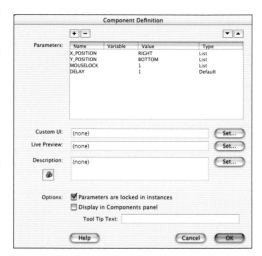

Figure 13.19
Use the Component Definitions window to define variables that are easily altered through the Clip Parameters panel.

Delete the **toolTip** movie clip from the stage (Flash has a bad habit of not updating component information), and then drag another instance of the **toolTip** movie clip to the stage. (Don't forget to give this new instance an instance name of *mc_toolTip* in the Instance panel.) When it's on the stage, right-click (Ctrl-click on the Macintosh) and select Panels>Component Parameters from the contextual menu. If you want a different delay time than 1 second, enter new values for those parameters now.

Taking this extra step means that any time during the production of your site, you can change the **_DELAY_** parameters without having to touch the code. It also means you can reuse this tool tip module in *any* future projects without adding a single line of code to the main tool tip file.

Figure 13.20
Use the Values editor to create drop-down lists of options.

One quick tip before signing off: If you plan to use loaded movies in levels rather than in movie clips (for example, if you use the `loadMovieNum()` command), you also will want

Figure 13.21
Using the Component Parameters panel, set the appropriate values for your tool tip.

to load the tool tips into a level; otherwise your loaded movies will appear on top of the tool tips, making them pretty useless. It's a good idea to load your tool tips on a very high level. If you don't, you run the risk of having to increase the tool tips' level later in the project rendering all of your calls to the function useless.

To do this, if you created your tool tips in an existing file, copy the tool tip and paste it into a new file called **toolTips.fla**, and then export the movie as **toolTips.swf** into your main movie, wherever that is. Add the following line of code to the first frame of the movie:

```
loadMovieNum(toolTips.swf, 1000);
```

The only other change you have to make is on the buttons themselves. Because the tool tips no longer reside on level 0, you must change the references in the code. For instance, what was

```
on(rollOver)        {
  _level0.mc_toolTip.showTip("Enter text here");
}
```

now becomes:

```
on(rollOver) {
  _level1000.mc_toolTip.showTip("Enter text here");
}
```

CONCLUSION   So you're done and you have a shiny new tool tip object that you can use in any of your projects without changing a single line of code. Exciting, huh?

Key Points/Don't Forget

- **Tool tips *do not* make up for poor interface design.** This cannot be stressed enough. A bad user interface with this tool tip object tacked on is still a bad user interface.

- **Be consistent and intelligent in your implementation of tips.** If you tip one button, you should tip all similar buttons. But don't get too carried away and tip everything. Most users will know how to use a scrollbar or an arrow button and won't thank you for telling them again.

- **Make the messages in your tips short.** You're trying to speed up users' movement through the site, not bog them down with reams of text. Make tool tips short, relevant, and informative.

- **Even if you don't use this code, use these tips!** At the time of this writing, tool tips seemed to be all the rage among ActionScript gurus, so there are some very cool tool tip-style smart clips and movie clips out there (probably even more now). If you find one that you like more than this one, make sure it's got all the features you need. Forgotten what they are? Here you go: time-delayed initialization, instant off, state maintenance, precise placement, message dependent, and mouse follow.

CHAPTER 14
The End...

So, you've made it to the end. Congratulations! Hopefully you've picked up a thing or two about usability along the way and can use that knowledge to create better, more user-centered interface designs for your projects.

If you've made it here from the beginning, you have covered a heck of a lot of stuff. If you skipped straight here, you can pick up some useful tips from this chapter; however, you might want to delve back into the book later to see how to make these principles work for you in practice.

KEY POINTS   Either way, here are a few key points to remember:

- **Usability is design.** There is a clear distinction between the visual design of a project and the interaction modeling of it. Don't forget, however, that both are design processes and born out of the same need to solve problems creatively and devise the best end product for the user.

- **Designing for usability doesn't negate creativity.** Just because you focus on the end users and making their experience better doesn't mean you are stuck designing gray buttons, beveled edges, and drop shadows. Work to design a creative approach to the usability problem. This is how innovation happens!

- **Usability isn't a weekend retreat.** This book is just the beginning of the journey for you. It's important that you continue to look into usability and interface design. Visit the sites listed in Appendixes B and C, read the books, and attend the lectures. Just as with software applications, you must keep up with the latest information to remain relevant.

- **Flash is not 99 percent bad; usability isn't a Flash issue.** Flash is a tool just like Photoshop, Director, and Freehand: You can choose to use it in a responsible way, or you can neglect your users. Don't take the critics personally when they bash Flash as being bad, but try to learn from their comments.

- **Know the rules; know when to break them.** Controversial though it may be, at various times during the production of this book, user studies have shown that the human interaction rules don't necessarily provide the solution to every problem. Just applying a rule without making sure it's valid is not much better than ignoring the rules completely. Intangible qualities such as enjoyment, entertainment, and appreciation are no less important than ease of use. Think of usability rules as guidelines. They're not cast in stone, they're just there to help you design with your user in mind. You never know, some users may actually want an interface that takes several minutes to explore and comprehend. The key, as always, is to leave your preconceptions, your ego, and your rigid design philosophy at the door and think about your users. Remember: *It's not about faster or easier, it's about better.*

We really hope these points can help to guide you in your efforts to improve the experience of your users and your client's users. Good luck.

APPENDIX A
What Every Interface Designer Should Know

Although far from a comprehensive look at all the laws, rules, and formulas of usability and interface design, this appendix contains a few of the most universally accepted concepts. You can use these ideas not only in your development of Flash (and web pages in general) but also as a starting point for further investigations into usability.

TEN USABILITY HEURISTICS

The following rules were developed by Jakob Nielsen and Rolf Molish in 1990, and were refined by Nielsen in 1994. Although they were directed primarily at the development of applications, the theory behind them applies equally well to Flash:

- **Visibility of system status.** The system should always keep users informed about what is going on, through appropriate feedback within reasonable time.

- **Match between the system and the real world.** The system should speak the user's language, with words, phrases, and concepts familiar to the user, rather than system-oriented terms. Follow real-world conventions, making information appear in a natural and logical order.

- **User control and freedom.** Users often choose system functions by mistake and will need a clearly marked "emergency exit" to leave the unwanted state without having to go through an extended dialogue. Support undo and redo.

- **Consistency and standards.** Users should not have to wonder whether different words, situations, or actions mean the same thing. Follow platform conventions.

- **Error prevention.** Even better than good error messages is a careful design that prevents a problem from occurring in the first place.

- **Recognition rather than recall.** Make objects, actions, and options visible. The user should not have to remember information from one part of the dialogue to another.

- **Flexibility and efficiency of use.** Accelerators—unseen by the novice user—may often speed up the interaction for the expert user such that the system can cater to both inexperienced and experienced users. Allow users to tailor frequent actions.

- **Aesthetic and minimalist design.** Dialogues should not contain information that is irrelevant or rarely needed. Every extra unit of information in a dialogue competes with the relevant units of information and diminishes their relative visibility.

- **Help users recognize, diagnose, and recover from errors.** Error messages should be expressed in plain language (no codes), precisely indicate the problem, and constructively suggest a solution.

- **Help and documentation.** Even though it is better if the system can be used without documentation, it may be necessary to provide help and documentation. Any such information should be easy to search, focused on the user's task, list concrete steps to be carried out, and not be too large.

INTERFACE DESIGN PRINCIPLES
Another good list of design advice is Brice Tognazini's Interface Design Principles at `www.asktog.com/basics/firstPrinciples.html`. These principles are much longer and more detailed than Nielsen and Molish's rules but cover some very important concepts (as discussed in the following sections).

Anticipation

Applications should attempt to anticipate the user's wants and needs. Do not expect users to search for or gather information or evoke necessary tools.

Consistency

These guidelines on consistency, taken together, offer the designer tremendous latitude in the evolution of a product without seriously disrupting those areas of consistency most important to the user. The importance of maintaining strict consistency varies. The following list is ordered from those interface elements demanding the most faithful effort to those demanding the least. (Paradoxically, many people assume that the order should be exactly the reverse, leading to applications that look alike, but act completely differently in unpredictable ways.)

- **Interpretation of user behavior.** For example, shortcut keys maintain their meanings.
- **In-house consistency.** Follow your company's style guidelines.
- **Platform consistency.** Keep within the established standards of the platform for which you're designing.
- **Invisible structures.** This refers to such invisible objects as Microsoft Word's clever little right border that has all kinds of magical properties, if you ever discover it's there. It may or may not appear in your version of Word. And if it doesn't, you'll never know for sure that it isn't really there, because it's invisible. That is exactly what is wrong with invisible objects and why consistency is so important. Other objects are, strictly speaking, visible, but do not appear to be controls, so users, left to their own devices, might never discover how the objects can be manipulated. The secret, if you absolutely insist on there being one, should be crisp and clean. For example, "You can click and drag the edges of current Macintosh windows to size them;" not, "You can click and drag various things sometimes, but not other things other times."
- **Small visible structures.** The appearance of such objects as icons, size boxes, scroll arrows, and so on need to be strictly controlled if people are not to spend half their time trying to figure out how to scroll or how to print. Location is only slightly less important than appearance. Where it makes sense to standardize location, do so.

Conversely, it is just important to be visually inconsistent when things must act differently as it is to be visually consistent when things act the same.

You should also avoid uniformity. Make objects consistent with their behavior. In other words, make objects that act differently look different.

Finally, remember that the most important consistency is consistency with user expectations. The only way to ascertain user expectations is to do user testing. No amount of study and debate will substitute.

Explorable Interfaces

Give users well-marked roads and landmarks, and then let them shift into four-wheel drive.

- **Mimic the safety, smoothness, and consistency of the natural landscape.** Don't trap users into a single path through a service, but do offer them a line of least resistance. This gives the new user and the user who just wants to get the job done in the quickest way possible a "no-brainer" way through, while still enabling those who want to explore and play "what-if" a means to wander further afield.

- **Sometimes, however, you have to provide deep ruts.** The closer you get to the naive end of the experience curve, the more you have to rein in your users. A single-use application for accomplishing an unknown task requires a far more directive interface than a habitual-use interface for experts.

- **Offer users stable perceptual cues for a sense of "home."** Stable visual elements not only enable people to navigate fast, they also act as dependable landmarks, giving people a sense of "home."

- **Make actions reversible.** People explore in ways beyond navigation. Sometimes they want to find out what would happen if they carried out some potentially dangerous action. Sometimes they don't want to find out, but they do anyway by accident. By making actions reversible, users can both explore and can "get sloppy" with their work.

- **Always allow an undo.** The unavoidable result of not supporting undo is that you must then support a bunch of dialogs that say the equivalent of, "Are you really, really sure?" Needless to say, this slows people down.

- **Always allow a way out.** Users should never feel trapped. They should have a clear path out.

- **Make it easier to stay in.** Early software tended to make it difficult to leave. With the advent of the web, we've seen the arrival of software that makes it difficult to remain. Having 49 options on the screen that lead directly to destruction of the user's work, along with 1 or 2 that just might help, is not an explorable interface; it is the interface from hell.

- **Choose metaphors well.** Use metaphors that will enable users to instantly grasp the finest details of the conceptual model. Good metaphors are stories, creating visible pictures in the mind. If you want something to be portable from one program to another, for example, consider using the suitcase metaphor. Bring metaphors alive by appealing to people's perceptions— sight, sound, touch, and kinesthesia—as well as triggering their memories.

Before you can apply any of these concepts, however, you really must have a firm grasp on what your users intend to do with your interface. You can help determine this through task analysis.

PROPER TASK ANALYSIS
Task analysis sounds technical, but it really is a basic necessity for every project. Interaction design starts by deconstructing the main goal of the site into specific tasks or steps that the user needs to accomplish to meet the goal.

Task analysis involves breaking down these tasks into the individual steps it takes to complete each task and analyzing them to determine their importance to the task. This process helps you to discover areas you may not have fleshed out as thoroughly in the initial concept. It also will help you to refine usability paths that are overly complex for the task the user is trying to accomplish.

COGNITIVE WALKTHROUGH
This is another complex sounding term that really is quite simple. A cognitive walkthrough is the process of evaluating the usability of an interface from the perspective of a first-time user. How easy will it be for the user to learn the interface? Does the interface promote exploring and is it easy to discover how the tasks help accomplish the user's goal? This process, although very similar to task analysis, really requires the tasks to have been analyzed so that you can determine how easily the tasks can be learned and the steps needed to complete them.

As mentioned previously, these tips were devised for applications. As you begin to focus your Flash design on the user's experience, however, you will realize how useful these ideas can be in Flash, too.

TESTING, TESTING...
Testing your interface is crucial—and it's not just about seeing whether what you imagined works for you and your colleagues. The more you can test it the better.

Testing can start as soon as you have an interaction model that you can sketch out on paper. Create wire frame sketches of your interface's interaction on paper and sit down with test subjects who match your client's target audience. Develop questions that don't focus on the buttons or specific usability terms, but give users a goal to accomplish. Have the users tell you what they are thinking as they complete the task, and observe their actions as they do so. This is a key time to catch design flaws in the interaction model. You haven't spent a lot of time creating extensive widget libraries or fancy mathematical algorithms for sliding images on and off the screen: It's a minimal investment for a huge potential return.

As you continue to iron out the interaction issues with your project and start to integrate the visual design with the interaction, work on still screens. Many times designers/developers get bogged down with trying to tweak code for buttons or smooth out the tweening of some transition. These are details that may affect the usability of your interface, but always design static screens first that you can export in order and test further with users.

At the 2001 Flash Forward conference in New York, our technical editor, Chris McGregor, suggested an excellent approach to finding people to help you in your testing stages. He had the audience stand up, turn to a person they had never met before, and exchange business cards. These are our testers. When you prepare a still screen prototype, email it with a detailed questionnaire to one of the people you may have met at a conference or online and get his feedback. These types of tests may not involve your exact target audience, but the feedback you get will invariably be beneficial.

While you are testing, remember a few things: Pay attention to what your test users are actually doing. They may be telling you that they are having trouble with one thing, but you may notice they are actually having difficulty as a result of something else in the interface. You need to interpret user actions and find the best solution for accommodating them.

Give the testers time. Don't stand over their shoulder and direct them every step of the way. Give them a clear goal and see whether they can execute it. If they get stuck, assure them that it is nothing that they are doing wrong, and that they are allowed to explore. If it's too hard for the user to accomplish their task, maybe you need to reevaluate your interaction model.

Take to heart any feedback you get, but don't be hasty to implement the solutions that may have been suggested to you. Go back to your wire frame interaction stage and make sure you have a solid big picture. Then you can solve the usability issue in question.

APPENDIX B
Usability Resources

Usability isn't a book, it's not a web site, and it's not something you can learn overnight. It's a continuous process of reading, learning, experimenting, revising, refining, and trying. To really dedicate yourself to usability, you have to immerse yourself in the community, read the books, visit the web sites, attend the lectures, and continue to do so. Usability isn't a weekend retreat.

There are many books, web sites, mailing lists, and conferences that focus on usability. One important thing to keep in mind is that you might not agree with everything (or even anything) that these books and web sites say. Often, heated debates occur between different camps of usability experts. The important thing is that you familiarize yourself with them and formulate your own opinions.

BOOKS
We can't stress enough that you should check out as many usability and interface design books as possible. Literally dozens of books on usability are on the market, and some of them are really good. Find the books that really speak to you and, most of all, teach you about designing for the user from the beginning of your project. Many of these books go into detail about how and when to conduct user testing, techniques that you can employ to help in the design process, and how to rally your coworkers and clients around the effort to improve usability.

Note that not all of these books are about putting pixels on the screen in a certain way. Many of these books explore the psychology of the user, the mechanics of the human body, even the culture a user is from and how it might affect their interaction with your interface. The field of human-computer interaction (HCI)—also known as computer-human interaction (CHI), human factors, or user-centered design—is vast and can include parts of anthropology, ethnography, and psychology.

You must step outside of the realm of the computer and look at the world around you for inspiration. Blenders, cars, crosswalks, VCRs; these are all items in our everyday lives that provide varying levels of usability. By observing the usability in these objects, you might find some correlation between them and the objects you create onscreen.

We really enjoyed the following list of books. These books inspired us (as they have many others).

The Inmates Are Running the Asylum
By Alan Cooper

The inventor of Visual Basic, Alan Cooper is both the founder of Cooper Interaction Design and a respected software designer and usability expert. *The Inmates Are Running the Asylum* captured the attention of countless software engineers and interface designers and has helped to raise the level of usability for software the world over.

This book really changed the way I think about interfaces. I always thought "cooler is better," or "I want to design something that is totally futuristic and cool!" After reading this book, however, I realized that there is really more to interface design than pretty pixels. It's about making something that someone else can use without cursing the designer who made it. Of course, I still make sites that are experimental and exploratory, but those are for me, not my clients.

Author Note: Michelangelo

About Face
By Alan Cooper

This is another excellent book by Alan Cooper. It doesn't refer specifically to Flash usability, but general points about interfaces made in this book should help Flash designers produce more usable sites.

The Humane Interface
By Jef Raskin

Jef Raskin was one of the original inventors of the Apple Macintosh in 1984, the computer that spawned the GUI revolution. In *The Humane Interface*, Raskin looks not only at what has worked in the past, but to the future and where computer interfaces should be headed. There's even mention of Flash toward the end of the book. Even though it's a bit math heavy in sections, it should be on your bookshelf.

Designing Web Usability
By Jakob Nielsen

Yes, you should read this! As stated in the book, this is not an "us against them" war. We should all be working together to better the web, not slinging insults and catchphrases back and forth. Read this, learn from it.

Flame Wars: The Discourse of Cyberculture
Mark Dery, Editor

Flame Wars is a collection of essays about the advent of online culture. It was written in 1994, only a year after the "graphical web" was born, so it is written by some fairly visionary people. Although the entire group of essays is worth reading, we specifically recommend "Techgnosis, Magic, Memory, and the Angels of Information," which looks at the development of GUIs from as far back as medieval times.

Being Digital
By Nicholas Negroponte

Nicholas Negroponte is the director of the MIT media lab and an all around super smart guy. *Being Digital* is one of the most fascinating books you will ever read; and although it has very little to do with usability today, seeing what the future holds for us should help to inspire you to explore new methods of usability.

Understanding Comics
By Scott McCloud

Understanding Comics is yet another book that is only tangentially related to the field of usability and interface design. Mr. McCloud's book is a fascinating read on the history of comics, from ancient Egypt up to today. Of course, comics are one of the most successful examples of information expressed in a visual manner.

Reinventing Comics
By Scott McCloud

This book is the follow-up to *Understanding Comics*. This book delves into comics and technology, specifically the Internet.

Envisioning Information
Visual Explanations: Images and Quantities, Evidence and Narrative
The Visual Display of Quantitative Information
All by Edward Tufte

These three books not only represent a brilliant look at visually displaying quantitative information, they surpass many design books in terms of quality and attention to detail. These are certainly the best looking math books we have ever seen. *Visual Explanations*, the second book, demonstrates how accurately presented visual information could have prevented the Challenger accident in 1986.

Ender's Game
By Orson Scott Card

Okay, so this is the least relevant book on this entire list; but believe it or not, there are a whole bunch of important lessons about usability in here. It's not in-your-face information by any means, but if you spend some time with this book you'll see what we mean. Plus it's a great read.

The Invisible Computer

Things That Make Us Smart

Both by Donald A. Norman

Donald Norman is another software usability guru whose book really hits home. He is one of the founders of the Neilsen Norman Group (along with Jakob Neilsen) and helps to pinpoint the pitfalls in the usability of today's computers and software. He explains how we can begin to drive a trend toward a better usability future. *Invisible Computer* discusses information appliances and the specializing of devices—some great stuff!

Snow Crash

The Diamond Age

In the Beginning Was the Command Line…

All by Neil Stephenson

Okay, we had to add these. Again, these are examples of books that might not directly relate to software usability. The first two describe some pretty exciting interfaces of the future. It's never too early to start thinking about that nanite-driven user interface! In *Command Line*, Stephenson takes a look at the advent of the operating system, from old teletypes, through the MacOS, all the way up to Linux and BeOS. Although his beliefs on user interface are in many ways antithetical to user interface design, he provides an interesting look at how gear-heads view the computer.

Techgnosis

By Erik Davis

Erik Davis' newest book was just hitting the bookstores as this volume went to the printers, so we can't include a review here. Needless to say, however, if it's half as fascinating as Mr. Davis' essay in the aforementioned *Flame Wars* collection, it's bound to be unique and well worth your time. Check out the *Skip Intro* web site for a full review.

WEB SITES

As always, the web offers a huge assortment of information, and it delivers much concerning usability. The great thing about these links is that they lead to sites that are published by many of the authors mentioned earlier. You'll find an endless assortment of articles, essays, research, and more that have influenced us and countless others. We like to keep the following list of links handy:

Skip Intro

www.skip-intro.org

Yes, the *Skip Intro* site is a great place to start. For more information and a full feature list check out the "What's on the Web Site" section at the back of this book.

Flazoom.com

www.flazoom.com

Our ultra cool technical editor, and author of the Macromedia white paper on Flash usability, has an excellent site with several great articles on usability and Flash.

Ask Tog

www.asktog.com

Bruce Tognazzini originally founded the Apple Human Interface Group and had a hand in many of the user interface features you still use today in the MacOS. He has some great insight into usability issues and is one of the principals of the Norman Neilsen Group.

Donald Norman's jnd web site

www.jnd.org

Donald Norman covers topics from video game interfaces for education to the poor usability of your stereo equipment. This is a great site from a respected usability giant.

Jakob Nielsen's web site

www.useit.com

This is where a lot of controversy begins! Jakob Nielsen cannot be accused of holding things back! In this site you'll find Nielsen's critiques on different software and web interfaces (including Flash) and suggestions for fixing the problems he finds. Many read Nielsen's articles and get defensive; if you take his comments to heart, however, you'll find that your interfaces may be better for it.

Usability First

www.usabilityfirst.com

This is a great resource of links to research, essays, books, and other things that all revolve around usability.

UIDesign.net

www.uidesign.net

This site offers some great strategies for improving web usability by changing the production process to be more user-centered.

Human Factors International

www.humanfactors.com

This is a user interface and interaction design company that sends out a great user interface design newsletter. Go there and sign up for it!

Webword.com

www.webword.com

Offers daily news on usability and the web. You also can sign up for a daily email with usability news.

NEWSGROUPS, EMAIL LISTS, ORGANIZATIONS

Newsgroups and email lists make for some great discussion on the topic of usability. Many of the industry usability gurus pop into these lists and are very eager to answer questions or just discuss the details of usability itself. You can learn a lot just by reading other's posts, which is all we have time to do anyway. If you're looking to get out of the house and away from that computer for a bit, try one of the special interest groups—they have some great events and inspiring speakers.

Comp.human-factors newsgroup

This newsgroup discusses usability in detail. Many very knowledgeable experts appear here. Check it out and get involved.

SIGCHI

www.acm.org/sigchi/

This is a special interest group that has brought together all the disciplines of computer-human interaction in an effort to improve the usability of the computer, as we know it today. Check out their Local SIGs link to see whether there is a chapter in your area.

BayCHI

www.baychi.org/

This is the Bay Area chapter of SIGCHI, a special-interest group that focuses on computer-human interaction issues. It's a great organization, and some of the speakers are just amazing.

CHI-WEB email list

http://sigchi.org/listserv/

This is a great list with many top usability professionals discussing anything relating to usability on the web. Examples of some great topics that have appeared on there recently are solving issues for the color-blind population, good and bad ways to conduct a live usability test, and the usability of scrolling and clicking.

Flash Usability

http://aether.ultraservers.net/mailman/listinfo/flashusability_emberton.com

A usability mailing list hosted by David Emberton of *Flash 4 Magic* and *Flash 5 Magic* (New Riders).

APPENDIX C
Flash and Design Resources

Like designing for usability, being a Flash developer and a designer in general is a continual process. You should always be learning and gathering new information. Part of the design process is about bringing all those things that inspire you together into one place and drawing from it.

This appendix lists some of the books and web sites we visit when looking for answers and inspiration.

WEB SITES   Are you looking for good Flash resources for code help, animation ideas, and plain old inspiration? The web's got it all! You can spend days and days checking out innumerable Flash code sites, artsy design sites, and discussion forums filled with useful tips and great ideas. After a while you'll settle on some really good sites that meet your needs. Alternatively, you could cheat and take a look at the following small selection of the sites that we try and hit daily.

Were-Here

www.were-here.com

One of our favorite Flash message boards on the Internet. Very friendly people, very helpful too, and there's an entire forum dedicated to usability and architecture with tons of Flash gurus there to help when you need it. Drop by and say "hi."

> My favorite, hands down. I'm always in there wasting far too much time.
>
> **Author Note: Duncan**

Flashcoders mailing list

http://chattyfig.figleaf.com

Wow! Branden Hall's Flashcoders email list is just amazing. If you're an intermediate or advanced ActionScripter, you might want to sign up for this mailing list.

Flash Code Hacks

www.flashcodehacks.com

Lots of great links to other sites about Flash, including a whole slew of links that relate to usability and Flash.

The ActionScript Dictionary

www.macromedia.com/support/flash/action_scripts_dict.html

This site is an online and, most importantly, up-to-date version of the ActionScript dictionary.

A List Apart

www.alistapart.com

Always an informative and interesting site. Apart from having a cool design, this site contains links to great articles about web development, dealing with clients, and selling standards.

Builder.com

http://builder.cnet.com

This site has plenty of great information. Check out the "References" section for some really well-displayed details on such things as CSS, XML, and more. There is also a list of sample contracts for designers and coders who are freelancers.

Webmonkey

http://hotwired.lycos.com/webmonkey

Another great general web resource. Here you'll find a great quick-reference section and an in-depth how-to section to help you on those late night projects! Keep this one handy.

Surfstation

www.surfstation.lu/frames.html

If you're in need of general artistic inspiration, this site's got a lot of it. This is one of many sites on the web that link to a plethora of Flash- and non-Flash-based web sites with great design work. This is the kind of site you'll want to check daily.

K10K

www.k10k.com

Another site great for checking out some inspiring web sites. You'll find links here to great artwork and design sites as well as articles on design. This has always been a great center for the online design community.

ThreeOh

www.threeoh.com

More artistic inspiration. This site works much like the K10K and lists some great Flash and DHTML sites. A lot of the work that shows up in this list is from company web sites from around the world, so you can keep up on those progressive Norwegian design shops!

Praystation

www.praystation.com

Okay, here's a guy who's fired us up more times than we can count! Joshua Davis is a crazy Flash designer who, although not totally focusing on usability, is busy providing wanton inspiration to the Flash community!

Yugop.com

www.yugop.com

Yugo is on an entirely different plane of Flash development. The work he produces continues to inspire the entire Flash community, and he doesn't show any signs of slowing down.

> (dm)
>
> I have to say that Yugo's site got me back into Flash design. I had given up on Flash and not used it in about year, missing Flash 3 all together. Someone pointed out the "liquid Mona Lisa" and I was blown away! I hadn't realized what could be done with Flash 4 and was totally inspired by what I saw there.
>
> **Author Note: Duncan**

BOOKS

In addition to consulting the web, you might want to check out these books for ideas and inspiration. You'll find ActionScript books toward the top of the list and design books toward the bottom.

New Riders books

This might sound like a cop out, or dancing for the man, but honestly every single one of New Riders books on Flash has been absolutely tip-top. New Riders really does understand that their authors have a unique voice, and that's what you (the readers) should get to hear, not just another code cookbook. You just can't go wrong with 'em.

Flash ActionScript for Designers: Drag, Slide, Fade
By Brendan Dawes

Brendan, the guy behind the Flash Psycho Studio, tackles ActionScript for designer types. An excellent place to start if you're new to coding.

Flash to the Core: An Interactive Sketchbook by Joshua Davis
By Joshua Davis

Okay, at the time we're writing this, Joshua's book isn't even out yet; but we did get a very funny email telling us what it was going to be like. We reckon it'll be pretty good.

Flash 5 Magic

By J. Scott Hamlin and David J. Emberton

The follow up to the much-adored *Flash 4 Magic*, this one goes much deeper and tackles some pretty complex issues.

They're not the only kids on the block, however; so here's list of other books we love.

ActionScript: The Definitive Guide

By Colin Moock

This book will take you to new levels of ActionScript. Colin spent a year and a half putting together this comprehensive guide to ActionScript, along with examples and a great web site to boot. You'll probably want to keep this book right next to ours.

JavaScript: The Definitive Guide

By Dan Flanagan

With Flash 5 switching over to an ECMA-compliant scripting language, JavaScript knowledge can be leveraged in the Flash 5 authoring environment.

These next few books are more design inspiration, or inspiration in general. Some of them may seem a bit off the wall but, hey, it's our book.

Maeda & Media

By John Maeda

Okay, there won't be too much about Flash or usability in this book, but John Maeda is a great digital artist and this is an inspiring book to flip through when you're stuck.

Noise 3, Noise 3.5, Noise 4

By The Attik

Just amazing design work: These books are very hard to come by and relatively expensive; but if you can find a copy of any of these, don't think, just buy. You won't be disappointed.

Soak Wash Rinse Spin: Tolleson Design

By Steven Tolleson

A look at the work of noted design house Tolleson Design. Very, very nice stuff.

Akira Vol 1-6

By Katsuhiro Otomo

Probably no book on the market better illustrates the benefits of paying attention to detail. The book is about 2000 pages long and was about a decade in the making. Every stroke of the pen was placed with purpose. Everything in this fictional world has been designed to function (at least on a theoretical level), even if it just makes a single frame appearance. We should all strive to be as attentive to detail as Mr. Otomo.

Oblagon

By Syd Mead

This could easily go in Appendix A, "Usability Resources." Syd's designs are so well thought out from a usability standpoint, one can't help but be inspired. Syd has worked on the design of everything from *Blade Runner* to *TRON* to Nissan cars.

> **(mc)**
>
> I love this book, and many others like it. I have a favorite art bookstore that I go to when I am in a rut and need inspiration, and I usually leave at least a good half day open to mulling around the shop, looking in all these books, and getting excited again. Everyone should find his own favorite bookstore, and add it to this list.
>
> **Author Note: Michelangelo**

Microserfs

By Douglas Coupland

An amusing, fictionalized look at a group of Microsoft castoffs who band together to form a startup software venture.

INDEX

Symbols

+ (plus sign), 53

A

About Face, 233
acceleration, gesture-driven scrolling lists, 65
ActionScript, LoadInfo Component, 41-42
The ActionScript Dictionary, 240
ActionScript Editor, context-sensitive, 21
ActionScript: The Definitive Guide, 243
adding
    auto-hide features to tabbed sliding panels, 151
    clip parameter variables to tabbed sliding
        panels, 152
    initialize function to tabbed sliding panels, 153-159
    invisible triangles to hierarchical menus, 185
    timer/state check to hideMessage(), 216
Akira Vol 1-6, 244
analyzing tasks, 229
anticipation, Interface Design Principles, 227
arrays, creating clip arrays, 69-70
Ask Tog, 236
attachMovie() command, 109
The Attik, 243
audiences
    finding for testing interfaces, 230
    knowing target audience to create effective
        designs, 14
auto-hide features, adding to tabbed sliding
    panels, 151

B

Back button, 176
Bandwidth Profiler, 47
BayCHI (Bay Area chapter of SIGCHI), 238
Being Digital, 234
Bell, Genevieve, 15
books
    Flash resources, 242
    usability resources, 232-235

branding, 175
breadcrumb trails, 177
bugs, 25. *See also* errors
Builder.com, 241
buttons
    creating for tool tips, 204-205
    for tabbed sliding panels, code, 140-141
bytes, downloading per second, 48

C

calling showMenu() function, 100
Card, Orson Scott, 234
cascading hierarchical menus, 181
case sensitivity, search fields, 165
case studies
    The Digital Museum, 33-34
        character profiles, 35
        defining goals for sites, 35-36
    GroceryClick.com, 129-130
        character profiles, 130-131
        goals, 131-132
    Wind-Automata Knowledge Base, 174-176
        character profiles, 176-177
        goals for, 177-178
challenging design usability, 13
changing cursors, 106, 112-114
character profiles
    GroceryClick.com, 130-131
    user of MODA, 35
    Wind-Automata Knowledge Base, 176-177
checking state of mouse cursors for gesture-driven
    scrolling lists, 74-75
checkTipState() function, 217-218
CHI (computer-human interaction), 232
CHI-WEB email list, 238
cleaning up cursors, 114-116
clicking, single-clicking versus double-clicking, 13
client-side "Find in Page" feature, 162
clip arrays, 69-70
clip parameter variables, adding to tabbed sliding
    panels, 152
clips, organizing list clips, 70-72
CLIP_BASE_NAME, 69
closing tabs, tabbed sliding panels, 146-150

245

code
for Find in Page searches, 165-169
for mouse under menus, 93
building menus, 94-95
changing from movie clips to components, 102-103
fading, 100-101
initializing, 93-94
mouse handling, 95-98
public functions, 98-100
for tabbed sliding panels
accessing move functions, 145
activating code, 159
adding auto-hide features, 151
adding clip parameter variables, 152
buttons, 140-141
closing tabs, 146-150
initialize function, 153-159
making code portable, 152
movie clips, 141-142
opening tabs, 142-145
setting initial positions, 144
setting up component clips, 159
for tool tips
creating buttons, 204-205
creating function bridges, 205
finishing touches, 218-219
hiding messages, 206-207
making code portable, 219-222
placement of tool tips, 210-214
setting height and width, 207-210
timed tool tips, 214-218
translating, 27
code errors, 23
coding, 26
comments, 23
Expert mode, 21
Hungarian Notation, 21-22
Normal mode, 21
speed at which code executes, 22
white space, 22
cognitive walkthroughs, 229
colors, tool tips, 202
commands
attachMovie(), 109
duplicateMovie(), 109
Load Order, 39
stop(), 138
commenting on code, 23
comp.human-factors newsgroup, 238
component clips, setting up for tabbed sliding panels, 159
Component Definition interface, 53
components
changing from movie clips (for mouse under menus), 102-103
cursors, 123
computer-human interaction (CHI), 232
consistency, Interface Design Principles, 227-228
CONSTANT_VARIABLES, 22
content areas, creating for tabbed sliding panels, 137-138
content windows for tabbed sliding panels, 137
context-sensitive, ActionScript Editor, 21

controlling
cursors, 106
streaming movies, 46-47
conventions for organizing files, 20-21
converting
search fields to lowercase, 165
text fields to movie clips, 203
movie clips to tool tips, 202
Cooper, Alan, 12, 233
"Navigating Isn't Fun", 134
counting frames, 50
Coupland, Douglas, 244
createClipArray function, 69
cursor cleanup, 107
cursor hog, 107
cursorCleanUp(), 115
cursors, 123
alerting users to additional functions, 107
changing, 106, 112-114
cleanup, 114-116
components, 123
controlling, 106
creating, 107-108
cursor libraries, 109-110
setting up events, 110
feedback, 106
hogging, 107, 116-117
installing, 110-111
key points, 124
libraries, 109-110
modifying, 118-123
mouse outs, 113-114
mouse overs, 112-113
moving, 111
overriding, 107
preparing to move, 110-111

D

Davis, Erik, 235
Davis, Joshua, 242
Dawes, Brendan, 242
declaring variables, 118
designing
better sites, 18
on paper, 13
for personas, 14
usability, 11, 224
***Designing Web Usability*, 233**
designs
effective designs. *See* effective designs
identifying bad designs, 12-13
***The Diamond Age*, 235**
differentiating variables, 22
dispatching menu clicks, Hierarchical Menu Component, 197
double-clicking, 13
downloads
estimating
download times, 47-52
time left in download process, 51

live feedback, 38
progress bars, 56-58
waiting for, 38
dragging menus with mouses, 95-98
drawing
graphics for tool tips, 202
menus, hierarchical menu component, 188-191
drawMenu(), 188-190
duplicateMovie(), 109

E

e-commerce. *See also* shopping carts
areas of, 129
tabbed sliding panels. *See* tabbed sliding panels
usability features, 131-132
effective designs, 14
knowing
goals, 15-16
market, 15
rules and mathematical forumulas, 16
target audience, 14
tools, 16
users, 14-15
your own personality, 17
simplicity, 14
else statements, indexOf(), 168
email lists, usability resources, 238
Ender's Game, 234
Envisioning Information, 234
eraseMenu(), 191
error messages, 168-169
errors
identifying, 24-26
logic errors, 23-24
preventing, 24-26
syntactical errors, 23
troubleshooting, 25
estimating
download times of streaming movies, 47-52
time left in download process, 51
evaluating interfaces, 13
events for cursors, setting up, 110
executing code, speed of, 22
exitTime, 217
Expert mode, 21
explorable interfaces, Interface Design Principles, 228-229

F

fading, 193-194
hideMenu() function, 101
hierarchical menu component, 196
of hierarchical menus, 181
feedback
cursor feedback, 106
elements of, 40
for users, 32
live feedback of downloads, 38
files, organizing, 20-21

Find in Page searches, 162
code, 165-169
creating
movie clips, 164
search fields, 163
error messages, 168-169
implementing, 163
find() function, 164-165
finding rate of downloads, 48
Fitts's law, 89
Flame Wars: The Discourse of Cyberculture, 233
Flanagan, Dan, 243
Flash
history of, 11
problems with, 10-11
resources
books, 242
web sites, 240-242
usability, 224
Flash 5 Magic, 243
Flash ActionScript for Designers: Drag, Slide, Fade, 242
Flash Code Hacks, 240
Flash Usability, 238
Flashcoders mail list, 240
Flazoom.com, 236
formatBytes(), 44-46
fps (frames per second), 23
frames, counting, 50
function bridges, 205
functions
checkTipState(), 217-218
createClipArray, 69
cursorCleanUp(), 115
drawMenu(), 188-190
eraseMenu(), 191
find(), 164-165
formatBytes(), 44-46
getBounds, 69
getBytesLoaded(), 44
getBytesTotal(), 44
getClipOffset, 69
getPinPosition(), 156, 158
getTimer(), 48
hideMenu(), 93, 99
fading, 101
hideMessage(), 207
hitTest(), 97
Hungarian Notation, 22
indexOf(), 166-167
initialize(), 153-154, 156-159
initMessage(), 206-207
itemMouseMoveFunc(), 97
itemMouseUpFunc(), 97
lastIndexOf(), 166-167
Math.floor(), 49
menuItemMouseMoveFunc(), 190-192
menuItemMouseUpFunc(), 190
menuMouseDownFunc(), 96
menuMouseMoveFunc(), 96
menuMouseUpFunc(), 96
modifyCursor(), 118, 122
moveCursor(), 111

openTab(), 144-145
pop(), 67
pressHandler(), 140, 142
private functions, 98
public functions, 98
releaseHandler(), 141-142, 145
restoreCursor(), 114
setCursorHog(), 117
setMessagePlace(), 219
setMessageWidth(), 207, 209
setPrimaryCursor(), 113, 119-121
showMenu(), 90, 99-100
showMessage(), 207
showTip(), 204
startDrag(), 152
stopDrag(), 148
swapDepths(), 94
switchCursor(), 112
trace(), 47
    streaming movies, 52-56
typeof(), 189
underMenuDispatch(), 97
unHogCursor(), 118
unloadMovie, 39
updateAfterEvent(), 111

G

gesture-driven scrolling lists, 62-64
clip arrays, creating, 69-70
components, creating, 85-86
creating, 66
handling offsets, 68-69
implementing, 64-66
list clips, organizing, 70, 72
mouse cursor, checking state of, 74-75
movie clips
    hiding, 67
    moving around, 76-79
private functions, 67
public functions, 67-68
speed of, 62
testing, 80-85
usability, 62
variables, initializing, 72-74
getBounds(), 69
getBytesLoaded(), 44
getBytesTotal(), 44
getClipOffset function, 69
getPinPosition(), 156, 158
getTimer() function, 48
gLoading, 43
global features, 88
global variables, 22
goals
for GroceryClick.com, 131-132
knowing to create effective designs, 15-16
for web sites, 35-36
for Wind-Automata Knowledge Base, 177-178
graphics, drawing for tool tips, 202

GroceryClick.com, 129-130
character profiles, 130-131
goals for site, 131-132
gTimeIn, 217-218
guidelines
for hierarchical menu component, 198
for LoadInfo component, 58-59
mouse under menus, 104
for searches, 170
for tabbed sliding panels, 160
for tool tips, 222

H

handling mouses, mouse under menus, 95-98
HCI (human-computer interaction), 232
height, setting for tool tips, 207-210
height property, 143
heuristic evaluations, 13
hideMenu() function, 93, 99
fading, 101
hideMessage() function, 207
timer/state check, adding, 216
hiding
auto-hide features, 151
messages for tool tips, 206-207
movie clips, 46, 67
hierarchical menu component
creating, 183-184, 187-188
    drawing menus, 188-191
    mouse handling, 192-194
fading, 196
guidelines for, 198
implementing, 182-183
menu clicks, dispatching, 197
movies, setting up, 184
packaging, 197
skinning the menu, 184-187
testing, 194-195
hierarchical menus, 177, 180-181
hierarchies, 180
histories, 177
history of usability, 11
hitTest() function, 97
hogging cursors, 107, 116-117
Human Factors International, 237
human-computer interaction (HCI), 232
The Humane Interface, 233
Hungarian Notation, coding, 21-22

I-J

ideas, sketching, 26
identifying
bad designs, 12-13
errors, 24-26
implementing
Find in Page searches, 163
gesture-driven scrolling lists, 64-66
hierarchical menu component, 182-183

LoadInfo component, 41
    mouse under menus, 91
    streaming movies, 41-42
    tabbed sliding panels, 135-136
    tool tips, 201
In The Beginning Was the Command Line, 235
indexOf(), 165-167
    else statement, 168
information objects, LoadInfo component, 41-42
initialize function, adding to tabbed sliding panels, 153-159
initializing
    code for mouse under menus, 93-94
    variables for gesture-driven scrolling lists, 72-74
initMessage() function, 206-207
    adding timer/state check, 215
initTimer, 216
The Inmates Are Running the Asylum, 233
installing cursors, 110-111
Interface Design Principles (Brice Tognazini), 227
    anticipation, 227
    consistency, 227-228
    explorable interfaces, 228-229
interfaces
    cognitive walkthroughs, 229
    evaulating, 13
    explorable interfaces, 228-229
    features, organizing, 88
    global features, 88
    task analysis, 229
    testing, 229-230
intuitiveness, 13
The Invisible Computer, 235
invisible triangles, 195
    adding, 185
itemMouseMoveFunc(), 97
itemMouseUpFunc(), 97

JavaScript: The Definitive Guide, 243
jnd web site, 236

K-L

K10K, 241
key points. *See* guidelines

lastIndexOf, 165-167
Linkage property, 109
List Apart, A, 241
list clips, organizing, 70, 72
live feedback, 38
Load Order command, 39
loadedBytes variable, 56
LoadInfo component, 40, 58
    guidelines for, 58-59
    implementing, 41
    information objects, 41-42
loadMovie, 39
logic errors, 23-24
lowercase, converting search fields to, 165

M

Maeda & Media, 243
Maeda, John, 243
mailing lists, Flashcoders, 240
markets, knowing to create effective designs, 15
Math.floor(), 49
mathematical formulas, knowing to create effective designs, 16
McCloud, Scott, 234
mc_movieClips, 22
Mead, Syd, 244
memory, streaming movies, 39
menu clicks, dispatching for hierarchical menu component, 197
menuItemMouseMoveFunc(), 190, 192
menuItemMouseUpFunc(), 190
menuMouseDownFunc(), 96
menuMouseMoveFunc(), 96
menuMouseUpFunc(), 96
menus
    hierarchical menu component
        drawing for, 188-191
        skinning, 184-187
    hierarchical menus. *See* hierarchical menus
    mouse under menus. *See* mouse under menus
methods, setSelection(), 166-167
mice
    cursors, checking state of, 74-75
    following tooltips, 219
    movements of hierarchical menu component, 192-194
Microserfs, 244
MODA (Museum of Digital Art), 35
    case study, 33-34
    defining goals for site, 35-36
    profile of user, 35
modifyCursor(), 118, 122
modifying cursors, 118-123
Moock, Colin, 243
mouse outs, 113-114
mouse overs, 112-113
mouse under menus, 89-90
    code, 93
        building menus, 94-95
        changing from movie clips to components, 102-103
        fading, 100-101
        initializing, 93-94
        mouse handling, 95-98
    creating, 91
        components, 92
        setting up movies, 91-92
    guidelines for, 104
    implementing, 91
    public functions, 98-100
MOUSELOCK, tool tips, 211
MOUSE_BUFFER, 72
moveCursor(), 111
movements of mouse for hierarchical menu component, 192-194

movie clips
    changing to components for mouse under menus, 102-103
    converting text fields, 202-203
    Find in Page searches, creating, 164
    hiding, 46, 67
    moving around for gesture-driven scrolling lists, 76-79
    tabbed sliding panels, code for, 141-142
    tabbedWindow, setting up, 138-140
movies
    setting up
        for hierarchical menu component, 184
        for tooltips, 202
    streaming, 38. *See also* streaming movies
        example of, 39-40
        implementing, 41-42
        memory, 39
moving
    cursors, 111
    tool tips, 201
The Museum of Digital Art (MODA). *See* **MODA**

N-O

"Navigating Isn't Fun", 134
Negroponte, Nicholas, 234
newsgroups, usability resources, 238
Nielsen, Jakob, 233
    useit.com, 237
Noise 3, **243**
Noise 3.5, **243**
Noise 4, **243**
Normal mode, 21
normal variables, 22
Norman, Donald, 235
    jnd web site, 236

Oblagon, **244**
OFFSET, tool tips, 211
Offsets, gesture-driven scrolling lists, 68-69
opening tabs of tabbed sliding panels, 142-145
openTab() function, 144-145
organizations, usability resources, 238
organizing
    features of interfaces, 88
    files, 20-21
    hierarchies, 180
    list clips, 70-72
Otomo, Katsuhiro, 244
overriding cursors, 107

P

packaging hierarchical menu component, 197
panels, tabbed sliding panels. *See* **tabbed sliding panels**
paper, designing on, 13
passing functions, 205
percentageLoaded variable, 55

persona concept, 12
personas, designing for, 14, 176. *See also* **character profiles**
placing tool tips, 210-214
PLAY_BYTES variable, 53
PLAY_FRAMES variable, 54
PLAY_PERCENT variable, 54
PLAY_TYPE variable, 53
plus sign (+), 53
pop() function, 67
portable code for tabbed sliding panels, 152
Praystation, 242
preparing cursors to move, 110-111
pressHandler(), 140-142
preventing errors, 24-26
private functions, 98
    gesture-driven scrolling lists, 67
progress bars, 56-58
properties
    height, 143
    of tabbed sliding panels, 136
    Stage.height, 143
public functions, 98
    gesture-driven scrolling lists, 67-68
    mouse under menus, 98-100

Q-R

Raskin, Jef, 233
rate of downloads, finding, 48
rebranding, 175
Reinventing Comics, **234**
releaseHandler(), 141-142, 145
resources
    about Flash
        books, 242
        web sites, 240-242
    about usability
        books, 232-235
        email lists, 238
        newsgroups, 238
        organizations, 238
        web sites, 236-237
restoreCursor(), 114
rules
    knowing to create effective designs, 16
    for usability, 226

S

scrolling gesture-driven scrolling lists. *See* **gesture-driven scrolling lists**
search fields
    converting to lowercase, 165
    Find in Page searches, creating, 163
searches
    Find in Page. *See* Find in Page searches
    guidelines for, 170
    server-side CGI, 162
server-side CGI, 162

setCursorHog(), 117
setMessagePlace() function, 219
setMessageWidth() function, 207-209
setPrimaryCursor(), 113, 119-121
setSelection() method, 166-167
shopping, tabbed sliding panels. *See* tabbed sliding
  panels
shopping carts, 129
  frusterated users, 128-129
  GroceryClick.com case study, 129-130
Show Streaming, 39
showMenu() function, 90, 99-100
showMessage() function, 207
showTip() function, 204
SIGCHI, 238
simplicity, effective designs, 14
simplifying web sites, 32-33
situation awareness, 38
size of tool tips, setting, 207-210
sketching ideas, 26
skinning menus, hierarchical menu component, 184-187
Skip Intro, 236
smart tool tips, 201
Snow Crash, 235
Soak Wash Rinse Spin: Tolleson Design, 243
speed
  at which code executes, 22
  of scrolling gesture driven lists, 62
Stage.height property, 143
startDrag(), 152
Stephenson, Neil, 235
stop(), 138
stopDrag(), 148
STREAM variable, 56
streaming movies
  controlling, 46-47
  creating, 43
    setting stage, 43-45
  example of, 39-40
  figuring out estimates of time to download, 47-52
  implementing, 41-42
  memory, 39
  progress bars, 56-58
  testing, 45
  trace() function, 52-56
Surfstation, 241
swapDepths() function, 94
sweepTimer, 115
switchCursor(), 112
switching between Normal and Expert mode, 21
syntactical errors, 23

T

tabbed sliding panels, 134-135
  code
    for adding auto-hide features, 151
    accessing move functions, 145
    activating code, 159
    adding clip parameter variables, 152
    for buttons, 140-141

    closing tabs, 146-150
    initialize function, 153-154, 156-159
    making code portable, 152
    for movie clips, 141-142
    opening tabs, 142-145
    setting initial positions, 144
    setting up component clips, 159
  content areas, creating, 137-138
  content windows, creating, 137
  guidelines, 160
  implementing, 135-136
  look of, 135
  movies, setting up, 137
  properties of, 136
  setting up tabbedWindow movie clip, 138-140
target audiences, knowing to create effective designs, 14
task analysis, 229
Techgnosis, 235
testing
  gesture-driven scrolling lists, 80-85
  hierarchical menu component, 194-195
  interfaces, 229-230
  showMenu() function, 100
  streaming movies, 45
  usability, 13
text box variables, 22
text fields, tool tips, 203
Things That Make Us Smart, 235
ThreeOh, 241
timer/state check, adding
  to hideMessage(), 216
  to initMessage(), 215
timing of tool tips, 214-218
Tognazini, Brice, Interface Design Principles, 227
Tognazzini, Bruce, 236
Tolleson, Steven, 243
toLowerCase(), 165
tool tips, 177
  code
    creating buttons, 204-205
    creating function bridges, 205
    finishing touches, 218-219
    hiding messages, 206-207
    making code portable, 219-222
    placing tool tips, 210-214
    setting height and width, 207-210
    timed tool tips, 214-218
  colors of, 202
  creating
    converting to movie clips, 202
    drawing graphics, 202
    setting up movies, 202
    text fields, 203
  following mouse, 219
  guidelines for, 222
  implementing, 201
  moving, 201
  placement of, 210-214
  smart tool tips, 201
  transitioning events, 200
  working tool tips, 200-201
  X_POSITION, 212
  Y_POSITION, 212

tools, knowing to create effective designs, 16
totalBytes, 44
TOTAL_CLIPS, 69
trace() function, 47, 52-56
transitioning events, tool tips, 200
translating code, 27
transparent error messages, 169
triangles. *See* invisible triangles
troublshooting errors, 24-26
Tufte, Edward, 234
typeof(), 189

U

UIDesign.net, 237
underMenuDispatch(), 97
Understanding Comics, 234
unHogCursor(), 118
unloadMovie, 39
updateAfterEvent(), 111
usability, 224
    breadcrumb trails, 177
    challenging designs, 13
    designing for, 11, 224
    features for e-commerce sites, 131-132
    Flash, 224
    gesture-driven scrolling lists, 62
    hierarchical menus, 177
    history of, 11
    identifying bad designs, 12-13
    resources
        books, 232-235
        email lists, 238
        newsgroups, 238
        organizations, 238
        web sites, 236-237
    rules for, 226
    testing, 13
    tool tips, 177
Usability First, 237
useit.com, 237
users
    alerting users to additional functions with
      cursors, 107
    feedback about downloads, 32
    knowing to create effective designs, 14-15

V

variables
    clip parameter variables, adding to tabbed
      sliding panels, 152
    declaring, 118
    differentiating, 22
    Hungarian Notation, 22
    initializing for gesture-driven scrolling lists, 72-74
    loadedBytes, 56
    percentageLoaded, 55

PLAY_BYTES, 53
PLAY_FRAMES, 54
PLAY_PERCENT, 54
PLAY_TYPE, 53
STREAM, 56
The Visual Display of Quantitative Information, 234
Visual Explanations: Images and Quantities, Evidence and Narrative, 234

W-X-Y-Z

waiting for downloads, 38
web sites
    The ActionScript Dictionary, 240
    Ask Tog, 236
    Builder.com, 241
    defining goals for, 35-36
    Flash Code Hacks, 240
    Flash resources, 240-242
    Flashcoders mailing list, 240
    Flazoom.com, 236
    goals. *See* goals
    Human Factors International, 237
    jnd, 236
    K10K, 241
    List Apart, A, 241
    Praystation, 242
    simplifying, 32-33
    Skip Intro, 236
    Surfstation, 241
    ThreeOh, 241
    UIDesign.net, 237
    Usability First, 237
    usability resources, 236-237
    useit.com, 237
    Webmonkey, 241
    Webword.com, 237
    Were-Here, 240
    yugop.com, 242
Webmonkey, 241
Webword.com, 237
Were-Here, 240
white space, 22
width, setting for tool tips, 207-210
Wind-Automata, Inc., 174-176
    character profiles, 176-177
    goals, 177-178
windows, content windows for tabbed sliding
  panels, 137
wire frames, 13

X_POSITION, 211-212

Yugop.com, 242
Y_POSITION, 211-212

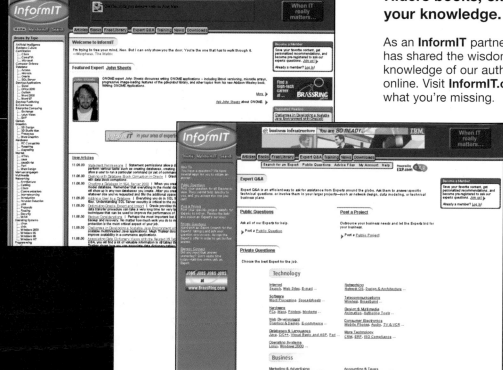

Publishing
the Voices
that Matter

OUR BOOKS

OUR AUTHORS

SUPPORT

::::: web development | **::::: graphics & design** | **::::: server technology** | **::::: certification**

NEWS/EVENTS

PRESS ROOM

EDUCATORS

ABOUT US

CONTACT US

WRITE/REVIEW

You already know that New Riders brings you the Voices that Matter.

But what does that mean? It means that New Riders brings you the

Voices that challenge your assumptions, take your talents to the next

level, or simply help you better understand the complex technical world

we're all navigating.

Visit **www.newriders.com** to find:

- ► Never before published chapters
- ► Sample chapters and excerpts
- ► Author bios
- ► Contests
- ► Up-to-date industry event information
- ► Book reviews
- ► Special offers
- ► Info on how to join our User Group program
- ► Inspirational galleries where you can submit your own masterpieces
- ► Ways to have your Voice heard

New Riders

WWW.NEWRIDERS.COM

VOICES THAT MATTER

HOW TO CONTACT US

VISIT OUR WEB SITE

WWW.NEWRIDERS.COM

On our web site you'll find information about our other books, authors, tables of contents, indexes, and book errata. You will also find information about book registration and how to purchase our books.

EMAIL US

Contact us at this address: **nrfeedback@newriders.com**

- If you have comments or questions about this book.
- To report errors that you have found in this book.
- If you have a book proposal to submit or are interested in writing for New Riders.
- If you would like to have an author kit sent to you.
- If you are an expert in a computer topic or technology and are interested in being a technical editor who reviews manuscripts for technical accuracy.
- To find a distributor in your area, please contact our international department at this address: **nrmedia@newriders.com**.

- For instructors from educational institutions who want to preview New Riders books for classroom use. Email should include your name, title, school, department, address, phone number, office days/hours, text in use, and enrollment, along with your request for desk/examination copies and/or additional information.
- For members of the media who are interested in reviewing copies of New Riders books. Send your name, mailing address, and email address, along with the name of the publication or web site you work for.

BULK PURCHASES/CORPORATE SALES

If you are interested in buying 10 or more copies of a title or want to set up an account for your company to purchase directly from the publisher at a substantial discount, contact us at 800-382-3419 or email your contact information to corpsales@pearsontechgroup.com. A sales representative will contact you with more information.

WRITE TO US

New Riders Publishing
201 W. 103rd St.
Indianapolis, IN 46290-1097

CALL US

Toll-free (800) 571-5840 + 9 + 7477
If outside U.S. (317) 581-3500. Ask for New Riders.

FAX US

(317) 581-4663

New Riders

WWW.NEWRIDERS.COM